From
College to Career

From College to Career

Entry-Level Résumés for Any Major

From Accounting to Zoology

Donald Asher

The **WetFeet.com** Career Management Series

WetFeet.com
609 Mission Street, Suite 400
San Francisco, CA 94105
www.wetfeet.com
415-284-7900

First edition published in 1991 by Ten Speed Press of Berkeley, California.
Cover and book design by Carpenter Design, Corte Madera, California.
ISBN 1-582-07079-2
Printed in the United States of America.

Table of Contents

Acknowledgments

First of all I must express my indebtedness to the thousands of students who sent me copies of their résumés, and to the directors of college career planning and placement who encouraged them to do so. College career offices are all too often understaffed and budget squeezed, and I have the highest respect for those who do so much for students with so little acknowledgment of their contribution. Let a student win a Rhodes scholarship or other academic laurels and the faculty comes forward to take a bow. Let a student win a highly coveted assignment, whether it is with a Fortune 500 company or with a global nonprofit, and few think of the office of career planning and placement, the source for that student's career strategy, résumé, interview technique, and guidance.

Some of the examples used in this book originally appeared in *The Overnight Résumé*. Some of the examples and narrative used in this book originally appeared in the career publications of *The Wall Street Journal*, including the *National Business Employment Weekly* and *Managing Your Career*. They are reprinted with permission of Dow Jones & Co., Inc. Some examples are adapted from the *Swarthmore College Guide to Writing Résumés and Cover Letters*, 4th ed.; they are used with permission of Swarthmore College. Special thanks to my associate, Chuck Klein, for his résumé for Clark Kent. I am indebted to Eric A. Grover, Esq., and the firm of Littler, Mendelson, Fastiff & Tichy, for counsel on employment law matters.

All the examples in this book are lifted verbatim or adapted from résumés from students and recent graduates. In some instances, dates, schools, locations, company names, and other details may have been changed at the discretion of the editors or by request of the individuals whose lives are chronicled herein. All addresses and telephone numbers and some names have been changed to protect the privacy of the contributors. Any employers wishing to contact candidates represented in this book may do so by writing to Donald Asher, From College to Career, c/o WetFeet.com, 609 Mission Street, 4th Floor, San Francisco, 94105.

I am indebted to my publisher, WetFeet.com. They are smart, fast and under the radar, and I like that about them. If you have a good career or business book idea, they're a great publisher. Their other titles focus on career launch and career development issues, and you might want to check out their web site at www.wetfeet.com.

For Elmer Otto Asher and Clyde Ulon Asher, two men, stalwart pillars upon which to build a family.

To your success.

How to Use This Book

WHO THIS BOOK IS FOR

This book is for college seniors, graduate students, recent graduates, and savvy college students at any level who wish to have a career and not just a series of jobs. If this is you, then this book is for you.

This book is just as useful for a postdoctoral fellow in theoretical physics as it is for an undergraduate with a major in business administration. While most of the résumé sections apply to everyone, sections on technical résumés and curricula vitae focus on designing and producing a compelling presentation for such possible futures as becoming an engineer, medical doctor, research specialist, or college professor.

The résumés prepared with this book will not only be used for jobs. Many will be used to gain entrance to graduate programs, to win fellowships and grants, and to participate in special projects. Anywhere and anytime you need to make a professional presentation of your educational and experiential background, this book will be of use.

Shortcuts

If you need a basic résumé and you need it fast, read Part I, "Getting Ready to Write," pp. two to seven, then read Chapters 4 through 10, pp. 36 to 97. This can be done in as little as two hours, including doing the exercises and drafting your résumé.

If you need a technical résumé, you need to read the above material on regular résumés and Chapter 12, "How to Write a Technical Résumé."

If you need a curriculum vitae, you need to read the material on regular résumés and Chapter 14, "How to Write a Curriculum Vitae."

If you need to plan and manage a job search, Part III, "Cover Letters, Interviews, and Job Search Tips and Techniques," provides a quick overview.

I have learned that a great many students sit down to write a résumé without a particular employer in mind. There are many shortcuts to writing a résumé and planning a job search, but you cannot eliminate envisioning that potential résumé reader. As you read this book, you will discover that there are a dizzying number of options as to what experience to include and how to feature it best; you cannot sort those options without reference to a potential reader.

Do the exercises. This is an action-oriented text. Exercises have been kept to a minimum and not one of them is superfluous. If you do the exercises as you come to them, your document will be drafted by the time you finish reading. So have a pen and a pad of paper ready at all times while you are reading.

The Book's Goals and Uses

This book's primary mission is to help you prepare a compelling résumé, technical résumé, or curriculum vitae—one that is so superior to the average product that your targeted reader puts down your résumé and immediately reaches for the phone, hoping to recruit you before someone else grabs you first.

Can a résumé do that? You bet it can. As part of a well-thought-out, systematic job search, a good résumé can vault you over piles of mediocre presentations and win you the job over better-qualified, but less-well-presented, candidates. In this book you will learn easy solutions to the challenges that most seniors and recent grads face: too little experience, unrelated experience, no permanent address, too many addresses, and a checkered or complex academic career. Parts I and II guide you from self-assessment through writing and editing to the final stages of design and printing.

This book's secondary mission is to teach you how to use your résumé or c.v. No matter how cogent your presentation is, you still need to know how to plan and orchestrate a systematic job search. Part III of the book is dedicated to this topic. Even if you only need a résumé for a class or as part of the on-campus recruiting program, be sure to take a look at the interviewing and protocol tips in Part III.

Finally, this book will teach you about modern careers and prudent career management. The process of learning to get a job is no longer a matter of crisis management. As the work world changes, the condition of needing a job is no longer an acute episode, a temporary condition to be survived or endured until you can return to the perceived security of a permanent position. Outside of some areas of academic or government employment, there are almost no permanent positions left in the American job market. Even tenure, that epitome of job security, is increasingly restricted or revoked under an "economic necessity" clause.

In summary, this book can help you prepare a highly competitive written presentation, use that presentation effectively, and become more sophisticated about the topic of careers in general.

This Book's Main Limitation

One thing this book cannot do, however, is tell you what career or job to pursue. It offers an excellent system for refining your career ideas, but you must provide the ideas to refine. This is a "how to," not a "what to." This book is a tool, a device, more a canoe than a map of any particular lake. More exactly, this is a tome on map-making rather than an atlas. You must supply the initiative and the direction, and this book will supply the means.

If you know exactly what you want to do, or have a rough idea of your career direction, you can use this book now. The tips and techniques will help you refine your target, pursue it, and obtain a first career job. If you do not know what you want to pursue, see your campus career counselor, take some assessment tests (interest and skills inventories), talk to your peers about their career plans, make an appointment to talk with your academic advisor about the career paths of alumni with your major, and read some good books like *What Color Is Your Parachute* and *What Can I Do with a Major In . . . ?: How to Choose and Use Your College Major.* Some key questions to ask yourself are: What have you dreamed about doing for a career? If money and preparation were no barrier, what would you love to do for a living? What would you do for free? Or, taken to the logical conclusion, what would you gladly pay someone else to get the privilege to do? What industries do you know about? What industries are people in your family involved in? What industries do your closest friends' parents work in? What industries are the hot growth industries today? You need to seek a match between your personality, your academic preparation, and your career target. Remember, even the most highly technical industries have many, many nontechnical career paths within them. Your first stop: your career counselor.

Some Assumptions about You

This book makes a few assumptions about you, the reader. The main one is that you are an intelligent, alert individual who is interested in having a successful career. Since you are either currently or recently a college student or graduate student, it is fairly safe to assume that you have a lot on the ball. Since you are reading this book, you are almost certainly interested in your career. You are probably interested in maximizing your career and making the most of your work life. Let's hope so.

It is explicitly assumed that you are paying attention. In the interest of brevity, some very important information is mentioned only once, and common sense interpretations are usually left up to the reader.

As mentioned above, it is assumed that you either have a fairly good idea of your career direction or are willing to propose an area of interest and pursue it.

It is assumed that you own a dictionary and are willing to use it as needed. On the other hand, it is not assumed that you are a grammarian or a polished writer, or that you have a secretary or unlimited resources. If you are able to think, follow directions, and apply general principles, you will be able to produce an outstanding résumé, technical résumé, or curriculum vitae.

A Note on Terminology

Since this book deals with three distinct types of résumés (traditional chronological résumés, technical résumés, and curricula vitae) the word 'résumé' is generally understood to encompass all three styles. This will spare you from reading down the laundry list of "résumé, technical résumé, or curriculum vitae" over and over again.

Likewise, whether you are an applicant for a scholarship or grant, entering the corporate working world, an artist applying for a show, or seeking a faculty or staff position in academe, most of the information addressed to the "student," "job applicant" or "candidate" and referring to the "potential employer" and so on, will apply to you. Applying for and lobbying to win a postdoctoral grant is a lot like executing a professionally conducted application for a coveted job.

Where This Book Came From

This book grew out of my experiences as a professional résumé writer and a counselor and coach in the job-search process. My service has traditionally focused on assisting fast-track professionals who engineer their own career paths, create their own success, and generally self-actualize their working life to suit themselves. I have worked with almost exactly 10,000 such individuals since I started in this business. The tips and techniques presented in this book are the collective experience of 10,000 highly motivated, highly intelligent, and creative people.

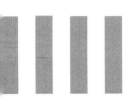

part

Getting Ready to Write

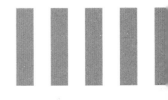

⇒ ⇒ ⇒ ⇒

CHAPTER 1

What Is a Résumé?

TERMS DEFINED

The terms "résumé," "technical résumé," and "curriculum vitae" are used throughout this book. The following may be more than you ever wanted to know about the terminology of job-search documentation, but it is important that you understand that these three terms all refer to different styles of the same thing, rather than three different things altogether. Besides, these terms have an interesting history.

The word résumé comes to us from the French verb résumer, which means to sum up or summarize. It has been in common use in the English language for almost two hundred years, but for the first hundred and fifty years of English usage, was primarily a literary term, meaning a short summary of a written work. Then, sometime after World War II, along with the rise of the use of résumés in the job-search process, the word came to be associated closely with job résumés.* This is now its most common meaning, although it remains a synonym for summary.

Incidentally, this latter fact is one reason that some purists object to starting a résumé with a section entitled SUMMARY, which would be a summary of a summary. As you shall see, I am not that much of a purist.

In current usage, a résumé is a brief written summary of a person's education, experience, and qualifications, usually used in application for a job, political appointment, or other dispensation.

The term curriculum vitae has an even more venerable history. It comes to us from the Latin, as you might imagine. The Latin word curriculum originally meant a race or a racecourse, and was derived from the verb currere, to run. Vitae is the possessive

---

*Before job résumés, most workers collected letters of reference from all past employers, a practice still common throughout Europe.

form of the word for life. Lexicographers usually give the Latin meaning of curriculum vitae as "the course of life," but the more exact translation would be "the racecourse of life," or, more loosely, "the rat race." So you may properly think of a curriculum vitae as a report on one's progress in the rat race.

The plural of curriculum vitae is curricula vitae. In academic circles and the top echelons of business you will occasionally hear the word "vita." To academicians vita is simply a synonym for curriculum vitae. To business people vita means something else entirely— an extremely short narrative biography used in place of a résumé or curriculum vitae, and sometimes as a source document to prepare an introduction for a speaker.

The term curriculum vitae has been in the English language for almost 100 years, but it has always meant the same thing: a document used in a job search to present one's employment history, education, and credentials. It should come as no surprise that the most conservative industries in America would retain this older term. Academia and medicine still use curricula vitae while the rest of the North American business world uses résumés.

Finally, a technical résumé is nothing more than a résumé for a person with a technical background.

In practice, résumés, technical résumés, and curricula vitae are different names for the same thing: a document used to present your education, experience, and qualifications. There are different styles for such a document, but the basic nature and purpose of the information are the same.

An Advertisement

It is useful to think of the résumé as an advertisement. A résumé informs employers of the services available from a candidate, and should generate interest and action from the employer.

Like other advertisements, résumés have the disadvantage that the best advertisement does not necessarily represent the best product. They have other advantages, however, that will ensure their continued use in any employment or selection process that involves judging a number of candidates by their educational and experiential backgrounds.

First and foremost, a résumé can be reviewed in seconds; interviews, even by telephone, take several minutes per candidate. Second, résumés allow one to consider a large number of candidates who may be geographically distant or otherwise unavailable.

4

Third, when databanked, thousands of résumés can be searched electronically to find exactly the candidates who meet the skill requirements for a position. And fourth, résumés allow a company to reject the overwhelming majority of candidates without having to say anything to them face-to-face. This reduces both management stress and potential legal liability. In this setting, it is easy to see the résumé's role as a screening device. In effect, an employer uses résumés to decide which candidates not to interview.

Employers use résumés to control their resources, to assemble a large pool of applicants without expending too much management time. They use résumés to decide exactly which of the candidates they will expend further resources on (i.e., interview). This is so efficient that résumés will never disappear from the hiring process, as long as employers insist on hiring the best candidates they can find.

Returning to our analogy, the résumé is an advertisement for further consideration; that is, for more management time. (Remember that "management" could refer to a faculty search committee, an engineering recruiter, the members of a collective, or anybody to whom you would submit your résumé. All organizations need to control their resources.)

The résumé's single most important function is to win an interview in head-to-head competition with other résumés. In this Darwinian selection process, it is the best résumé, not the best candidate, that survives. A candidate who ignores or maligns the résumé's role in this process is at considerable risk.

A Conversation Piece and a Proxy

Occasionally, candidates will assume that since they already have an interview, or are assured of getting one, the résumé is a "mere formality" on which they need spend little energy. This is almost always an error, as very few candidates have no competition. The résumé is an important factor at all stages of the decision-making process, and can help or hurt as long as the employer has more than one candidate.

After winning the initial interview, the résumé:

> Structures the interview

> Reminds the interviewer of you later

> Justifies the hiring decision to others

Most interviewers refer constantly to a candidate's résumé during an interview, reviewing the material from top to bottom. This means that a résumé structures the interview since it is the central conversation piece and focal point. A strategically arranged résumé can even control the interview, guiding the topic of conversation onto subjects the candidate chooses and skipping quickly over topics he would rather avoid.

A résumé should serve to pique rather than satisfy interest. Any major topics that you would like to discuss should be mentioned at least briefly. Contrary to what some résumé guides claim, there can even be a valid role for "human interest" listings.

After providing a focus and structure for the interview itself, the résumé reminds the interviewer of the candidate later. Few candidates realize how important this role is. Employers may interview dozens of people in a single day, or spread their interviews over a span of many days or weeks. The interviewer needs résumés to refresh her memory. In fact, studies show that a résumé can overcome the employer's memory of the actual interview. A neat and well-presented candidate with a weak and sloppy résumé is remembered after a few days as a sloppy and ill-kempt individual, and a poorly presented candidate with a crisp, well-written résumé is remembered as articulate and professional. An experienced interviewer will take a few notes, but the résumé becomes her main reference when considering a candidate later.

Another little-considered role of the résumé is to justify the hiring or selection decision to third parties, senior managers, and others whom a candidate may never meet. Other parties almost always review such decisions, and the better you look on paper, the more comfortable both the hiring manager and the third parties will be with this decision. Your résumé should represent you as well as you can represent yourself in person.

Résumés are central to the hiring and employment process. Employers expect them. They will ask for them, and tend to be suspicious of potential employees who try to circumvent the process. Résumés almost always become part of an employee's permanent personnel file, which is an exceptionally good reason to be sure to tell the truth and nothing but the truth. A lie on your permanent record can come back to haunt you when you least expect it, years and years later, perhaps after you have risen into management and can no longer afford to start over.

Perhaps the Greatest Benefit of All

Perhaps the greatest benefit of preparing an outstanding résumé has nothing to do with the actual document. The very act of assessing and articulating your strengths, your accomplishments, and your qualifications for a job and career path is both cathartic and preparatory. When it comes time to verbally present your candidacy in an interview, you will have already done your homework. You will have a more detailed idea of what you have to offer, and it will be on the tip of your tongue. Your interviews will go much better than if you had prepared a cursory presentation.

The act of preparing a résumé, a good résumé, is a focusing and clarifying experience. You should not launch a job search without the benefit of this process. This is a hidden benefit, and it is one often overlooked by even the most qualified of candidates.

Benefits in Order of Magnitude

While the benefits will vary for each individual, this list shows the most common benefits to taking the time and energy to write and use a good résumé, in order of magnitude:

1. Prepares the candidate mentally to present a strong and focused candidacy

2. Wins the interview in direct, head-to-head competition with the résumés of many other highly qualified candidates

3. Structures the interview in your favor

4. Reminds the interviewer of your best points

5. Justifies the hiring decision to third parties

These are pretty important benefits. In my personal opinion, most people who denigrate résumés and the role of résumés in the selection and hiring process simply do not know how to develop a highly compelling document, either for themselves or for others.

In this book, you will learn how.

CHAPTER 2

Know Your Target Market

THE RÉSUMÉ AS PERSUASIVE WRITING

Before you write a résumé, you should consider your target. Who is your reader? What is important to her? What is she looking for? What will turn her off?

Résumés are a form of persuasive writing—writing that is intended to influence the reader and incite action. Other forms of persuasive writing include sales brochures, advertisements, press releases, and almost every speech written since Pericles.

Persuasive writing requires a special knowledge of its reader. No politician would stand before a hall of people without knowing something about the audience. No Madison Avenue wizard would begin crafting a new ad campaign without reviewing a vast amount of demographic and product positioning data. Likewise, no résumé writer should begin to write without identifying and assessing his potential employer.

Before we discuss this process, you should be familiar with a few terms and concepts that will be used throughout the book. Then you need to define your job target. In the next chapter we will come back to your résumé's reader and try to define her interests and relate them to your background.

Job vs. Career

There is a considerable difference between a job and a career. A job is a title, a place on the flowchart, a collection of responsibilities. A job is what you go to work and do every day, whether you are a volunteer, a freelancer, or the owner of a company. By contrast, a career is a collection of jobs that compound and complement one another to advance you into increasingly responsible positions. A career designed correctly brings ever-increasing satisfaction, challenge, and intellectual achievement. You cannot apply for a career; you must build it one job at a time.

Anybody who is employed has a job, but only those with a sense of purpose have a career. A gardener can have a career, while an accountant might very well just have a job. An acquaintance, a highly placed professional, once confided, "I don't have a career. I have a lifestyle." He had no plan for further advancement, and while his job was not onerous he derived little satisfaction from it.

In this book, it is assumed that you are interested in having a career. Therefore, virtually every reference in this book to a "job" refers to a job that will contribute to the creation and advancement of your career.

Career Paths and Positioning
A career path is the sequence of jobs that advance one's career. In the long run, almost all career paths will be singular and particular. For instance, the route to CEO will have been different for each person in that position. Many highly successful individuals make radical career shifts between college and retirement. In the short- to medium-term, however, most career paths will be fairly typical: associate attorney leads to partner, staff accountant leads to senior staff accountant, sales assistant leads to account executive leads to sales manager leads to vice president of sales.

A savvy careerist is always thinking in terms of career paths and positioning: "Which job or assignments will position me for the next step on my projected career path?" Sometimes your best choice is to take an otherwise undesirable assignment if it will position you better for your next move. For example, I have known clients who took a cut in pay in order to double their salaries, or who went to a business Siberia to prove they could open a branch office and launch a new territory. Every company has established career paths and plenty of exceptions to the rules. Try to avoid assignments that will not advance you.

A classic case study in career paths is how grocers discriminated against women: Stockers were promoted to manager and managers were promoted into the parent company; checkers were promoted to head checkers, where they could stay until they died. Of course, grocers claimed a stocker had to have a Y chromosome to lift those heavy boxes. Women should be suspicious of any gender-specific career path. If you are told that the way to become an account executive at an advertising agency is by starting as a receptionist or secretary, ask if that's how the men start.

Industry vs. Function
Once again, a major assumption made in this book (and the main reason it isn't 495 pages long) is that you have a fairly good idea of what you want to do, what kind of function you want to perform and in what kind of industry.

Functions are categories of jobs, industries are categories of companies. Sales, accounting, writing and editing, mechanical design, computer programming, teaching, illustration, and production planning are all functions. Aerospace, manufacturing, banking and finance, retailing, advertising, food service, agriculture, education, and the federal government are all industries.

If you can identify at least one target function and industry, you can start your job search. If you cannot, you will not succeed in your search until you do. The main reason people launching new careers fail is the lack of a clear job target and ultimate career path. In other words, they don't get anywhere because they don't know where they are going.

In employment, "function" has a narrow definition: Functions are categories of whole jobs. In other words, full-time jobs are dedicated to performing these functions, and nothing else. If you ask a group of students to write down the functions they are interested in, someone invariably writes down something like, "working with people." While that is certainly a useful job interest, it is not a category of whole jobs. Working with people is only one aspect of a whole job. Counseling and sales are both functions, but "working with people" is not.

Here are more functions: event planning, financial analysis, personnel/human resources administration, training, recruiting, outplacement, mechanical/industrial/ electrical/chemical/software/hardware and all the other kinds of engineering, materials management and distribution, marketing, merchandising, customer service, business analysis, strategic business planning, tax management, risk management, purchasing, facilities management, client relations, public relations, operations analysis, quality assurance, computer and information systems management, records administration, credit, collections, equal employment opportunity representation, employee assistance program counseling, regulatory compliance, security, telecommunications management, labor relations, legal affairs, and so on, ad infinitum.

Finally, you need to know that a job's name is its title. Even if you know a job exists out there at some junction of function and industry, you need its name before you can do anything about it. Be careful with titles! At different companies the same job might be called controller, accounting manager, head of accounting, or full-charge bookkeeper, but there is always a world of difference between an assistant editor and an editorial assistant.

The whole point of all this is that having a fairly good idea of your desired function and industry will help you identify specific jobs and companies to target. This is the key to launching your job search in a systematic and ultimately successful manner.

Make a List of Jobs You Want

Before reading any further, get a pen and a pad of paper. First, we are going to define the specific job titles you want in specific companies or industries. Then we will add geographic considerations, company size, and other parameters that you may wish to apply to your own case. The goal is a list of well-defined job targets, or objectives.

For those of you who know exactly what you want to do, this might be terribly easy. You may have already written objective statements as precise as these:

> Assistant buyer in the management training program at Bloomingdale's

> CAD specialist for an electrical engineering company located in the Silicon Valley (preferably a start-up)

> Financial analyst position in the rating department of a public utility (energy)

Note that these are clearly defined jobs in specified industries. You need industry, function, and title to define a job, and you must identify jobs before you can develop a job target and launch a job search.

Remember, you cannot apply for a career, an industry, or a function. You can't even apply for a job if you don't know its name. "Advertising" might be all you know about your future career goal, but you cannot apply for "advertising." You'll need to learn about "assistant account executive," "copywriter," "traffic," and "assistant media buyer" before you can get past the front desk.

If your job search target is not as exact as the three objective statements above, it must be refined. Start with what you know: List the industries and functions that interest you. Some people will have a stronger and more definite list in one category than in the other. That's fine. It is also fine if you have divergent or even mutually exclusive interests. The next step is to flesh out each listed function and industry until it is as separate, distinct, and finite as possible. The more specific you get, the easier it will be to identify viable job targets or pursue further research.

For example, "real estate" is too vague. Something like "residential real estate development" or "commercial real estate leasing and sales brokerage" would be more useful. Finally, try to identify and define typical entry-level jobs in those areas.

You can't just list "work in a museum," as that only specifies an industry—and a rather diverse one at that. "Docent in a museum," or "assistant curator in a museum" would be places to start. "Docent in a modern art museum" of "assistant curator in the musical instruments section of an internationally recognized museum" would be even better. Do whatever research is necessary to identify specific job titles.

You may be sure of your desired function—maybe you are trained as a tax accountant or know that you would excel in sales—but unsure of which industry to target. You have to decide before you can identify appropriate jobs and apply for them properly.

Some industries are very difficult to break into, and students think they will have better luck if they just "apply for anything available." This approach is particularly common when applicants approach "glamour industries" such as new media, advertising, publishing, television, film, and music businesses. The problem with this strategy is that such employers are looking to hire gofers, secretaries, accountants, production assistants, promotion assistants, writers, and a host of highly skilled technicians. No employer sees her needs in terms of opportunities to offer young careerists. Employers see their needs in terms of specific jobs that need to be filled—and you must too if you want to be successful.

If your ultimate goal really is to break into a particular industry via any entry-level job, then discover and define every entry-level job in that industry. Until we get down to grouping jobs by related skills clusters later, each one of those jobs should be treated as a separate target. You most certainly can pursue several related or unrelated objectives at the same time, but each objective should be a specific job, with a title, in a specific industry.

In recent workshops with soon-to-graduate students (both undergraduate and graduate), participants in this exercise came up with these objective statements:

> First choice: laboratory assistant with biotechnology companies. Second choice: technical sales professional for other life sciences companies, such as pharmaceutical or instrumentation manufacturers.

> Assistant director of financial aid at an Ivy League school, or other college or university with both an outstanding academic reputation and sound fiscal standing.

> Chemical engineer with waste management companies, either solid waste management companies with emphasis on recycling or wastewater engineering firms with an environmental ethic. Geographical preference: New York, New Jersey, Connecticut, or California.

> Counselor position in a substance abuse prevention or recovery program, preferably working with women, including single mothers.

> Public relations or lobbyist position for a cause like Greenpeace, Amnesty International, Oxfam, or the ACLU.

> Economist for a legal consulting firm, with emphasis on real estate valuation modeling and demographic and population studies.

> A teaching position; specifically, high-school teacher of math and/or physics, within a reasonable commute of my wife's job, or in Minneapolis.

> A position as reporter for a suburban newspaper or as a writer/editor for a trade magazine or online 'zine.

> Legislative assistant to a Republican state senator. Second choice: campaign assistant for a nonincumbent in a national or statewide race. Third choice: teach English in Japan.

> A tenure-track position in the psychology department of a highly selective college or university; probably U.S., but maybe Canada, New Zealand, or Australia.

> A job, any job.

> Analyst on Wall Street. Would consider position as sales assistant or assistant trader.

> Staff accountant with a Big Five firm. Second choice: join the Air Force (may join the reserves anyway). Last choice: join my father's firm.

> Civil engineering position with major international design/building firm, hopefully with immediate overseas assignment.

Such targets will become mission statements, which can structure and guide your entire job search—starting with writing your résumé. If you cannot generate at least one target statement that is at least as specific as these (excluding "a job, any job"), then you should not try to write a résumé. There are no shortcuts to this process. A job search without an objective is like a chicken with its head cut off. It may run around for a while, but it's not going to get very far.

Still Unsure of Your Direction?
Some of you already know all about your targeted job and employer from your work experience, family background, or prior research. If you are dead certain of your career choice and what it entails, then you can skip to the next chapter, "Know Your Product."

13

14

If you don't know exactly what career or job you want to pursue, you have three choices: put off your job search while you do some research, arbitrarily decide on a job target and go after it, or pursue jobs and research careers simultaneously.

If you are unsure of your career interests, skills, or strengths, then you are not ready to write a résumé. You should consider continuing your research via aptitude testing, informational interviews (see below), career counseling (either through your college or from a private practice), reading career books (see Bibliography), and most of all, by talking to lots and lots of people about their jobs and their careers.

Although it can be successful, it is rarely a good idea to arbitrarily pick a job target just to launch a job search. You will probably get a job, but are unlikely to launch a career, and may end up truly miserable. Making an arbitrary career choice is about as sensible as making an arbitrary decision to marry someone.

If you can identify at least a few interesting jobs that would contribute to your goals, you can pursue them while refining your knowledge of industries, functions, and jobs. In fact, everyone can and should research her career options while conducting a job search. Researching careers and applying for jobs are separate, distinct tasks, but they are complementary and synergistic.

Do not be afraid to approach the job market with less than total certainty! Although you do need an initial job target, looking for employment is always a process of discovery. A rigid dedication to your initial target is not only unnecessary, but often unwise. Allow happy accidents to happen. There are jobs and careers out there that you have never dreamed of, that you won't find until you blunder onto them. Tomorrow's hot growth and glamour industry is almost certainly hiding out there somewhere now, totally

15

overlooked by the media and your peers and waiting for you to stumble onto it. The job you will love may very well never show up in the U.S. Labor Department's *Dictionary of Occupational Titles*. Although you do have to start somewhere, it's a good idea to be flexible.

Further Research to Identify Viable Jobs and Career Paths
If you want to know more about a particular career path or job, find someone who knows more about it and talk to her.

Although you can probably find someone in the job you want now, why not talk to people who have the job you want in two years, five years, or ten years? Ask them how they got into the field, what the keys were to their career advancement, what they would do differently if they had it to do over again, and what specific advice they have for you. People are almost always willing to talk about themselves, but you should still be prepared for this conversation. The more you know about the industry, the entry-level position, and the career path you want, the more someone like this can help you.

The above is a classic example of "informational interviewing," and job candidates never really outgrow the need for it. Even division presidents seek guidance and counsel from CEOs when considering a possible career move. Don't be intimidated by the term informational interviewing or its cousin, networking; these are just two more ways to say "talking to people."

Job seekers are often daunted by the notion of seeking out mentors and advisors. Start with your family, your friends, your friends' parents, your parents' friends, your professors (if appropriate), and so on. Be sure you stop by the office of career planning or the alumni office to get a list of alumni who are in the industries you want to check out. They can be a gold mine of friendly information—just call them all up and ask for advice. You don't need to buy anybody lunch, but you do need to be ready to ask a series of questions similar to the ones two paragraphs back.

Do not confuse informational interviewing with applying for a job. If you begin a meeting simply asking for information and suddenly switch to applying for a job, your credibility is shot. Besides, how strong a candidate could you be for a position if you start by asking for basic information? Informational interviewing is useful for gathering intelligence—over the phone and in personal meetings—on jobs, career paths, industries, and functions. Applying for jobs is the packaging and presentation of your candidacy for specific openings or specific types of openings; it is an entirely different process that is covered later in the book.

16

Should you find yourself invited to apply for a job as a result of an informational interview, that is another matter. If it fits your career path, go for it. Alternately, if you discover an interesting job in the course of an informational interview, be professional and ask, in as formal a tone as you can, "That sounds like a very interesting opportunity. How would I go about applying for a position like that? May I use your name?" Then, make your formal application later. Even if no opening is mentioned, leave the door open by saying something like this: "Ms. Wong, this interview has certainly been very interesting and confirms my original impressions about ___. If my other investigations and research also confirm this career direction as the best one for me, you can bet that you will be hearing back from me."

Be sure to observe standard business protocol; send everyone who helps you a brief thank-you note or card. Take every opportunity to compile leads, such as the names of people who could help you later when you launch your actual job search (see Chapter 16, "Planning and Organizing a Search"). The naïve student turns informational interviews into job interviews, but savvy careerists turn job interviews and meetings of all kinds into informational interviews. They go to interviews for jobs they have no intention of accepting in order to extend their contact network and knowledge of their industries. Never pass up an opportunity to learn more about viable career options.

Read all the magazines and newspapers that cover your future industry, whether that means *The Wall Street Journal* or *Automotive News*. (If you don't know where to look for these publications, *The Gale Directory of Publications* is a good place to start.) If you read about someone who is doing something of interest to you, call her up: "Hi. My name is Andrea Tipton and I'm a student at Brown University. I saw your name in a recent article in *Asian Antiquities* and I was wondering if you had a few moments to answer a question I have." Who could say no to that? "I'm a senior in anthropology, and I was fascinated by the dig you were on. I was wondering, how does a recent grad get a job on a dig like that?"

A way to meet seemingly impossible-to-meet people is to attend one of their lectures. During intermission or before or after the lecture, walk up to the speaker and make your inquiry. Get right to the point, however, as you probably will be able to complete only a very short exchange. In this way, you may find out how to become an NPR reporter, or how to join the foreign service, or whether you really need a degree to become a fashion designer (you don't). I think you get the point.

If you are still a student, my favorite technique for learning more about a particular job or industry is the "I am writing a paper" approach. In fact, I think any student who doesn't do this is wasting a golden opportunity. Call up the targeted individual, preferably someone like the director of recruiting in the human resources department, and find a way to ask, "What are you looking for in a new hire?"

For example, you might say, "Hi. My name is Lisa Mahdi. I am in a senior-level class in materials science at M.I.T. I understand your company has hired a lot of engineers from M.I.T." If Ms. Mahdi has done her homework, the answer will be yes. "I am preparing a report on current applications of materials science in industry, specifically concerning lighter metals and composites. What particular areas do you see as growth areas as far as your own company is concerned?" Be sure to be ready with a series of follow-up questions, as well.

Or, working with the sponsorship of a professor or your college career center, you can use a form like this to survey employers:

Senior Survey
Date
Maureen Bigshot [do your best to identify exact person by name]
VP HR [or similar-level company officer]
Company
Street Address
City, State Zip

Dear Ms. Bigshot:

I am a senior at [name your school], and I am conducting a research project to survey employers in [targeted field here]. My goal is to improve the match between employer's needs and student expectations. The result of my survey will be presented to [a study group sponsored by the career center or, alternately, any specific, senior-level class].

Would you please take just a moment to help me? If you would fill out the following questionnaire and return it in the enclosed postage-paid envelope, I would be very appreciative.

1. Does your company ever hire new college graduates?   ☐ Yes   ☐ No

2. If yes, for what positions or types of positions?

_____

_____

_____

_____

3. Which of the following skills, talents, traits, and abilities are very important to you in a new hire?

☐ A positive attitude and a good nature.

☐ The ability to answer the phone in a professional manner.

☐ The ability to take direction and follow instructions.

☐ The ability to work directly with clients.

☐ Punctuality.

☐ Knowledge of standard office suites, including word processing applications.

☐ Knowledge of standard office suites, including spreadsheet applications.

☐ Computer skills in general.

☐ The ability to learn new computer skills without formal training.

☐ Programming experience.

☐ Skills in financial and statistical analysis.

☐ Professional dress.

☐ Customer service skills, including the ability to take a complaint.

☐ The ability to make a presentation to a group.

☐ The ability to write well.

☐ Sales talent, in the sense of managing existing relationships.

☐ Sales talent, in the sense of cold-calling for new relationships.

☐ The ability to do practical research, to "find things out" on one's own.

☐ The ability to perform formal, library, database, and Internet research.

☐ Foreign languages, especially _____.

☐ Honesty and trustworthiness.

☐ The ability to make decisions with incomplete information.

☐ The ability to function on a team, and resolve minor interpersonal issues independently.

☐ Willingness to work overtime as needed.

☐ Negotiating talent.

☐ Ability to unjam a printer, copier, or fax without running for help.

☐ Ability to organize and plan work, including projects.

☐ Ability to train and motivate others.

4. Which of the above or other skills, talents, traits, and abilities are most important to you in a new hire?

20

_____

_____

_____

_____

5. What, in your opinion, are the best reasons to hire a less experienced person?

_____

_____

_____

_____

6. What do you find least appealing about new hires? What could they do better?

_____

_____

_____

_____

7. What is your "hiring cycle"? When do you first begin to look at student résumés for hiring each year's new crop of college graduates?

☐ Sep–Nov   ☐ Dec–Jan   ☐ Feb–Mar   ☐ Apr–May   ☐ Anytime

8. To which person and/or to what office do you prefer entry-level candidates apply?

Name _____

Title _____

Department _____

Address _____

9. Do you have any advice for me and my fellow students about to launch careers this year?

_____

_____

_____

_____

10. May we call you to discuss your hiring needs and processes further?

    ☐ Yes, call me at this number _____.

    ☐ It's better if you call

    Name _____

    Title _____

    Department _____

    Number _____

Thank you! Thank you! Thank you!

◉ ◉ ◉

This survey form works best with smaller organizations or with specific departments within larger ones, and won't work at all if you send it to VPs of HR at Fortune 500 companies.

You can also conduct the survey by phone. Used correctly, this survey will work for undergraduate and graduate students in any major. "Hi. My name is George Plimpton and I am in a graduate seminar in journalism at Columbia University. I'm going to be giving a presentation on the country's top sports journalists, and I was wondering if you could take a moment and tell me how you got into the business." Of course she can!

If you use this technique, be sure that you actually write the paper or give the presentation or do whatever it was you said you were going to do. You may very well be calling this person again in a few months to ask about concrete job opportunities, and she will almost certainly ask to see the paper or inquire how the presentation went. Never tell a lie in a career-related setting. If you discuss this project with the appropriate professor in advance, you should have no trouble getting him to endorse it.

You may have to do some sophisticated telephone work to reach these people, but the most effective technique is exceedingly simple: persistence. Fewer than seven attempts to complete an unsolicited telephone contact is simply not enough. (More telephone techniques are in Chapter 18, "Cold-calling, Interviews, and Closing the Deal.") Learn to call strangers fearlessly and you gain one more key to success. This will serve you well when launching a career and in advancing that career later.

You can also learn about entry-level opportunities in some industries through various publications. This is not as good as talking to people, but it can be a good place to start. If you were interested in advertising, for example, you might read *So, You Want to Be in Advertising: The WetFeet.com Insider Guide* or *How to Get Your Book Together and*

Get a Job in Advertising. An excellent introduction to thirty different industries is *WetFeet.com's Industry Insider Guide.* Public libraries are often full of such guides, although sometimes they are out of date, as well as the *Dictionary of Occupational Titles, The American Almanac of Jobs and Salaries,* and similar reference works. WetFeet.com publishes a wide variety of guides for different industries, including *Insider Guides to Jobs in the Entertainment, Biotech and Pharmaceuticals, Computer Hardware, Computer Software, Insurance, Investment Banking, Management Consulting, Mutual Funds,* and *Venture Capital* industries; you can order these guides at www.wetfeet.com. The department of employment development or its equivalent in many states publishes pamphlets describing entry-level job options in various industries. Finally, some trade and industry associations publish career pamphlets, and many provide pages at their website, that are specifically aimed at college students and recent graduates. Examples include the *Young Professionals' Aerospace Career Handbook* ($9.95; free to members) published by the American Institute of Aeronautics and Astronautics (800-682-2422) and the online pamphlet on "Careers in Public Relations," by the Public Relations Society of America, at http://www.prsa.org/careers.html, to name but two.

To find additional industry information, look in the *Encyclopedia of Associations* for appropriate organizations, call the organization's national office, and ask if they have any such pamphlets or can refer you to pertinent books or reference materials. Your research should make good use of the phone, a sympathetic reference librarian, and the special-order desk at your local bookstore. See the Appendix for more books that may be of interest to you.

CHAPTER 3

Know Your Product

YOU, THE PRODUCT

If your résumé is an advertisement and your targeted employer is the potential customer, then you are certainly the product. How saleable are you? A quick look at product development may provide the answer.

The two main types of product development are engineering-driven and market-driven. In engineering-driven development, designers and engineers allow the available technology to shape the product. They do what's easy or obvious, avoiding major obstacles or challenges. When dealing with proprietary or brand-new technologies, this can be very efficient. If you are the first one in town to invent ice cream, you don't need extra flavors. Likewise if you are the only one licensed to sell ice cream. Everybody gets vanilla, and you go to the bank just as though you had thirty-one flavors—like Henry Ford who said the consumer could have any color of car he liked, so long as it was black.

In market-driven product development, engineers go into the field and ask consumers what features they would like to see on a new widget. They then get consumers to rank those features. For example:

1. Essential "gotta have this feature, or I won't buy it"

2. Preferred "would pay an extra 15 percent for this"

3. Extra "wouldn't pay an extra 15 percent, but would like to see it"

4. Fanciful "always wished I could find a widget that did this, but I've never seen one"

The engineers then go back to the laboratory and design the product that the consumer wants. In a mature, open, or highly competitive market, market-driven product development wins every time. Guess which one wins in the job market.

Most students are an engineering-driven product. Their education molds and shapes them into predictable forms. A modern university education is not by nature particularly market-responsive; nor should it be. Universities should provide a liberal education, not vocational training. The solution is to give students tools for interfacing with the job market, rather than highly specialized job preparation that will be obsolete before their careers are even halfway launched.

The Ideal Candidate: A Market-Driven Product

Recent graduates often try to sell themselves to employers using the same value system that was important in college. This is a bad idea. The skills and achievements that were most important in college may be irrelevant to employers, or even entirely unsalable in the job market. Such students compound the mismatch between their engineering-driven education and the needs of employers.

(As counterintuitive as it may seem, a significant minority of recent college grads don't even try to sell themselves to employers at all; instead, they ask employers, "what can you promise me?" If you are selling a proprietary or brand-new, much-in-demand product, you can get away with this approach—until somebody makes it in chocolate.)

Employers often complain that students don't understand the language of business, and given my experiences lecturing in both business and academic settings, I have to concur. The language of academia is based on truth, validity, principle for principle's sake, and knowledge. The language of business is profit contribution, the bottom line, competitiveness, cost vs. benefit, and results. In the academic world, the unspoken but ever-present question is "what and whom do you know?" In business, you will be asked quite straightforwardly, "what can you do for me, my department, and my company?"

It is easy to see the potential for culture clash! Maybe you find business repugnant and are going into social services. There is a language for social services, too. Likewise for politics, the military, and so on. Remember, you cannot fight a fact; you have to deal with it. In this case, it means learning to present yourself in terms that will make your future employer most comfortable talking shop with you.

You do not need to reengineer, reeducate, or redevelop yourself to enter the job market, but you may need to reconsider exactly what it is you have to sell. You need to prepare a market-driven presentation for the product.

Most students and recent grads start by asking themselves, "What do I have to offer?" That is the wrong question. Your first question should be, "What do my targeted employers want?" The follow-up question, of course, is, "How can I show them I have it?" If you get nothing else out of this book, get this.

Employers buy skills. It's that simple. If you present the right skills in the right language, you look like a viable candidate. If you highlight the wrong aspects of your background or use language that is foreign to your employer, the hiring manager will not see a match.

This chapter will help you to predict your targeted employer's needs, and then help you scour your background for the features that relate to those needs. We will examine what employers are looking for on a résumé, and prepare to translate your candidacy into the employer's language. This process works identically for all employers, whether they are research universities, major defense contractors, or nonprofit environmental organizations.

Q: What Does the Employer Want?

A: A Skills Cluster

In the last chapter you identified and developed objectives—specific jobs in specific companies or industries. Employers are seeking candidates with the skills to excel in the positions they are hired to fill. From the employers' point of view, every job has a set of skills associated with it, and all candidates are measured against this desired skills cluster. To present distinctly different skill clusters, you will need distinctly different versions of your résumé. Jobs that are substantially similar will require the same skills cluster, and you can use the same résumé for all of them.

For example, looking back at the target listings in Chapter 2, it should be obvious that "laboratory assistant in a biotechnology company" would have a different skills cluster than "technical sales professional for a pharmaceutical company." It may not be as obvious that "sales assistant, assistant trader, or assistant portfolio manager for a Wall Street firm" should not be combined into one objective. Why? The skills cluster required for each of these brokerage jobs is different. While they are all entry-level brokerage jobs, a hiring manager is not looking for the same sort of candidate to fill all three of these openings. She is looking for a round peg for the round hole, a square peg for the square hole, and a triangular peg for the triangular hole.

To the candidate, these three jobs are related. To the employer, they are not. Many students strongly resist thinking about their potential employer's point of view, but I can assure you that the employer is not seeking a "sales assistant, assistant trader, or assistant portfolio manager." You can combine targets like these if you insist, but it isn't the best way to present your candidacy.

Go back to your list of objectives and pick your first choice. Be sure it is a specific job in a specific company or industry. Write it at the top of a fresh sheet of paper. The more narrowly you have defined your target, the easier it will be to predict an employer's needs. Your goal is to come up with the desired skills cluster, a list of the educational background, experience, talents, and skills that would be of interest to your first-choice employer.

Forget about yourself entirely and focus on your potential employer. Anticipate her needs and requirements, imagine her criteria, think her thoughts relative to your job objective. (Concentrate only on one objective for now; you can perform this exercise later for your other interests.) What is she looking for? How will she measure your candidacy? List each facet of this skills cluster down the left-hand side of your paper, leaving the right side blank for a later exercise.

Do not read ahead in the book until you finish this list. Keep your items as concrete as possible. "Good communication skills" is meaningless; "fluency in written/spoken French" is not. "Laboratory experience" doesn't tell us much; "knowledge of electron microscopy and photo spectrometry laboratory techniques" does. Be as specific as you can, and concentrate on essential skills—those skills and abilities that are critical indicators of your ability to excel in your targeted position.

You should note that some recent grads can apply for a wide range of entry-level positions with the same résumé, particularly generalists seeking positions where intelligence and aptitude are more important than specific skills. Ironically, most high-level managers, presidents, and CEOs are also generalists; they don't usually have to prepare more than one version of their résumés either. But don't label yourself a generalist to avoid learning about specific jobs or avoid considering the employer's point of view. A targeted résumé is a more powerful résumé, and a targeted, focused candidacy is a more powerful candidacy. As your actual job search progresses, your résumé(s) will evolve. Plan on it.

If after an honest effort you absolutely cannot name the specific skills needed for your future job, keep going. You probably need to do some more research, but finish this chapter first. You may find it easier after the next exercise.

Goal: demigod

Criteria:
1. *Knows several gods*

2. *Very powerful, almost all powerful*

3. . . .

4. . . .

5. . . .

6. . . .

7. . . .

8. . . .

Profile of the Ideal Candidate

In addition to the specific skills cluster that you developed above, most employers are also looking for a general set of aptitudes and personality traits. Here is a laundry list of more general attributes that may be important to your next employer:

> Ability to acquire new technical, analytical, or computer skills quickly

> Teamwork skills

> The ability to sell ideas and persuade others

> Creative problem-solving talents

> Ability to follow orders

> Leadership aptitude

> Drive, stamina, and a strong work ethic

> Intelligence

> Diligence, "stick-to-itiveness"

> Initiative

> The ability to acquire foreign languages

> Ambition

> Reliability

Some of these may be fairly specific to the job or industry you are targeting. For example, "compassion and a desire to help others" would be a preferred trait for certain jobs with certain employers, but irrelevant or negative for others. There are thousands of other attributes that your employer may be interested in, such as a good memory, the ability to read and summarize reams of written material, or the physical strength to lug around heavy sample cases.

Think long and hard about your future employer and what person she might consider ideal for the job you have targeted. Write these attributes down on the left-hand side of your page, underneath the specific skills cluster (continue to keep the right-hand side blank). Stay focused! Remember, do this for only one target at a time, one specific job in one specific industry.

The initial skills cluster and this expanded list of general attributes should combine to create a profile of your future employer's ideal candidate. Do not read ahead in the book until you have created this profile of the ideal candidate. Incidentally, it's a good idea to try ranking these attributes as essential, preferred, extra, or fanciful.

Our goal, of course, is to present you as the ideal candidate, or as close to as is honestly possible.

Note: Some students have reported that they were unable to build this profile because they simply didn't know what the prospective employer was looking for. If your preliminary research doesn't provide a clear picture, use your imagination. A profile of the ideal candidate is integral to the résumé-writing process. Do not go forward in the book without completing it. It should take no more than about twenty minutes the first time you do it. If you aren't totally happy with your list, set it aside, talk to somebody who knows about jobs in your future industry, and come back to it later.

Evaluate All Your Features before Writing Your Advertisement

The last step before you begin writing is to consider the total universe of possible résumé topics and pick the ones that will be most meaningful to your prospective employer. Here are a few categories to consider:

> Work history (work of all kinds, paid and nonpaid)

> Classroom work, special projects, and other educational experiences

> Research (consider this separately from the above)

> Publications and presentations

> Licenses and credentials

> Honors and awards

> Activities

> Sports

> Travel

> Community service

> Family background

> Languages and special skills

> All your computer skills, learned in class, at work, or on your own

Students usually consider too narrow a range of material when writing their résumés. Employers are happy to consider any concrete evidence you can present related to a skills cluster and the general attributes they want. In other words, if you have any experience anywhere in your background that relates to your profile of the ideal candidate, you should consider putting it in your résumé.

I recently heard of one candidate who prepared a résumé as part of her application for a grant in biology. She had dutifully listed her employment and her education, but failed to mention going to Africa to participate in research on gorillas with the group continuing Diane Fossey's work. She didn't think that spending months in the jungle on internationally renowned research was important, because, as she put it, "I was just a volunteer."

Candidates almost always have more to offer than they think they do.
Briefly go through each skill or attribute on your profile of the ideal candidate, using the right-hand side of the paper to jot down anything in your background indicating that you have that skill or attribute. Don't just consider whole jobs and whole classes; break each one down into tasks, responsibilities, or projects that concisely demonstrate that you have the desired skill or attribute. Also, remember that you could have gained a valuable attribute in an area of your background that is totally unrelated to your future job and industry—you could have learned how to be reliable when you held an early morning newspaper delivery job for several years, or perhaps you learned to supervise others when you worked at a sandwich shop one semester.

Employers like concrete examples, and are usually unimpressed by unsubstantiated claims. The table you are creating, listing desired skills on the left and corroborating evidence on the right, structures your background in a reader-oriented format. It helps you think about the employer's interests, and will be crucial in writing your résumé.

Catalog of Résumé Topics

While working on the exercises above, you should also make the following brief lists. These lists form your catalog of possible résumé topics which we can draw on in the coming chapters.

Work experiences. Work is a category that goes well beyond paid employment. In fact, many students and recent grads find that paid employment is not their most impressive experience. Include nonpaid work, volunteer work, part-time and temporary positions, internships, unstructured work, self-employment, odd jobs, and miscellaneous informal services you may have provided to your department or a favorite professor. Remember, you are searching your background for any and all evidence that you possess the specific skills cluster and general attributes that an ideal candidate should have. List employers, your title, and the approximate dates. Jot down how the job may support your candidacy. Be brief, however, as we will certainly come back and do more with these listings later. Here is an example:

> Professor T. L. I. Fitzsimons
> Teaching Assistant, Test Proctor, Grader (unpaid)
> Spring 2000
> Indicates scholarship, teaching ability, integrity

Classroom experiences. Of course you should list your degrees, the exact names of your theses and dissertations, and any other major academic milestones. Start by making a list of courses you have taken that relate to your targeted job objective (regardless of

your major). Then go beyond the classes. List any major papers or research projects that might be of interest to your employer. List any in-class presentations you have made over the years. Mention any academic conferences you may have presented at or even just attended. Be sure to list academic honors and accolades, including those that you think are "no big deal." Listing courses is particularly effective, as we shall see later, in technical résumés or when you have done coursework that is directly related to the line of work you are pursuing. Remember, focus on educational experiences relevant to your future employer, not those you enjoyed the most or made the best grades in. In the following example, a student explains his major in a way that is much more compelling to an employer than just listing the degree; he is speaking in the employer's language:

B.A. Economics and B.A. Geography, University of Massachusetts, 2001

- Completed six years of focused study leading to expertise in urban and land-use geography and real-estate economics. Earned two degrees simultaneously.

- Gained advanced research, analytical, and reporting skills.

Research. Even undergrads often perform highly interesting research projects. Make a list of those that might demonstrate a desired skill or attribute to your potential employer. Of course, if you are applying for a teaching or scientific position, you will want to catalog all your major research, published and unpublished. For example:

Assisted Prof. B. Smelley in her ongoing research into the forward and reverse reactions of dimerization of pyrimidine bases. Assembled and modified apparatus, conducted experiments, obtained and verified quality of data, prepared initial analysis.

Publications and presentations. This could include everything from a letter to the editor published in your school newspaper to your internationally lauded breakthrough article in *Science* magazine. Your preliminary list could include publications unrelated to your current job search, depending on how they can be presented. Make a complete list; later chapters will discuss what to include. Be sure to present the information in the standard citation format for your discipline. For example:

> The Pharmacokinetic of Vecuronium During Liver Transplantation in Humans, J. D. F. Gordon, M.D., J.E. Caldwell, F.F.A.R.C.S., M. C. Prager, M.D., M. L. Sharma, Ph.D., L. D. Gruenke, Ph.D., R. D. Miller, M.D., *Anesth Analg 2000*; 70: "S432 (abstract, presented at the IARS 64th Congress, Honolulu, Hawaii, March 13, 2000).

Licenses and credentials. Are you a CPA? NASD Series 6? Member of the Bar? Do you have a commercial passenger driver's license? Community college teaching credential? EPA certificate in hazardous materials handling? FAA single-engine aircraft pilot's license? Make a list.

Honors and awards. Even an award that you won just for having a heartbeat and being in the right place at the right time can look very impressive on a résumé. Make a complete list, and don't forget to include civic or community service awards received outside of college.

Activities. List clubs, fraternities, sororities, committees, participation in special events, speaking engagements, outside consulting engagements, and so on. Hobbies are almost never mentioned on modern résumés, but you may wish to make a list of them anyway and consider whether they are relevant later.

Sports. It's not always a good idea to list participation in sports, but it can be. Again, make the list now and we will consider the pros and cons in later chapters.

Travel. Where have you been? What did you do there? This could be of interest to an employer either as a work qualification or as a topic for casual conversation in an interview.

Community service. Almost everybody is involved in community service, whether he thinks of it in those terms or not. Include tutoring, peer counseling, fundraising and philanthropy, services in kind, and other things you do to brighten the lives of others.

Family background. Is there anything from your family background relevant to your candidacy? Suppose your mother was a foreign correspondent and you spent 12 years of your youth in various South American countries—this could be of great interest to some companies.

Languages and special skills. Fluent in Japanese? Able to untie tiny knots with your toes? This is your last chance to survey your background for potential résumé materials.

In compiling these lists you have built the foundation for your whole job search, and your résumé is practically written. It can be very fulfilling to review and catalog your life to date, so take your time with this; don't be in a rush.

Do not read ahead until you have finished this complete review of your background and how it relates to your future employer's needs.

Review

So far, you have made a list of viable job targets; answered the question, "What does the employer want?" by creating a profile of the ideal candidate; prepared a table of evidence to prove that you have the education, experience, skills, and personal attributes your future employer desires; and reviewed the accomplishments of your lifetime.

In the process, you have learned the basics of career planning and probably have begun to think about your career more seriously—and more realistically. You are now ready to make an articulate presentation of your candidacy, in a résumé and in person.

You've already done the hard work; everything else in this book is easy.

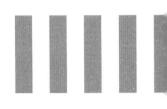

Writing Résumés, Technical Résumés, & Curricula Vitae

CHAPTER 4

The Structure and Style of a Modern Résumé

STANDARD COMPONENTS

A résumé doesn't have to follow any hard and fast rules. Legally you can put any information on it that you want, and should include any information you think will increase your chances of being selected for an interview, hired for a job, designated to win a grant, chosen for a faculty position, or whatever your goal may be. And just as with regular advertising, there is no rule of résumé-writing that cannot be broken with good cause.

Before you go out there and make a pie chart of the economic value of your skills or introduce your résumé with a long story about your first dog, Sparky, you should know that there is considerable consensus on what exactly a résumé or curriculum vitae should look like and the type of information it ought to contain. Every hiring manager in the world has a drawer full of weird résumés that she has collected over the years, but all of the people who wrote those résumés work somewhere else, if at all.

In this chapter and the seven that follow, we will consider the standard business résumé; later chapters will cover technical résumés and curricula vitae. "Business résumé" is perhaps a misnomer, as it refers to the most popular résumé style in the world, the standard for job applications in everything from nonprofit charities to political espionage.

This book does not cover functional résumés or narrative biography-style vitae. Narrative biography vitae are used only by senior executives, major political and social figures, and people on the speech and lecture circuit. For examples of functional résumés or narrative biography-style vitae, see my book *Asher's Bible of Executive Résumés and How to Write Them*. Functional résumés are structurally different from curricula vitae and standard chronological résumés. They are best used by job seekers who are attempting a major career switch, or those with a diverse or spotty work history or something to hide. Although they can be very clever and useful documents, they are not what many employers will expect from qualified college graduates. If you want to learn how to write them anyway, read Yana Parker's *Damn Good Résumé Guide*. There are also examples in my book, *The Overnight Résumé*.

It is important that your résumé have the right look as well as the right information. This book is designed to guide you through creating your résumé one component at a time, with clear descriptions of how each component should look. Chapter 10 shows how to pull it all together, and Chapter 11 is filled with samples illustrating these points.

The modern résumé is designed to provide relevant information in the order the employer wants it and in language she can grasp and use immediately. You will learn how to accomplish this component by component. If you follow these guidelines and think as you compose, design, and edit your résumé, you will create a document that is a showcase for your candidacy.

The components of a standard business résumé are:

> Heading

> Skills profile or objective (optional)

> Education

> Experience

> Activities and extras (optional)

Two to five years after your last degree, education will usually be given less weight than experience. This means you have two to five years to capitalize on your education before it ceases to be a salable aspect of your background. Activities and extras can be mixed in under education or pulled together and presented at the end. The skills profile has taken the place of a firmly specified job objective, although some employers prefer to see an objective and some schools ban both profiles and objectives from résumés used for on-campus interviewing. We will debate that in Chapter 6, "Profile: Winning in the First Ten Lines." We will also discuss résumé strategies that are particularly useful for students and recent grads, such as adding a section for SPECIAL PROJECTS, or separating out activities and featuring them under EXPERIENCE.

As a general rule, experience should be presented in reverse chronological order, which just means that your current or most recent job is listed first, the prior job next, and so on backward in time. There are many good reasons to organize your experience out of chronological order, as we shall see.

Use Insiders' Language

Use the language of those who are already employed in your target industry. This includes acronyms, universally understood abbreviations, and phrases that are peculiar to that industry.

Don't be afraid to use commonly understood acronyms in your résumé. For instance, some business terms, such as CPA, ROI, CEO, and P&L, are almost universally understood. It is unnecessary to write out these terms in full. Besides, why slow your reader down reading words that do not sell your candidacy?

Jargon that identifies you as an insider is a fine example of using the employer's language. No one in employment benefits would write out Employee Retirement Income Security Act; everybody in that role simply says "ERISA." Some acronyms and abbreviations are so common in a specific industry that they are better known than the terms they represent. Everyone in retail knows what a SKU is, but few could tell you what it stands for (it stands for stock keeping unit and is pronounced "skew").

On the other hand, you should avoid jargon unique to your college or former employers; "the C-5 cluster of required courses" is likely to be an unintelligible reference outside the ivy-covered walls of Elite College.

Résumé Ingredients Rule

You may be a product, but your résumé is not a label for a can of soup. The FDA does not require that you list the ingredients of your education and experience in order of volume or by weight. You have the right to present your label of "ingredients" in any way that you choose, including deciding what information needs to be on the label at all, and in what order.

You may have been a clerical assistant at your last job, but you are applying for an opening as sales assistant at your first-choice company. Your description of that clerical job had better go on at length about client contact, public relations, problem solving, and serving as a buffer between the executives and clients. All of this may have been only 15 percent of your duties, but you can devote 85 percent of your résumé to these relevant duties before you bother to mention organizing and filing—briefly if at all.

As you construct your résumé, keep this principle in mind: Organize the information on your résumé in accordance with your desired impact on the reader. This should govern which information you present and the order in which you present it. Here is the rule, stated another way:

Put your information in order of interest to the targeted reader.

If you follow the instructions in this book, you will soon have entirely too much material for your résumé, even if you have never worked a day in your life. This Résumé Ingredients Rule is a very handy guideline, a tool to use in deciding what to include on your final draft.

Not a Place for Modesty

A résumé is no place for modesty. If you don't tell your potential employer about your skills and accomplishments, how will they know? They want to know how wonderful you are! If you fail to discuss all of your strengths, you are depriving employers of the very information they want most.

If you are shy, reticent, or self-deprecatory, you must overcome these personality traits long enough to let your qualifications be known. On some college campuses, it is anathema to brag about your intellectual feats or other successes. On a résumé, however, it is de rigueur. Force yourself to take some credit. Imagine how your closest relative or friend might describe your academic and work accomplishments.

Remember that you are just presenting the facts, the employer is very interested in the facts you are presenting, and the job will go to someone less qualified if you don't talk about who you are and what you can do. Modesty in a résumé does no service to anyone.

Never, Never, Never Tell a Lie

At the other end of the spectrum from the overly modest are those who make claims on their résumés that are unsupported by fact. It is extremely easy for employers to check the basic facts on a résumé, especially education, official job titles, dates of employment, and salary. Reference checking is a sort of hobby for many employment professionals, a game at which they take pride in excelling.

In the end, lying may be worse for you if you succeed than if you had been caught in the act. Your résumé almost invariably becomes part of your permanent personnel file; you have no job security whatsoever as long as your permanent file contains an out-right lie. Most companies have few ironclad personnel policies, but they almost always address the issues of theft and lying. Most companies will discharge you at once if they discover an act of theft or intentional misrepresentation, even after years of faithful service. It's not worth it.

In any case, lying shows a failure of imagination. Any problem you feel compelled to lie about can be solved another way. If you need some experience related to your targeted industry, you don't need to make some up, go get some! Volunteer, ask to go in and observe, get an internship, or whatever. If you need one more class to finish that degree, use one of the strategies presented in Chapter 7, "Education: 1001 Ways to Sell Education." You can present your education in a positive light without lying about your degree. Then finish that class. If you need some more activities to demonstrate your well-rounded personality, go out there and get involved. It's never too late to add some true credentials to your résumé, and it's never a good idea to lie.

Résumé English Grammar: Same as It Ever Was

Résumé grammar is the same as any other English grammar, except that the first-person nominative pronouns, most articles, and most helping and being verbs are omitted. First-person nominative pronouns are I and we. Articles are a, an, and the. Helping and being verbs are have, had, may, might, am, is, are, was, and were.

Résumés are written in the first person, which means that you, the candidate, will be the subject of most of the sentences. If you are still employed, your ongoing duties will be in the present tense, and completed projects will be in the past tense. Your first draft can read just like a letter to a friend. For example:

I manage the box office for the I.Q. Zoo, the largest trained-animal show in the world. I supervise six cashiers. I set up the cash drawers, balance cash-to-sales, and prepare the bank drop daily. Occasionally I dress up in a gorilla suit and play the piano. Some of my accomplishments are that I trained the baboon to wait tables, allowing the elimination of two paid positions, and I taught the zebra to do algebra, gaining national press coverage.

Next, take out the first-person nominative pronouns and as many articles and helping verbs as possible. You may need to combine, rearrange, or otherwise adjust some of the sentences slightly to retain their meaning. Here is the résumé version of the above paragraph:

Manage the box office for the I.Q. Zoo, the largest trained-animal show in the world. Supervise six cashiers, set up cash drawers, balance cash-to-sales, prepare bank drop daily. Occasionally dress up in gorilla suit and play piano. Accomplishments: trained the baboon to wait tables, eliminating two paid positions, and taught the zebra to do algebra, gaining national press coverage.

Finally, incorporate design considerations (discussed in full later on). For example, this is an excellent way to show the break between ongoing duties and special accomplishments:

Manage the box office for the I.Q. Zoo, the largest trained-animal show in the world. Supervise six cashiers, set up cash drawers, balance cash-to-sales, prepare bank drop daily. Occasionally dress up in gorilla suit and play piano. Accomplishments:

- Trained the baboon to wait tables, eliminating two paid positions.

- Taught the zebra to do algebra, gaining national press coverage.

Passive verb constructions are to be avoided (pun intended). Avoid phrases like "responsible for . . ." and "duties included . . ." Use hard-driving language, avoid wordiness and circumlocutions, eliminate most adverbs and adjectives, eschew obfuscation, and start each sentence with an active verb. Keep your résumé spicy and fast-paced. Never say "served on a committee to . . ." when you can say "marshalled support for . . ." Never say "handled" when you can say something like "orchestrated." Use vivid, evocative language whenever possible, although the language in your résumé shouldn't overpower the accomplishments and experience being presented.

Remember: Since the first person pronoun, "I," is understood, you can start each sentence with an action verb. On this page is a table of effective résumé verbs. You should not limit yourself to these words, but consider them when replacing more mundane terms.

42

Achieve	Convert	Finalize	Orchestrate	Select
Act	Coordinate	Forecast	Organize	Sell
Administer	Counsel	Found	Originate	Simplify
Advise	Create	Generate	Overhaul	Solve
Allocate	Decrease	Guide	Oversee	Spearhead
Analyze	Delegate	Head	Plan	Specify
Approve	Demonstrate	Identify	Prepare	Start
Assess	Design	Improve	Present	Stimulate
Assign	Develop	Increase	Prioritize	Streamline
Attain	Devise	Initiate	Produce	Strengthen
Audit	Diagnose	Inspect	Project	Supervise
Balance	Direct	Install	Promote	Survey
Calculate	Document	Institute	Propose	Teach
Chair	Draft	Instruct	Quantify	Test
Clarify	Edit	Integrate	Recommend	Train
Classify	Eliminate	Interview	Reconcile	Translate
Coach	Enable	Investigate	Recruit	Troubleshoot
Collaborate	Engineer	Introduce	Reduce	Update
Compile	Enhance	Market	Recruit	Upgrade
Compose	Enlist	Marshaled	Reorganize	Verify
Conceive	Ensure	Maximize	Research	Write
Conceptualize	Evaluate	Monitor	Resolve	
Conduct	Expand	Motivate	Revitalize	
Consolidate	Expedite	Negotiate	Schedule	
Contribute	Facilitate	Obtain	Screen	

Length

No matter how complex your background is, if you are a college student or recent college graduate, your résumé should be exactly one page long. The reason for this is simple: universal convention. If you submit a two-page résumé or otherwise deviate from this norm, you are inviting the round file treatment for your application. Employment managers from coast to coast and in all industries agree that an entry-level résumé should be one page long. Résumés for graduate students and curricula vitae are often much longer than this, but entry-level business résumés and technical résumés are not. (There will be exceptions, however, and there are even a few two-page entry-level résumés among the samples in this book.)

If you have too much information to fit onto one page, and you are positive that all of it is relevant and of interest to your potential employer, you can offer to present it on request. The résumé you initially submit, however, should still be one page long. You can refer to additional information, enclosed or to be presented later, with listings like these:

HONORS & ACTIVITIES:
List of undergraduate honors and activities provided on request.

ADDITIONAL SALES EXPERIENCE:
Prior sales experience described on request.

RESEARCH:
See addendum, "Research and Publications."

Promising such data is often more impressive than actually providing it, implying that there is more to you than could possibly fit onto one page.

Of course, you should always keep a list of impressive information that didn't make it onto your résumé, so that you can bring it up in the course of natural conversation during an interview.

Later in your career, after you have ten years of experience or a diversified and complex background, a two-page résumé will be perfectly acceptable. In fact, in most industries a two-page résumé is standard for any candidate with several years of management experience. When you get ready to write that mid-career résumé, read my book, *The Overnight Résumé* and if you do really well read *Asher's Bible of Executive Résumés*.

Layout and Presentation
In general, your résumé should resemble the samples in this book. The past 10 to 15 years have seen only four major changes in business résumés: the evolution of objective statements into profiles (as covered in the next chapter), the removal of dates from the left margin to the right, the advent of word processing and laser printing as the standard for presentation, and the rise of the e-mail résumé. Regarding this fourth change, the principles of a good résumé still apply—the only change is how you send it (and you'll still need good-looking, paper backups).

English readers read from left to right, so the left margin is an area of tremendous importance. Twenty years ago, a candidate's stability and work ethic were measured by longevity, and dates were featured along the left margin. As dates have become less important to employers, and less of a selling point for candidates, they have retreated from this position of prominence. They are now relegated to the right margin, and sometimes omitted altogether.

44

Line up all headings to the left margin! Headings in the center of the page make your résumé hard to read efficiently. Do everything you can to ensure that your résumé conveys information easily.

Your résumé should be word-processed and laser-printed on 8 ½ x 11 paper. If you do not have access to a computer, call the campus computer center or a copy shop (many have computer services). Although it doesn't matter how you compose your rough draft, you will need to see what it will look like before you can edit it into its final form. Design is a very important part of résumé presentation, and you will not be able to see the actual design until you have specified all the fonts and type sizes. Incidentally, avoid the temptation to use microscopic type so that you can cram more onto one page. The standard size is a twelve-point font, eleven point is okay, and ten-point type is probably the smallest you will want to use on a résumé.

You should consider the full set of design features, including variable type size, italics, boldface, and so on. Incorporate these features into your design as you compose your résumé. Do not mix too many different forms of emphasis on the same page or your presentation will look busy. The final product should not resemble a piece of junk-mail with screaming headlines and words underlined, in italics, underlined and in italics. . . . I think you understand what to avoid. Later chapters will discuss how you can use these features to control emphasis—and what the reader sees. Think about design constantly. Ask yourself, "How should this look?" as you are writing. Think like a poet. Be aware of how the material will look on the page.

Long before you print your résumé, you should make a special trip to a paper supplier to buy a heavier weight of paper. Most copy shops carry nice-looking paper, but it is almost always too lightweight. Several years ago, *The Wall Street Journal* noted a study in which the same résumés were printed on different colors and weights of paper. The correlation between paper weight and selection was conclusive; a heavy paper denoted a more serious candidate. Unless you are in the arts, keep the paper color to beige, grey, or white. The nice thing about white is it can be faxed, scanned, and copied with no loss of clarity. There are many interesting types of paper being manufactured today, but before you use one of the more exotic ones, get advice from your career counselor.

Review: What Your Résumé Can Do for You

As you compose your résumé in the coming chapters, keep in mind the functions you want it to perform. We will be constructing your résumé one component at a time: heading, profile, education, experience, and activities and extras. Each component should contribute to the efficacy of your résumé, or you should rewrite it until it does.

Once again, here is what your résumé should be able to do for you:

> Prepare you mentally to present a strong and focused candidacy

> Win an interview in direct, head-to-head competition with the résumés of many other highly qualified candidates

> Structure the interview in your favor

> Remind the interviewer of your best points

> Justify any hiring decision to third parties

Good luck, and good writing!

CHAPTER 5

Heading: Make It Easy to Reach You

COMMUNICATIONS IN A MODERN WORLD

Your résumé's heading is more important than you might think. For one thing, it is critical that prospective employers be able to reach you easily. No matter how impressive your résumé is, no employer will want to do any research to contact you. They need at least your name, mailing address, e-mail address, and phone number. Most recruiters will call or e-mail rather than write, and most will call or e-mail only once. If you consider yourself a job applicant at all, you absolutely must have a working e-mail address and telephone line with a reliable message system in operation at all times. If your roommates seem to have selective amnesia or your answering machine has electronic Alzheimer's or your e-mail server has too much personality, you have a serious problem.

If you need to, rent a voicemail service, get a cell phone, or adopt a standalone e-mail address for the duration of your job search, and list this contact data on your résumé. In addition to e-mail and home, office, cell, and voicemail phones, you may consider listing a fax number. E-mail and fax contacts are particularly important for international applications, as these prospective employers need to be able to reach you without worrying about time differences. E-mail is in fact becoming the medium of first choice for contacting job seekers everywhere and anywhere in the world. By the way, if your screen name is foxxx or randyman or suprfrky or drugsRus, it's time to change it to something more mature, at least until you get a job.

If you list a communication method on your résumé, it must be viable. Listing the message and fax numbers at Red Eye's All Night Copy Emporium is of little use if you fail to check with Red Eye himself at least once a day. In this increasingly international and instantaneous world, listing "24-hour" next to a message or fax number is a good idea. Anything you can do to make it easier to reach you is probably a good idea. I even heard of one student who purchased a toll-free "800" number for the duration of his job search.

Permanent, Temporary, Local, and Mailing Addresses

In addition to multiple phone numbers, student résumés commonly list more than one address. Anytime you can list an address in or near the community where a targeted job opening is, you enhance your candidacy. Who would believe that an applicant from Barnard College in New York City really wants a job in Atlanta unless she listed a permanent address in Georgia? On the other hand, if you are a Barnard student from Atlanta looking for a job in New York, you'd better see if you can come up with a New York City address, even if you have to borrow one from a friend.

You can use the addresses and phone numbers of family members, close friends, and even mailbox rental services to prove your geographic attractiveness. (Incidentally, you can also choose whether to list your high school for the same reason.) Unless you have the same last name as the person receiving your mail, it is a good idea to send a postcard to the person's local post office alerting them that you will be receiving mail at the address, or list your address with a c/o designation, as in: c/o Asher. Also, remember that your Aunt Marlene may be no more reliable than Red Eye when it comes to letting you know right away when you get a letter or a call.

Demonstrating an investment or substantiating an interest in the community where the job is makes you a much more attractive candidate than someone who may be applying for jobs from coast to coast with little idea of the differences between Spokane and Jacksonville.

What's In a Name?

You are not required to use the full name that appears on your birth certificate. If everyone in the world knows you as "Buddy Watkins" rather than "William Langhorn Zebulon Watkins," it's better to call yourself Buddy. Likewise, if your name is terribly difficult for others to remember or pronounce, you may wish to list a nickname in quotation marks or parentheses, for example: Talalkaiam "Tom" Saif or Talalkaiam (Tom) Saif. Avoid listing your names with just initials, as in: F. K. R. Tong. This technique conceals your gender, which will make employers reluctant to contact you because they don't know if they are calling for a Mr. or a Ms. If you choose to use a name with an unknowable gender, then place a small Mr. or Ms. after the name, in parentheses, as in: F. K. R. Tong (Mr.). If an employer doesn't know your gender, they will be uncomfortable calling you, and that discomfort may cost you an opportunity.

Note that all of these techniques are designed to elicit the maximum possible interest from your résumé reader. Remember the Résumé Ingredients Rule: Select and organize the information on your résumé in accordance with desired impact.

Titles for the Document

You do not need to title your résumé RESUME; the document should obviously be a résumé. You can, however, title a curriculum vitae CURRICULUM VITAE; doing so is often subtly impressive. In most cases, however, your name will serve as the only title, as you will see in the examples later in this chapter.

Electronic résumés, however, usually begin with the word Resume (no accents) and end with the words End resume, sometimes in parentheses. You'll see more on this later.

Half-Life of a Résumé: Longer Than You Think

You want all the data at the top of your résumé to be valid for a least the duration of your job search. A résumé that lists your college address becomes useless if you are still looking for work after graduating, and all your prior effort will have been squandered. Be sure that you have valid lines of communication for every contingency during your job search.

Résumés can last a long time, especially when you have unusual talents. I know of one candidate who borrowed a friend's phone number and address and sent out a few dozen copies of his résumé. A year later this friend was still getting a few straggling calls and letters about the candidate. The tragic part of this story was that the candidate had moved on to another state, still unemployed. He left no forwarding number with his friend and undoubtedly missed several viable job opportunities.

I know of another recent graduate who applied for several top jobs in Washington, D.C. She didn't get a single call before graduation, so she left on a cross-country driving trip with her husband. A prestigious public agency called her with a job offer, but no one in her family knew how to reach her for several days. During that time, the job offer expired.

Make sure that everyone associated with your job search knows how to reach you at all times.

Examples

Here are a few examples of résumé headings. Note the border-to-border demarcation line underneath each heading. This design device allows the reader to skip the heading altogether, focusing instead on your skills, education, and experience.

Look over the samples and then write out your own heading. Do not spend a lot of time on this as you can always change it later. You have much more important things to spend your creative energies on than creating fancy designs for phone numbers.

BARTON FREDERICK JEFFERSON III
bartnosimpson@aol.com

East Coast Address:
190 Eldridge Street, #4-S
New York, New York 10002
(212) 555-4179

West Coast Address:
6608 Hollywood Boulevard
Hollywood, California 90028
(213) 555-8506

[Résumé starts here; reader starts here.]

49

◎ ◎ ◎

ROXANNE L. MORIARTY
Roxy11@hawaii.net

Local Address:
270 Holokai Place
Honolulu, HI 96825
Message: (808) 555-6210

Mailing Address (until June):
196 Framingham Street, #1-B
Cambridge, MA 02125
(617) 555-3063

Permanent Address:
2238 East Circle Drive
Palos Verdes, CA 90274
(310) 555-2931

[Résumé starts here; reader starts here.]

◎ ◎ ◎

JORDAN T.W. ROBERTS
boberts@sunnyu.edu

Sand Towers, Apt. 623
38011 S. Old Shipwreck Road
Ft. Lauderdale, Florida 33310

Telephone: (305) 555-7192
24-hour Message: (305) 555-3928
24-hour Fax: (305) 555-7193

[Résumé starts here; reader starts here.]

CHAPTER 6

Profile: Winning in the First Ten Lines

STAYING IN THE "YES" PILE

To excel at résumé writing, you have to understand how employers read résumés. Typically, they sit down with a pile of them and make the first cut by skimming, or reading as little of each résumé as possible to assess whether that candidate meets the minimum qualifications. Those that don't are relegated to oblivion. They might elicit a polite but vague letter of acknowledgment, but basically they are not reviewed by human eyes again.

This process of skimming means that no matter how many hours and weeks you labor over your résumé, it will be judged, initially at least, in as few as three seconds! Recently, while waiting for a meeting to begin, I watched a corporate recruiter sort a stack of applicants for a specific opening. Quite a few résumés were rejected in three seconds, a few were reviewed for as long as two minutes, but the overwhelming majority were assessed in five seconds to forty-five seconds—less than a minute per person.

That's just the first cut. There may be three or more cuts before a single candidate is called for an interview. In Part III of this book, you will learn how to make sure that your résumé bypasses that sorting pile entirely. In any case, no matter whose desk your résumé lands on, you should always expect a rather cursory initial examination.

Generally, résumés are really not "read" until an employer is ready to decide whom to interview. Interviewers don't like wasting time on unqualified applicants, so the decision of whom to interview is usually made by the hiring manager or someone who understands the job opening intimately. The earliest cuts, however, might be performed by the company's most inexperienced employee. This is not a good business practice, but it is done every day.

Clearly, the faster you can establish your credentials, the better. There are two main ways to make the information on your résumé more accessible: Put a profile of your skills and qualifications or keywords at the top, or design your whole résumé very carefully so that desired information can be picked out easily. Of course, whenever possible you should do both. We will be reviewing design considerations throughout the book; this chapter covers ways to deliver crucial information in the first few lines of your résumé.

First Impressions: Objective Statement vs. Skills Profile or Keywords Lists

Since employers don't read résumé headings, the section directly underneath the heading will be read first. This fact alone makes it the single most important section of your résumé. The first rule, then, is obvious: Don't put anything negative or weak right at the top of your résumé.

Until recently, this first section was almost always reserved for an objective statement specifying which position or type of position the candidate was seeking. Here is an example:

Objective: A position as staff accountant with a major public accounting firm.

Such a statement might help someone sort your résumé, but it does little to establish your credentials and qualifications. In addition, the last clause, "with a major public accounting firm," is at best superfluous and at worst, disqualifying. The people to whom you mail your résumé know who they are. Duh!

Even worse, however, is the fact that objective statements tend to degenerate into shopping lists of demands, as in this sample:

> Objective: A challenging and rewarding position with a progressive company that rewards outstanding performance with rapid advancement and continuing opportunity for personal and professional growth.

Do you want any potential employer's very first impression of you to be a list of demands? Admittedly, this last example is almost a parody of bad writing, but every phrase in it is common in objective statements written by real job applicants. Objectives reached their nadir with lists of both immediate and long-term goals. Can't you just imagine an employer reading all that and then saying, "That's nice. Now, what can you do for me?"

Another great sin of objective statements is that they may not identify a job target at all. Read that last objective again. What is the candidate applying for?

I am most bothered by a more subtle problem. Objective statements are written from the wrong point of view. These statements are all about what the applicant wants, not what the employer wants. Your objective is not going to be that interesting to an employer. She wants to know about her objective: To find and hire a candidate who has the skills cluster required to excel in the position.

Instead of an objective, begin with a skills profile or a keywords list, a quick summary of your credentials and qualifications written specifically to target the skills cluster your potential employer is seeking. Such a list will establish that you possess the ideal candidate traits in the first ten lines; this means:

> Your résumé can be sorted into the "yes" pile without even being read.

> Your résumé can be routed to the hiring authority without even being read.

> When it is read, it can be reviewed with sincere interest right from the top.

Although they haven't caught on with everyone, profiles have for the most part replaced objectives on résumés. A profile is a compelling opener that can perform all the same functions as an objective, plus many more. For one thing, the information a potential employer desires the most is immediately accessible. The ideal profile is a combination of skills claims and experience claims. Here is a sample profile:

SPECIALTY:

T.E.S.L. & T.E.F.L.
Considerable success teaching students lacking in first language skills. Intern with Los Angeles Unified School District. Experience with students of Laotian, Vietnamese, Bosnian, Kosovar, and Central-South American origin, children and adults. Proficient with audiolabs and fully computerized classrooms. Can customize or write new curricula to meet class challenges. Fluent in Spanish; proficient in Nepali and Quechua.

Problems with Profiles
As useful as profiles can be, they do have a few drawbacks. First, you need to know as much as possible about the targeted job and the targeted reader in order to write a compelling profile. Often, candidates only have vague ideas about the jobs they are applying for, making it difficult for them to write an effective profile.

Second, the profile may limit your résumé to the area targeted in the profile. Students often want to be able to use one résumé for a lot of different applications, or to approach a company about one position without excluding themselves from consideration for another. In these cases a profile can be too delimiting.

Third, employers and college employment counselors rightfully complain that they often see profiles full of vacuous self-promotions, self-aggrandizements, and other fluff. This is the simplest problem to solve—just use the tips in this chapter to craft a substantive profile.

Finally, a few college placement services ban both objectives and profiles from résumés used in the on-campus interview process and the college's résumé bank or annual résumé book. The main rationales for this are: a desire for all the résumés to look the same; to maintain a "level playing field"; the fear that students might exclude themselves from consideration by potential employers who read and use the databank or book; and a dislike for the sort of fluff mentioned above.

I spoke with one MBA student who ignored the ban on profiles and got her résumé into the program's résumé book without a hitch. She explained that the profile was needed in her case to explain her narrow area of interest, radio station management. In the end, she believes that she caught the eye of her current employer precisely because she did have a profile. Of course, you can always comply with your career office's résumé guidelines and then use an alternate version for your self-directed search efforts.

At the least, you need a solid idea of your career direction to use a profile effectively. I usually suggest that everyone write one because even if you decide to delete it from your final draft, it can be used almost verbatim in cover letters. Besides, the act of writing one forces you once again to think about that potential employer and to anticipate his requirements. Writing a profile clarifies your thinking, helps you develop job-search strategies, and contributes to good interviewing later.

How to Write a Profile

A profile is your claim that you have a certain set of related skills. The more closely your profile resembles the profile of the ideal candidate you wrote in Chapter 3, the stronger your candidacy will be. Go back to your notes on the ideal candidate's profile and write a new profile, this time for yourself.

The profile section of a résumé can have any of the following headings. Just pick one, write it on your paper, and keep going. You can always change it later if you decide that another is more appropriate for you and your background.

> PROFILE

> OBJECTIVE (yes, same old heading, but new information after it)

> PROFESSION

> INTERESTS

> AREAS OF INTEREST

> STRENGTHS

> AREAS OF SKILL & KNOWLEDGE

> KEYWORD LIST or KEYWORDS LIST

> SKILLSET

Underneath that, write a subheading that describes your functional area of interest, experience, or knowledge, such as "Sales/Business Development/Account Management" or "Corporate Accounting." If you are sure of a particular job objective, you can sometimes just list the title straight out: "Production Assistant." Be sure to present your background with a slant to your future career direction. You can easily say: "INTEREST: Real Estate Sales" even if your entire sales background is in retail stores. In fact, you can follow the INTEREST heading with anything whatsoever.

The paragraph that follows, the narrative of your profile, should answer this question: What educational background, experience, skills, talents, personality traits, and other attributes do you have that will be of direct interest to the targeted employer for the targeted job? If you did the exercises in Chapter 3, you have basically done this already; if not, you can do it right now. Just write out what you have to offer relative to the targeted job.

Remember, you are the subject of these sentences. "I have the ability to," "I have experience in," "I can," or "I have a knowledge of." Avoid words like "expertise," "exceptional," and "outstanding," and adjectives and adverbs in general. Tell what you have to offer, but don't be pompous or grandiose. Be as concrete and factual as you can. Do not claim any skill you do not have or overrepresent the skills you do have, but tell the employer what you can do for him.

"Expert in small-business accounting" is almost unbelievable, but if you took a few accounting courses, surely you could say this:

> Knowledge of A/P, A/R, P/R, G/L accounting, state/local/federal taxation, and cashflow analysis. Some knowledge of how to conduct business valuation studies. Experience with several accounting and spreadsheet applications. Can set up new files and accounts. Always available for overtime as needed.

There's no fluff to that. This is all information of material interest to an employer.

Suppose you have no business background at all, and you're saying to yourself, "This looks great for business majors, but what about me?" You, too, can make a profile, using your knowledge of the targeted field and your knowledge of yourself. To spur your thinking, review the senior survey on p. 18, which lists skills of interest to employers. Then, think carefully about what skills, attributes, abilities, and traits your future employer would be interested in. Finally, survey your entire background for experiences that offer evidence that you possess the skills employers want. Remember, often the skills you want to discuss were obtained in out-of-classroom experiences. As an example, here is the profile of a philosophy major applying for a position as a marketing assistant.

55

> Ability to organize a large mass of information, identify important items from distracting and irrelevant data, and present pertinent findings orally or in writing. Knowledge of statistical analysis gained from classes in social sciences. Ability to write persuasively, with attention to connotations and subtext. Some understanding of demographics and psychographics. Able to work independently, and make decisions based on incomplete data sets. Proven talent for producing in a deadline environment where accuracy is a must. Computer skilled.

No matter what your major, it is your knowledge of your future employer and your knowledge of yourself that will allow you to write a good profile. If you don't know enough about your potential employers, you need to do some informational interviewing and visit with your career counselor.

One problem with profiles is they sometimes sound a little fluffy. Imagine someone else reading your profile. What would sound boastful to her? Take that part out or rewrite it. With a little work, your profile will be free of fluff and it will be a highly efficient presentation of exactly the information your employer is interested in reading first.

Next, rank the information in the order of greatest interest to your potential employer. Of course you cannot know this exactly, but your job as a résumé writer is to imagine it. Then rewrite your profile to present the information with the most interesting first. Keep it short! Ten lines is almost too long. Do not be a perfectionist about this. Just write an acceptable draft and go on to the next chapter.

The fastest way to establish your credentials and qualifications is just to hand them over, and a profile section accomplishes that. The fact that employers skim résumés becomes an advantage, rather than a liability, when you have a good, tight profile. Remember that even if you decide the profile is not appropriate in your particular case, you will have learned something just by writing it. Being able to articulate exactly what you have to offer in just a few sentences is a valuable talent for any job seeker.

Profile What You Have to Offer

If you are unable to project exactly which job you will be discussing with a particular employer, write a more general profile of what you have to offer, or what you think will be of interest to that particular employer, without relating the information to a particular position. If you can target the job as well as the employer or industry, your profile is likely to be more compelling and motivational to the employer. Sometimes résumé writers find that the process of résumé-writing itself helps to clarify their goals. Do not allow yourself to be cowed by the process of writing a profile; just plow on through and write one.

Remember that employers will know you are a student or recent graduate. They will also know that many of your skills claims will be theoretical, i.e., you studied this in school but have never done it "for real." They know this, so relax and be sure to profile what you have to offer, even if it is something you "just" studied. Use these qualifiers: "Exposure to," "Some understanding of," "Proficient in" or "Basic proficiency in," "Knowledge of" or "Basic knowledge of." This lets them know that you are not trying to claim advanced expertise, but that you are ready to attempt to use these skills on the job. Be brave. It is expected.

It May Be Entry-Level to You . . .

By now you should understand why you would never use the term "entry-level" any-where on your résumé: It is the wrong point of view. A position may be entry-level to you, but to the hiring manager it is just another opening that needs to be filled. Hiring managers are looking for talent, not warm bodies with a sheepskin. There are no unimportant positions as far as hiring managers are concerned; no proving grounds that exist for the sole purpose of testing your potential for later, more important, positions. Every entry-level position requires performance in that position, and the hiring manager is looking for evidence of aptitude for that position.

Students have more talents than they may realize. A technical understanding of English grammar is appreciated by employers, the ability to write a logical report incorporating financial data is valued, any experience working with clients in a professional business environment is desired, the ability to plan and organize a project is sought after, and the ability to work closely with others on a team project is a big plus. Whether your major is religion or biomechanics, you have skills to offer an employer.

Profile Samples

Here are some examples, all from the résumés of seniors, recent grads, and grad students. Note the range of different approaches to profile presentation:

OBJECTIVE	**Environmental Consulting, Civil Engineering, Grade Engineering**
PRIMARY SKILLS:	Stream and small basin discharge analysis.
	Erosion and slope control management.
	Environmental rules and regulations.
	Leveling and topographic mapping.
	Aerial photo interpretation and analysis.
	Manual and computer cartography.
	Planning analysis and principles.

57

⊙ ⊙ ⊙

EXPERTISE **Training & Development Management**
Effective combination of strengths: technical knowledge of human performance improvement theory and practice, some experience in training and corporate education, some management experience, good business acumen and organizational skill. Areas of advanced study: (a) employee skills training, (b) management development programming, (c) customer/client training. Includes documentation and collateral materials design. Senior project: HPT/Training consultant on organizational development team.

Additional strengths: human resources generalist prior to specialization in training, education and development. Skills: staff forecasting, job design/redesign, salary/benefits, EAP, recruiting, and other areas.

Computer skilled with MS and Corel office suites; basic understanding of PILOT (computer-aided instruction) and similar CAT/CAI/CBT/WBT applications.

⊙ ⊙ ⊙

PROFILE Over four years full- and part-time experience planning, developing, and managing public school, playground, and community center activities and recreational programs for boys and girls ages 6–18. Skilled coach and referee for football, softball, baseball, soccer, basketball, hockey, field hockey, and tennis. Also: commercial passenger driver's license and perfect driving record.

◎ ◎ ◎

SKILLSET HTML, web design, online transaction systems, intranets, converting marketing and content ideas into technical realities.

◎ ◎ ◎

KEYWORDS **Senior Web Architect**
Oversee project from engineering perspective at a high level, fitting software components together to fulfill business requirements of the project. Experience with multiple enterprise databases, including Oracle, Informix, and Sybase; familiar with application servers including Cold Fusion, Web Objects, Web Sphere; skilled at performance analysis, system integration, and tying website into backend legacy system, including IBM mainframes and non-Web technology.

◎ ◎ ◎

HIGHLIGHTS Specialized study in cultural adjustment counseling and diversity sensitivity training.

> Produced and tested AFL-CIO training module in crosscultural and nonverbal communications, with emphasis on integration of women and minorities into apprenticeship programs.

> Co-authored handbook on approaches to diversity training for corporate directors of HR/training.

> Co-designed predeparture programs for American high school students leaving on one-year foreign exchange programs.

> Teaching experiences in Japan, U.S., Switzerland. Fully fluent in French and German; conversationally fluent in Spanish; some basic Japanese.

◎ ◎ ◎

You can see how critical a focused objective is to write a compelling profile. The more you know about your target industry and the job you want, the better your profile will be. Whatever your objective may be, try to write a profile now. (You should note that many candidates who have a targeted résumé with a profile also make a second version of their résumés without the profile. They use the second version whenever they need a more general presentation.)

Write a profile before you go on to the next chapter. Don't worry if you can't do a perfect job of it on your first try. Just get down a first draft and keep going. You can decide whether to retain the profile after you have assembled your complete first draft.

CHAPTER 7

Education: 1001 Ways to Sell Education

HALF-LIFE OF A DEGREE: SHORT

If you are a recent or about-to-be graduate, education is the number-one item on your list of product features. This is just as true for someone with a bachelor of arts in philosophy as it is for someone with a master's degree in corporate taxation. Your education is what you have to put up for sale. Employers do like to see your education tempered with some experience and exposure to their industries, but the main reason employers will hire you and put you on a career track is because of that degree.

Before we go into the best ways to present education on a résumé, one warning about the salability of education: A recent graduate has one to two years to sell her education before her "real world" experience becomes the (overwhelmingly) dominant factor in evaluating her candidacy for a position. If you have a degree in international relations and you want to work for the IMF or an international trading company, you have only one year—two years at most—to make that move. You should not work at some unrelated job "for a while," planning to try it later. Your education is your ticket onto a career track, and it expires sooner than you think.

In fact, if there is anything you've always wanted to do, do it now. If you want to teach in Alaska, or write for a small-town newspaper, or be a naturalist for the U.S. Park Service, or take some wild commission-only sales job to see if you have what it takes, do it now. Over the years, I've worked with a lot of people on their careers. Most of these careerists were very happy, but a significant minority were not. The main cause of unhappiness was always the same thing: The person didn't do what she really wanted to do. Instead, she did what was easy, what she thought she ought to do, what her parents thought she ought to do, what paid the most, what her dog wanted her to do—anything but what she wanted to do.

There is no better time than right after graduation to be terribly idealistic, uncompromising, and gutsy. My advice is simple: Go for it. Life is not a game to be won; it is a game to be played. To the players go the game.

Listing Degrees

If your degree is recent, education should usually be listed before experience, even if you have a strong experience section. If you just want to list your degree(s) and go on to the next section, you can do so like this:

M.B.A., Howard University, Washington, D.C., 2000
B.S., Economics, Duke University, Durham, North Carolina, 1996

Or like this:

Bryn Mawr College, Bryn Mawr, Pennsylvania
B.A., Classics, 2001

If you want to put more emphasis on your degree than your school, or vice versa, control your reader's eye by strategic use of bold lettering. These next two listings are structurally identical, but dissimilar in impact:

The University of Arkansas, Fayetteville, Arkansas
B.S., Chemistry, 2000

◉ ◉ ◉

STANFORD UNIVERSITY, Stanford, California
B.A., Art History, 2000

Of course, if your degree does not support your job objective, you can just leave off the major:

B.A., Brown University, Providence, Rhode Island, 2000

If you have not yet graduated and do not want to draw attention to that fact, you can list the degree and your status as a candidate. Remember, what you put in bold lettering is what is going to register with the reader. Here are three suggestions:

New York University, New York, New York
B.S. Candidate, **Business Administration,** 2002

◉ ◉ ◉

61

B.A., Marketing, S.U.N.Y., Buffalo, expected 2004

☉ ☉ ☉

B.S.E.E. (Bachelor of Science in Electrical Engineering), ongoing
GMI Institute, Flint, Michigan

If you are just about to enter a program and for some reason you would like to list it on your résumé, you can always list yourself as an enrollee. This can be particularly useful if you want to win an internship or get related volunteer or work experience before classes start.

M.S.S.W. (Master of Science Program in Social Work), enrollee
B.S. (Bachelor of Science in Psychology), 2000
University of Texas, Austin

If you did not finish a program, do not reveal that you were a degree candidate who dropped out. Avoid listings like "M.B.A. Candidate, 2000–2001." Instead, point out what you got out of the program while you were in it:

Graduate Studies in Business and Finance, 2000–2001
Golden Gate University, San Francisco

If you have not finished your thesis or dissertation, you can use the ABT (all but thesis) or ABD (all but dissertation) acronyms:

Ph.D. (ABD), Anthropology, University of New Mexico, Albuquerque 2001
B.S., Life Sciences, University of Hawaii, Honolulu, 1995

☉ ☉ ☉

Sometimes you will want to omit some of your education. If you went to five under-graduate schools before you managed to graduate, do yourself a favor and just list the school granting the degree. If you have an associate's degree, omit it unless it adds something to your bachelor's degree. If you have any unrelated certificate or degree that will confuse your reader, skip it.

Do not, however, list an advanced degree without mentioning the preparatory degree. Citing a master's without mentioning the qualifying bachelor's degree may invite skepticism and suspicion. There are schools in the United States that grant such degrees, and some of them are less than reputable.

High School

Should you list a high school diploma? That depends on where you went to high school and what you are applying for. In most of the United States, you should not list a high school diploma on a business résumé. If you are applying overseas, however, you should know that one's high school is normally listed on the résumé or c.v. in Europe and throughout the Pacific Rim countries.

If you went to a renowned prep school, public or private, and you are applying for a job in the academic world, it would be wise to list it. In the Northeastern urban corridor (Boston-New York-Washington, D.C.) it is traditional to list private high schools on one's business résumé, especially if you work in any area of financial services. List high school education in the same format as college. Here are two examples:

The American College of Switzerland, Leysin, Switzerland
Diploma, college preparatory, 2000

◎ ◎ ◎

The Deerfield School, Leverett, Massachusetts
Diploma, college preparatory, 2000

If you have a truly unusual or outstanding accomplishment from high school, sometimes it is worth listing the school to provide a platform for presenting the activity.

El Dorado High School, Domino Hills, Colorado
• All-State Champion, High School Wrestling, 2000.
• Also won a writing contest and became weekly columnist, "Scenes from the Western Slope," for the local paper, Domino Daily, while still in high school.

Finally, some people discreetly choose to omit prep schools from their EDUCATION listings, and instead mention them under headings such as AFFILIATIONS or VOLUNTEER EXPERIENCE:

Form Agent, Treddle Academy, Concord, New Hampshire, 2000–2001
• Fundraising and event planning for the alumni organization.

63

Education, the Super Rubric

Your education section can include a large range of curricular and extracurricular listings, including several of the categories from the catalog of résumé topics you prepared in Chapter 3: classes, special projects, research, dissertation and thesis titles, other publications, in-class presentations, honors and awards, computer skills, grades, scholarships, sports, community service, social-fraternal affiliations, professional affiliations, and committee service. It is important to note that you can also convert information from the education rubric to the experience rubric. We will address that issue in the next chapter.

If you won honors, be sure to list them prominently:

B.S., Anthropology, *magna cum laude,* 2001
University of California, Berkeley

Many students also feature their GPAs. If you do this, however, you should know that there are so many people walking around with stellar GPAs that even a 3.5 isn't very impressive anymore. Of course, you can be selective in reporting your GPA; you can report GPA for your major only, for your last two years, or even for classes that meet after two in the afternoon. GPA is usually noted underneath the degree and school:

Cornell University, Ithaca, New York
B.S., Computer Science, 2000
• GPA in Mathematics and Computer Science: 3.78

I know this may be shocking, but employers aren't as interested in your grades as you may have feared or hoped. They are looking for skills, personality, career savvy—in short, a package. Grades alone are not a dominant factor in evaluating that package. Of course, any employer who knows your grades will consider them. On-campus interviewers tend to be more sensitive to grades than outside employers whom you contact through your self-directed search efforts. In any case, don't worry if you choose not to list your grades. It was optional in the first place.

If your classroom education is a qualification for the job you are seeking now, it can be very persuasive to list actual classes on your résumé. I prefer to use the word "coursework," allowing you to paraphrase class titles into more accessible terms. This technique is particularly useful for featuring classes you may have taken or skills you may have picked up outside your major or across disciplinary lines. Here is an example citing both classes and computer skills:

B.S., Business Administration, 2001
Michigan State University
Coursework included:
• Financial & Management Accounting
• Corporate Finance
• Statistics & Statistical Analysis
• Principles of Sales Management
• Marketing Strategy & Planning
• Marketing Research

Computer skills:
• HTML, MS Office, ACT, WordPerfect

You can also list class projects, thesis titles, and any similar data that might be of interest to your targeted employer. Major class projects that required the same set of skills as the job you are applying for can be very effective additions to your résumé. Below are two examples.

The Academy of Art College, San Francisco, California
B.F.A., Interior Design, expected 2003
Heald Technical Institute, San Francisco, California
A.S., Electronics Technology, 2000

Projects:
> • Won open ASID competition for light fixtures for the Sal Suisse Hall of the
>   Los Angeles Museum of Corporate Art.
> • Won AALD "Best New Concept" design award for gas plasma lighting system,
>   prototype installed in lobby at PG&E headquarters, San Francisco.

◉ ◉ ◉

Reed College, Portland, Oregon
B.A., Philosophy-Religion, 2001
> Senior Thesis: *Platonic Soul Theory in the Middle Dialogues:*
> *The Phaedo, The Republic, The Phaedrus*

◉ ◉ ◉

In spite of what they told you on pledge night, you should think carefully about how to list a nonacademic sorority or fraternity. If you can demonstrate leadership or service in an officer or committee chair position, then be sure to feature that, but mere membership is a mixed bag. If you happen to be applying to a brother or sister, then by all

65

means, list it in bold. In all other cases you run the risk of applying to a boss affiliated with a rival house or one of the majority of college graduates who never pledged or someone who has read too many articles about hazing and alcohol abuse. If you are the social chair, forgeddaboudit. Even though you may have managed a large budget, you don't want to have to talk about where that budget went. . . .

More Samples

Following are a few more education listings to give you an idea of different layouts and possible contents. Remember, two to five years after you graduate, this much detail under the education heading would be inappropriate. Along the same lines, do not let a string of details from prior degrees eclipse your latest academic activities. A stellar undergraduate career followed by a more mundane graduate school performance is not something you would want to emphasize visually by devoting the bulk of your education information to ancient history. Also, don't make a reader pick through your educational background to find your degrees; they may not bother. Note how the next example features subheadings on the left side and strategic use of bold lettering to guide the reader to her degrees:

EDUCATION

Architecture   **UNIVERSITY OF CALIFORNIA, BERKELEY**   Berkeley, CA
       Master of Architecture   2001
       • Architectural Consultant to Berkeley Cohousing Group,
         a pioneer of cohousing in the United States
         (design/build of a 15-unit development).

       UNIVERSITY OF CALIFORNIA, LOS ANGELES   Los Angeles, CA
       Graduate School of Architecture and Urban Planning   1998–99
       • Completed 1st year curriculum
       • Curriculum Committee
       • Admissions Committee

       COLUMBIA UNIVERSITY   New York, NY
       Architectural Design Studio   1997
       PRATT INSTITUTE   New York, NY
       Architectural Design Studio   1997

Undergraduate   **WELLESLEY COLLEGE**   Wellesley, MA
       Bachelor of Arts
       • Double Major: Art History & Political Science

◎ ◎ ◎

EDUCATION

B.S. Management, with honors, Trinity College, Dublin, Ireland, 2001

Emphasis: **Consumer Products Marketing,** with strong research orientation.

Thesis: *Discriminant Analysis and Psychographic Profile of Consumer Market for Pre-mixed Ethnic Culinary Ads.*

- Invited by marketing director and marketing manager of the country's leading food and spice distributor to present dissertation findings.
- Advertising intern, The Innovation Group, Cork, Ireland, 1999. Comprehensive introduction to advertising agency operations under the mentorship of agency director.
- Student representative, College of Marketing and Design (senior year).

◎ ◎ ◎

EDUCATION   **PEPPERDINE UNIVERSITY,** Malibu, California

Bachelor of Arts, Organizational Communication, 2001

- **Minor in Business**

Grade Point Average: 3.81 (cumulative); 4.00 (in major)

Honors: Graduated magna cum laude

National Dean's List, eight semesters

Outstanding Senior Student, Communication Division

Los Angeles Philanthropic Award for Scholastic Achievement and Community Service

Activities: President, Student Government Association

Chapter Founder, Phi Alpha Delta Professional Fraternity

Vice President, Theta Alpha Phi Sorority

Vice President, Students for a Better America

Participant, Year-in-Europe Program, Heidelberg, Germany

Tutor (to juvenile offenders), Camp David Gonzales

◎ ◎ ◎

Johnson & Wales University, Providence, Rhode Island
Candidate for the B.S., Hotel & Restaurant Administration
- Dean's Honors
- St. Tropez Scholar
- Hotel Association
- Eta Sigma Delta, International Hospitality Management
  Honor Society Vice President
- Professional Convention Management Association
- Champion, Intramural Tennis

◉ ◉ ◉

68

Georgetown University, School of Law, Washington, D.C.
Juris Doctor Candidate, expected 2002
Honors: Marshall Honor Society
                    Moot Court (won oral argument)
                    Ranking: Top 10% (tentative)

Activities: Law Review (appointed)
                    Health Law Association
                    Student Affiliate, NBA

◉ ◉ ◉

The Colorado College, Colorado Springs, Colorado
Bachelor of Arts, Classics-History-Politics, 2000
Honors: Phi Beta Kappa
                    Bramhall Award for outstanding Senior Thesis in Political Science:
                    *The Role of Leadership in the Political Thought of the Federalists and the
                    Anti-Federalists*

Activities: Co-Leader, Political Theory Senior Honors Seminar
                    Student Representative, Political Science Curriculum Committee
                    Secretary, Political Student Union

Florida State University in Florence, Florence, Italy
Semester Abroad, Italian Language, Art & Culture, Fall 2000
Activity: Organized "Grand Masters" Tutorial (permanently adopted by
                    the program)

◉ ◉ ◉

New York University, New York, New York
B.A., Accounting, *cum laude,* December 2001

        Edmund Celeski Award (Top Class Ranking)

GPA: 3.7/4.0 (3.85/4.00 in major)

Honors: Merit Scholar, 2000
           New York State Grand A (Academic), 2000–2001

Activities: President, NYU Accounting Association
           Campus Representative, Becker CPA Review
           Tutor, Project Read
           Tutor, NYU School of Accounting

Credential: Scheduled for CPA Exam, May 2002

69

◎ ◎ ◎

Write up your education section now, before reading further. Include any honors, activities, special projects, and so on, that you think may be of interest to your potential employer. After learning the strategies in the next chapter, you may choose to write up some of these listings into more full presentations under the EXPERIENCE or SPECIAL PROJECTS headings, but for now, just write the best EDUCATION section you can.

CHAPTER 8

Experience: Paid and Nonpaid, Formal and Informal

YOU HAVE MORE EXPERIENCE THAN YOU THINK

Your experience and education sections make up the heart of your résumé. The success of your presentation depends on a show of strength in both areas. Students and recent grads often fail to make an effective presentation of their experience because they use too narrow a definition of work experience. Even if you have never worked for pay one day in your life, you can make a compelling presentation of experience as a qualification for your targeted job.

First of all, relevant "work" experience is in no way limited to paid employment. As mentioned in Chapter 3, the experience section of your résumé can include nonpaid work, volunteer work, part-time and temporary positions, internships, unstructured work, self-employment, odd jobs, and miscellaneous informal services you may have provided to your academic department or a favored professor.

Before you begin to draft your experience section, search your background for anything that relates to the specific skills cluster and general attributes your future employer is seeking. Open your mind to evidence from all areas of your background, then consider the Résumé Ingredients Rule: Which items will be of interest to your potential employer, and in what order?

The two keys to a successful experience section are creativity in selecting experiences and ruthless application of the Résumé Ingredients Rule.

You might be surprised at what this process reveals about you. A traditional, non-targeted, and non-thought-out résumé might list all paid employment under experience, even if that employment undermines your candidacy. Your three years of restaurant management experience might be totally irrelevant when applying for a position as a laboratory technician. Your experience as a security guard supervisor might well be seen as evidence against your ability to supervise in a white-collar environment.

On the other hand, full descriptions of the laboratory experience that you gained as part of your curriculum might be very persuasive in an application for a laboratory position. And a discussion of your experience as editor of the student newspaper, an unpaid position that involved managing a body of temperamental volunteers, might be a much better indicator of your ability to supervise in a professional, team-oriented environment.

Before you begin to write, take the material you have compiled and ruthlessly apply the Résumé Ingredients Rule. If an experience does not demonstrate a skill valued by your future employer, consider omitting it no matter how important it may have been to you at the time. If any experience does demonstrate such a valuable skill, then consider featuring it even if it seems unorthodox. Remember, put your information in order of interest to the targeted reader.

Elected, Appointed, and Volunteer Positions

The following are examples of nonpaid, nontraditional experiences written up just like paid employment. These students are describing elected, appointed, and volunteer positions as if they were jobs, demonstrating a range of skills that simply could not be inferred from activities listings like "President, Student Environmental Association (SEA), 2000."

Black Student Union, University of New Hampshire (UNH), 1/00–12/00
Founder and **President**

- Conceived, created and promoted a new Black Student Union after a twenty-year hiatus at UNH. Created necessary articles of incorporation and lobbied the university administration and student government for official recognition. Designed fliers and promoted information meetings. Arranged private reception with Angela Davis as guest of UNH Women's Commission. Developed successful shoestring budgets. Obtained press coverage in *Concord Monitor, The New Hampshire, Portsmouth Herald,* and *Rockingham Gazette.* Speaker and panelist, UNH Diversity Conference, November 2000.

☉ ☉ ☉

71

Sigma Epsilon Chi Sorority, UCLA, Los Angeles, California, 1999–2001
Chapter Treasurer and **House Manager**

• Prepared and administered $82,400 annual house operating budget. Produced financial reports and submitted them to the chapter Board of Governors and the National Treasurer. Collected and deposited chapter monies from all sources and for all purposes. Audited all house committee financial activities. Analyzed overhead and set rent payment amounts. Contracted for supplies and services.

• Special accomplishment: Created formalized purchasing process and reviewed all vendor relationships; reduced budget by 19% with simultaneous increase in goods and services provided. Won annual "House Service Award" from sisters.

• Wrote training and procedures manual. Trained new Treasurer.

Central Everglades Wild Animal Rehabilitation Clinic, Miccosukee, Florida
Veterinary Assistant (Volunteer), Summer 2000

- Provided emergency care to injured wildlife, nursing care to convalescing animals, and physical therapy and behavior modification to animals that were potentially releasable. Learned to handle raptors, seabirds, alligators, and other wild animals. Attended at surgeries. Part of the capture crew, responding to reports of both injured animals and wild animals exhibiting dangerous/aggressive behaviors.

◉ ◉ ◉

Office of Admissions/Physical Education Department, Aug–Sept 1999 and 2000
Orientation Coordinator (Public Relations)

- Conceived role of public relations representative for the Sports Complex to the orientation process; was appointed by the A.D. as "Czar of PR."

- Won approval for Sports Complex as site of "Bop Tilya Drop" orientation bash.

- Convinced cheerleaders (male and female) to lead Sports Complex tours.

- Increased Sports Complex utilization by over 15% in first year alone. See enclosed letter from A.D. citing my contribution as key to exempting S.C. from budget cuts.

Pay particular attention to this last example. This student created this project for a lark. The only pay was a few extra perks around the gym. "I just did it to meet the best-looking new students," he told me, but look how well it turned out on his résumé. Many students do something for their departments, for some branch of student government, or for some student organization. Sometimes this kind of unstructured "work" can round out the rest of your experience rather nicely.

Employment Listings: Company, Title, Dates, Scope, Accomplishments
If your experience from any source supports your job objective (that is, demonstrates skills and talents of interest to your targeted employer) then by all means list it. Now that you are convinced of this, you need to decide whether to list it along with paid employment or separate it out under its own heading. Before we consider other options, let's review the classical presentation of paid work experience: List the company name, your title, the dates of employment, the scope of your job, and your accomplishments in the position.

73

Company name is pretty much a given. However, if you worked for a subsidiary and the parent company is better known, you might choose to highlight the parent company. Here is an example:

INTERNATIONAL BUSINESS MACHINES, San Jose, California
Avionics Applications Group, Inc. (a wholly owned subsidiary)

As a general rule, list the city where you worked along with the company name. Remember, use bold lettering to control what your reader notices; don't use bold lettering for cities, dates, or unimportant information; reserve it for key data only. Of course, you must be consistent; you cannot bold one company's name because you think it is impressive and not bold the others as well.

If you worked for an impressive company through an employment agency, you can list that fact like this:

Lucent Laboratories (Technical Contract Services, Inc.), Boston, Massachusetts

If the companies you served through a temporary agency are not so important, feature the agency itself and describe the types of assignments you had.

Your *title* is not as much of a given; it can be listed several ways. You can list your official title with a more descriptive or functional title in parentheses, or vice versa. Here are some examples:

Senior Technician (Laboratory Manager)
Business Analyst (Intern)
Sales Associate (Acting Assistant Manager)

Whenever possible, dates should be rounded off to years. You want your reader to be concentrating on your responsibilities and accomplishments, not calculating how many minutes of experience you might have. Dates should be deemphasized. You can list them by the right margin, to the right of your company or title, or even as the very last thing at the end of a narrative job listing. Here are two examples, and there are plenty more throughout the book:

ABC Alphabet Soup Company, Reading, PA, 2000–2001
Speller

ABC Alphabet Soup Company, Reading, PA
Speller, 2001–Present
Taster, 2000–2001

In rare cases, you can even omit the dates altogether. For example, if all of your experience is over ten years old because you were in prison, then raised a family, and then went back to college, listing your dates could be counterproductive. Don't do anything different; just omit all dates.

The scope of your job is a combination of your place on the corporate flowchart, the nature and size of your organization, the number and nature of employees reporting to you, and the volume and nature of your responsibilities. Scope is a sort of snapshot of your job. Quantify this information whenever possible. Identifying your employer as a "plastic pipe manufacturer" is not as descriptive as calling it a "$12 million plastic pipe manufacturing company with four plants in Louisiana and Texas, and a total of 322 employees." Notice how exact the sorority treasurer above is in specifying her budget responsibility as $82,400. It is always helpful if you specify to whom you reported (by title, of course, not by name). Your reader should literally be able to picture you at work and imagine your work environment.

Accomplishments are everything you did for your employer above and beyond showing up at work every day. What contributions did you make, what problems did you solve, what money did you save, what procedures did you invent, what special training or travel did you have, what did you do above and beyond the call of duty, what separates you from everyone else who ever held that position and had those responsibilities? Again, quantify this information whenever possible. Note how the treasurer mentioned in the last section reports a 19 percent reduction in overhead. That 19 percent, because it is so exact, is actually more impressive than claiming 20 percent. Nineteen percent sounds like a number lifted off a financial report; 20 percent sounds like a wild guess, perhaps unsubstantiated.

The classic formula for reporting accomplishments is PROBLEM $\rightarrow$ SOLUTION $\rightarrow$ RESULT. For example, you might report:

> Conducted a survey and discovered that students would use the bookstore more if it were open later in the evenings and on weekends. Realigned store hours with student needs, reduced full-time staff and increased use of peak-hour employees. Achieved a 17% increase in gross revenues with a concurrent decrease in actual labor cost as a percentage of gross sales.

75

In practice, however, there are thousands of ways to present your contributions. The above PROBLEM → SOLUTION → RESULT accomplishment might be more impressive if it just listed the solution and result, "By reorganizing store operations, created a 17% increase in gross revenues," or, just the result, "Achieved a 17% increase in gross revenues."

Avoid descriptions of routine duties. The less you say about duties that are probably obvious to your reader, the more room you have to discuss your accomplishments.

Whenever possible, use a superlative in reporting your accomplishments: "Achieved the highest gross sales in the history of the store, a 17% increase over prior manager." Anytime you can use words like first, only, most, best, and highest, your reader will be more impressed. Here are some more examples using superlatives:

- Youngest member of the New Business Development Task Force.

- Only student representative on the Curriculum Policy Subcommittee.

- Highest paid rookie sales rep in the history of the company.

- First undergraduate ever selected to serve as research assistant to the chairman of the department.

- Sales associate in the fastest growing unit in the chain.

- Co-author of the winning business plan, the only one ever funded 100% by the coalition of business professors who sponsor the competition.

Not all jobs will have accomplishments you can quantify and report, but whenever possible, do so.

The following is an excellent example of an experience listing, with company, title, dates, scope, and accomplishments:

Scheering Mechanical, Inc., Dearborn, Michigan, Summer 2000
Engineering Assistant, Quality Assurance

Conducted materials testing for compliance to procurement specifications on precision-machined bearings and sheet metals for this manufacturer of factory-floor conveyor systems, a $70 million company founded in 1937. Reported directly to the Chief Engineer, Quality Assurance, and indirectly to the Purchasing Manager. Inspected $2.8 million per month in incoming materials from 28 suppliers in the

U.S., Mexico, Korea, and Japan. Also served as member of production engineering team convened to improve manufacturing processes.

Accomplishments:
- Proposed new crimping technique for manufacturing wheel bearing housings, achieving 4% reduction in cost. Co-named on company patent. Won $500 cash award. Only intern ever named on patent application from this company.

- Identified cause of excessive bearing failure rate at customer site as a defective lubricant provided by the customer, averting $80,000 product lawsuit.

Make Everything Relevant
When dealing with unrelated work experience in your background, you have two options: make it relevant or leave it out. If you have plenty of relevant material, the obvious choice is to leave it out. With a little creativity, any job experience can be made relevant to your new objective.

There are two ways to make a seemingly unrelated employment listing relevant to your targeted objective: describe the job in the language and terms of the targeted industry, or don't describe the job at all and just tell what you learned that would be applicable in the new industry.

The following is one example of telling what you learned in your old industry that might be applicable in your targeted new industry. In the restaurant industry, the standard way to describe a position is to describe the menu, the number of tables, or "covers," and the volume, i.e., gross sales per annum. To interest a corporate recruiter for marketing and sales, though, you would have to use entirely different language. This candidate makes restaurant experience relevant to her future career goals:

Neptune's Sea Palace, Miami, Florida, Summer 2000
Food Server

- Acted as a "sales representative" for the restaurant, selling add-ons and extras to achieve one of the highest per-ticket and per-night sales averages. Prioritized and juggled dozens of simultaneous responsibilities. Built loyal clientele of regulars in addition to tourist trade. Used computer daily.

You could do a similar "conversion" of any experience if you just take the time to think and be creative. The following student makes a very compelling presentation of her part-time business selling T-shirts. In many cases it would be better to omit such seemingly trivial employment, but this student does an outstanding job of using the right language; she makes this job entirely relevant to her ability to perform in a business environment. Note how she conveys her quantitative and analytical skills without referring to them directly:

Owner, Sunny Sports, USC, Los Angeles, California, 2000–2002

Launched and ran highly profitable part-time business selling T-shirts at campus events. Commissioned original designs from art majors, projected sales two months in advance, identified and bought stock directly from a Hong Kong supplier, hired sales staffs of up to nine, liquidated surplus for a profit to the campus bookstore.

Results:
• Achieved margins as high as 48%.
• Earned net proceeds of $2,312 in first year, $6,683 in second year.
• Sold business after graduation for $500, even though the business had zero tangible assets.

You can also get away with listing a job without describing it at all. In place of the expected scope and accomplishments sections, you simply list what you gained from the experience that is relevant to your new objective. Even if the job is terribly mundane you can still use it to sell yourself, as in this example:

Marblehead Financial Consultants, Chicago, Illinois, Summer 2000
Receptionist

• Proved ability to deal with a wide range of individuals, including high-net-worth investors and institutional money managers, in a stressful and time-sensitive environment. Gained knowledge of financial markets and instruments, especially stocks, bonds, futures, and options. Excellent recommendation available.

I would not recommend this technique for every job in your experience section, but it is an effective way to get extra mileage out of a few positions.

If you have a strong education section and you are using your experience section for little more than to establish your work ethic, you can be exceedingly brief, like this recent grad:

EMPLOYMENT:
R.S. Saulz, Inc., a Professional Corporation, San Pablo, California, 2000–Present
Database Manager for Independent Sales Professional
• Systems administrator (MS Suite, A-C-T, Fourth Dimension).

Arctic Camps and Equipment, HQ: Anchorage, Alaska, Summers 1998–2000
Assistant Field Supervisor and **Heavy Equipment Operator**
• Sixteen-hour work days.

Any Mountain, Denver, Colorado, Winters, 1998–1999, 1999–2000
Ski Equipment Salesperson
• Top sales producer.

TGI Fridays, Denver, Colorado, 1997
Opening Team Member, Service Trainer, and **Food Server**
• Silver Star and Merit Awards.

Alyeska Ski Club, Girdwood, Alaska, Winter 1998–1999
Race Program Director and **Coach**
• Co-developed Club's first-ever beginning-level junior race program.

Organizing Sub-Headings of Experience

Your experience section can have any of the following main headings:

> EMPLOYMENT
> EXPERIENCE
> PROFESSIONAL HISTORY
> HIGHLIGHTS
> BACKGROUND

You can also separate your experience section into sub-sections. For example, instead of listing several less-relevant jobs before those you think will be of preeminent interest to your potential employer, lead with RELATED EXPERIENCE; after you have established your main credentials, you can list everything else in ADDITIONAL EXPERIENCE. Other divisions students and recent grads have used to their advantage are PROFESSIONAL EXPERIENCE and ADDITIONAL EXPERIENCE; MANAGEMENT EXPERIENCE and SALES EXPERIENCE; INTERNSHIPS and ENTREPRENEURIAL EXPERIENCE, and so on. Don't let a rigid adherence to chronology keep you from putting your best foot forward.

Here are two example of using subheadings to effectively organize a presentation of experience:

CORPORATE
EXPERIENCE

Empire Hardware & Supply, Inc., Albany, New York, Summer 2000
Business Analyst, Special Assistant to the Chairman

- Assisted Chairman in analysis of corporate structure prior to reorganization of this retail chain with 6 company-owned and 17 franchise units. Conducted comprehensive study of management and hourly positions at corporate level. Analyzed financial and work flow data, developed recommendations for major organizational and personnel changes, wrote and presented report to executive management.

- Represented corporation in meetings with dissatisfied franchise holders, presented overhead reduction plans, coordinated problem resolution with individual franchises.

- Reassessed corporate-to-store materials distribution system; negotiated new transport contracts decreasing costs by 21%.

ENTREPRENEURIAL (Earned 100% of College Expenses via the Following Enterprises)
EXPERIENCE

Number Systems, Binghamton, New York, Summers 1998, 1999
- Developed concept, established company as legal entity. Hired and trained crew of high school students in painting house numbers on curbs. Established sales quotas, pricing, and work standards.

Sales Technologies, Syracuse, New York, Summer 1997
- As a territory subcontractor, hired, trained, and organized a door-to-door sales force selling newspaper and magazine subscriptions.

1936 Modern Hauling, Bath, New York, Summer 1996
- Sold and performed moving and transport services using 1936 12′ flatbed truck. Managed advertising, accounting, collections, etc.

◎ ◎ ◎

80

EXPERIENCE: **Three Stars Leasing,** Hollywood, Florida, 1997–1998
professional   **Sales Representative (Management Trainee)**
- Consistently ranked in the top five out of 170 sales representatives. Performed marketing/outside sales of car leasing services. Targeted, contacted, and made presentations to car dealerships, repair shops, insurance companies, and corporate fleet representatives.
- Received award for Outstanding Sales & Service.
- Selected to train, orient and supervise new management trainees.

while student   **Hertz,** Newark International Airport, New Jersey, 2000–Present
Hiker
- Relocate rental cars to Hertz locations throughout the region.

Surfside Marina, Seabright, New Jersey, Summer 1999
Mechanic & Boat Rigger
- Maintained and repaired diesel and gas marine engines.

81

Separate Headings for Special Projects and Research

Instead of treating volunteer and nonpaid experience like paid employment, you might want to create headings such as SPECIAL PROJECTS or RESEARCH to convey such information without converting it into a traditional job format. Such a heading can be particularly effective when it falls between the EDUCATION section and possibly less relevant paid employment under an EXPERIENCE heading. Following are two examples of this technique:

PROJECTS
- Analyzed all sectors of the Norsk Hydro conglomerate of Norway, including industry and competitive trends, financial and management strengths, corporate infrastructure, and historical performance.
- Prepared comprehensive country profile of Brazil's business climate as part of feasibility analysis of investment and joint-venture potential.
- Developed study of crosscultural organizational behavior investigating corporate communications protocols using Pakistan as a model.

RESEARCH
- Fellowship, Pfizer Central Research, Novel Drug Delivery Systems Division. Only chemist on a team of medical researchers seeking to develop new methods of maintaining therapeutic levels of various drugs for extended periods. Results proprietary.
- Undergraduate recipient of National Science Foundation grant. Conducted research in the area of chemical carcinogens under auspices of the Dartmouth College Department of Chemistry. Abstract available.

Note that research and special projects such as these can be presented under EDUCATION, EXPERIENCE, or, as we have shown here, a separate-but-equal heading prior to EXPERIENCE. In the next chapter, we will discuss using yet another heading at the bottom of your résumé. You will need to consider all of these options to get the maximum impact on your particular reader given your particular background.

Experience Summaries
In order to squeeze every last drop of credit out of your background, you may want to refer to additional experience without giving a full description of it. Here are three different approaches to this technique:

ADDITIONAL EMPLOYMENT:
- Bank One: branch to general ledger reconciliations and variance analysis.
- The Sink Factory: established cost-of-manufacturing system for ceramics manufacturer.
- East Town Deli, Inc.: established accounting system for owner/manager, including design of cash control measures for staff.

⊙ ⊙ ⊙

PRIOR:
Three years additional experience in sales and sales management in insurance and retail environments. Details provided on request.

⊙ ⊙ ⊙

Additional employment as a bouncer, painter, carpenter, ski instructor, and sailing instructor.

Sorting Through Your Options

By now you should realize that you have a virtually unlimited number of qualifying experiences, and a virtually unlimited number of options for presenting that experience. You need to make a list of your options, and then reassess them in light of the Résumé Ingredients Rule.

Several years ago, I worked with a recent graduate who had an outstanding education in international affairs. He had internships at the United Nations and with a U.S. Senator. His senior research project had earned him accolades. While he was amassing these credentials, he had worked his way through college at a small retail electronics supply store. When the store's owner died, the widow asked this student to stay on as manager.

He was proud of his "real world" work experience and featured it in his résumé, mentioning his degree almost in passing. The bulk of his presentation was dedicated to resistors and oscilloscopes, and the travails of squeezing a profit out of an independent retail store. Few approaches could have shown less of his potential. His résumé evoked visions of a young man in a short-sleeve shirt and polyester tie with a massive pocket protector and vinyl shoes.

We completely restructured his résumé to feature his research, internships, and related employment; the electronics store earned a very brief mention at the bottom. Needless to say, he finally began to get interviews for positions commensurate with his potential.

At this point, you are very close to having completed a rough draft of your résumé. Make sure that it includes the right ingredients. Omit or redraft listings that do nothing to advance your candidacy. Be creative in what you consider experience, and be especially wary of paid employment listings that can damage your candidacy. Concentrate on your future; this is no time to get sentimental.

Before you go on to the next chapter, write up all the experiences you plan to include in the rough draft of your résumé. You can polish it later, but get down a solid first draft before continuing on.

83

CHAPTER 9

More Activities and Extras

LEAVE NO STONE UNTURNED

So far you have written descriptions of your skills, education, experience, and various kinds of special projects. Review your notes from Chapter 3, "Know Your Product." Any material left over from your Catalog of Résumé Topics which is pertinent to your objective should be worked into your résumé now.

Résumés for recent graduates can be rather flexible in their organization. For example, research can be listed under EDUCATION, SPECIAL PROJECTS, or RESEARCH, in a BIBLIOGRAPHY, or even referred to by a notation such as "see attached addendum." You will have a chance to reassess the organization and order of your material in the next chapter.

First, be sure everything is in that you want to include. Don't worry if your first draft is too long—that just gives you more to work with when it comes time to refine and polish. Check to be sure you have not left out material that can sell you, such as:

> Internships

> Scholarly presentations

> Teaching; serving as teaching assistant, proctor, lab instructor, tutor

> Articles, monographs, major class papers, and publications of any kind

> Sports

> Conferences, symposia, exhibitions, workshops, and retreats

> Travel, adventure, and foreign study

> Committee service

> Associations; scholarly, professional, and social affiliations

> Leadership role in social fraternity or sorority

> Foreign languages

> Computer skills

> Military history

> Certification, licensure, or placement exams

> Scholarships, fellowships, honors, prizes, and awards

> Writing, compositions, musical works, or art projects

> Hobbies, personal interests, and special talents

85

This type of information can often be listed quite simply, for example:

LANGUAGES
Fluent in Hungarian, German, Russian, and English.
Basic understanding of French and Spanish.

⊙ ⊙ ⊙

CONFERENCES
Magazine Writers' Symposium	Fall 2001
Aspen Writers' Conference	Summer 2001

⊙ ⊙ ⊙

TRAVEL
Kenya, Nepal, India, Europe, Iceland, Canada, Mexico, North Africa.

⊙ ⊙ ⊙

MILITARY

U.S. NAVY, 1998–2002, Honorable Discharge.
Assistant to the Division Head

COMPUTER SKILLS

Mac and PC experience running most common business applications.

Sometimes you can combine unrelated information under a heading such as ADDITIONAL or SPECIAL INTERESTS. Here are three rather different examples:

ADDITIONAL

Lived in Japan from age six to age twelve; fluent in Japanese; understand Japanese culture. NAUI and PADI Certified Scuba Instructor. Special interests include Japanese history, marine science, and adventure travel. Seeking a company where innovation and constant learning/self-teaching are expected.

ACTIVITIES

Alfred E. Neuman School of Business
Annual Economics Workshop, Summer 2001
Chairman of the Board
Led project on simulated International Trade Commission. Examined and assessed "fairness" of various options in context of conflicting economic interests as presented by fellow students. Judged and determined equitable trade laws and practices.

Varsity Lacrosse
    Most Valuable Player, 1999, 2000, 2001
    Acting Head Coach, 2000
    All America Honors, 2001
    All North Coast Athletic Conference Team, 2000, 2001
    National Collegiate Lacrosse Championship Playoffs, 1997, 1999, 2000

ADDITIONAL EXPERIENCE

Database Design Experience

Planned, organized, and created a statistical program for the Sandlot Baseball League. Devised program from scratch. Generated weekly statistics. Wrote documentation. Taught coaches and parents how to maintain program. System has been incorporated by other Parks & Recreation programs.

Tax Preparation & Compliance

Formulated corporate tax returns, item deductions, capital gains/losses, and P&L for a mock-up business organization in a senior finance seminar. Exposed to full gamut of complex tax issues. Earned highest grade in the class for saving company in excess of $1.2 million liabilities.

References

References should not be listed on your résumé itself, no matter how good they are. If you wish to refer to them, put REFERENCES ON REQUEST at the bottom of your résumé. It is understood that your references are available on request anyway, so such a line is purely optional, and perhaps annoying.

If your references are one U.S. Senator and two CEOs of Fortune 500 corporations, then it might be a good idea to include them with every résumé you submit, but not on the résumé itself. We'll consider this again in Chapter 17, "Cover Letters, Thank-You Letters, and Reference Sheets."

The Human Interest Factor

Not everything on your résumé has to be strictly business. Most corporate recruiters have to read dozens and dozens of résumés at a single sitting. Sometimes they even interview more than a dozen candidates in a single day. A strictly business presentation has to be pretty outstanding to get noticed. It can pay to be a little different, but not too different. If your résumé indicates that you might be interesting to talk to, recruiters will seek you out over other candidates. You can use such headings as ACTIVITIES, INTERESTS, and ADDITIONAL to report unusual sports records, extracurricular activities, and even jobs that will pique an interest in you as a person.

One college football player told me that he always ended up talking football in his interviews. Being a serious business major, he got tired of the distraction and took the sports listings off his résumé. After that, he felt his selection rate dropped off a little, and his interviews definitely were not as friendly. He decided to put the football listing back and just made sure that he emphasized his solid GPA and other qualifications.

An American physician with extensive research and postgraduate education listed his musical background like this: "Certified Grade VII (Final) 'with distinction' in violin, Board of Royal College of Music, London." In spite of all the research listed on his curriculum vitae, the first interview question was inevitably about this accomplishment from his youth.

A newly graduated attorney with the usual compendium of legal experiences retained a job listing from his undergraduate days to set himself apart from the other new Harvard J.D.'s: "Farmer, summers 1997, 1998, 1999. Operated 200-acre farm on profit-sharing basis. Drove and maintained all equipment. Made crop marketing decisions. Earned full tuition for junior and senior years of college, and first year of law school."

Like other résumé extras, human interest listings should be very brief. They do not need to tell the whole story; their purpose is to set your résumé apart from all the others, and to spark conversation in an interview. They should invite further inquiry, inciting rather than satisfying curiosity.

For example, under ACTIVITIES one student listed a summer outdoors trip that elicited highly favorable comments from reviewers. The listing was exceedingly brief—"Solo cross-Canada canoe trek, summer 1999"—but her interviewers never failed to bring it up.

◎ ◎ ◎

Before you continue on to the final editing stage, be sure that everything you want to include in your résumé is there on your first draft. You may rearrange and redesign the résumé, but no new data should be required after this stage.

CHAPTER 10

Editing: Second Draft to Final Form

OCCAM'S RAZOR: THE RÉSUMÉ INGREDIENTS RULE
If you have been following the guidelines in this book, you should have more than enough material for your résumé. You have searched high and low for evidence that you possess the desired skills cluster, and made seemingly unrelated experiences relevant to your current goals. Now you need to reassess your résumé's content and organization one last time before preparing a final draft.

Once again, we will sort and order this excess of data by using Occam's razor in the form of the Résumé Ingredients Rule: Select and organize the information on your résumé in accordance with desired impact. Ask yourself which material will be of interest to the potential employer, and in what order will it be of greatest interest?

For example, if computer skills are required for the types of position you are seeking, they should go in a PROFILE, SKILLS, KEYWORD LIST, or TECHNICAL SKILLSET section near the top of your résumé. If they are not required but you want to list them, consider listing them at the bottom of the résumé in a less-emphasized SKILLS or ADDITIONAL section.

Remember that you can break your background up into RELATED EXPERIENCE and ADDITIONAL EXPERIENCE, and even insert sections such as SPECIAL PROJECTS in the middle. You can also abandon chronological order entirely, arranging your jobs in order of perceived interest to your targeted employer.

Sometimes you must be rather ruthless in applying the Résumé Ingredients Rule. I know of a film major who worked her way through college by running the candy department at one of the country's largest drugstores. She was in charge of a business generating over a million dollars a year in revenues; had responsibility for employees, buying, business analysis, and the management report; worked eight years for this drugstore and had an excellent recommendation from them. But this job did nothing toward helping her land an entry-level film or media job. In fact, it counted against her.

Her potential employer might well think: "How can I send this woman out to get lunch and wash the blood off Dracula's cape after she's been in full charge of a million-dollar business?" or "Eight years with one employer? Hasn't this woman ever done anything else? She must be afraid of risk," or, worst of all, "Candy? That's obviously this woman's greatest strength, but we don't use a lot of candy around here."

This candidate should omit the job entirely. She should feature the fact that she wrote two feature-length scripts, directed six student films, wrote a computer application to break down a script into shooting sequences, won several awards, can sew, and is perfectly willing to get lunch and wash cars with her tongue to break into the business.

Take another look at your résumé. Do you emphasize candy jobs when you should focus on student films?

Things to Omit
In the bad old days, résumés were often part of a discriminatory hiring process in which managers actively sought to hire people of a certain sex, age, race, educational, and/or socioeconomic background to fill their openings. Those days are over, and employment laws protect you from having to reveal your age, race, religious affiliation, marital status, "family plans" (i.e., childbearing plans), parenthood status, and a good deal of other information that has absolutely nothing to do with your ability to perform on the job. If you ever experience discrimination or harassment—as an employee or as a candidate—be sure to report the incident to your state fair employment department.

Do not list your age, date or place of birth, height, weight, race, marital status, health, or similar personal information anywhere on your résumé or curriculum vitae!

Do not attach a picture of yourself to your résumé to show that you are white, black, grey, brown, or good looking.

(You can, however, include any kind of a photo on your personal homepage, and refer potential employers to your homepage anywhere on your résumé. By the way, take another look at that homepage. If you have a list of every person you've ever had sex with or a diatribe against the government or formulae for pipe bombs, be sure you don't send an employer to the site or shut it down for the duration of your job search.)

Some other information is better omitted because it is irrelevant, can be obtained more appropriately later in the employment process, or may be used to discriminate against you. Do not list your social security number, the street addresses or phone numbers of employers, the names of supervisors or references, your salary history, or reasons for leaving each job.

On the other hand, immigrants or foreigners with valid visas or work permits should be sure to state that clearly at the bottom of any résumé. For example, "Canadian Citizen since 1992," or "U.S. Resident Alien, valid Green Card. Qualified for immediate employment." Employers are often reluctant to pursue all the paperwork required to employ you legally if you are not already qualified. Don't give them any reason to hesitate.

If you are not legally qualified, say nothing on your résumé. Wait until the interview before you try to convince the employer that they will benefit from sponsoring you. You might also offer to pay any legal fees yourself, offer to pay them if you leave the company within a given time frame, or negotiate other contingencies to improve your attractiveness.

You should note that in Europe, the Pacific Rim, and in many other countries, it is de rigueur to list date of birth and marital status.

Throw-Out Factors

Candidates often unwittingly present damaging information in their résumés guaranteeing it receives immediate round-file treatment. In résumé-writing jargon, these items are known as throw-out factors, because they will cause a prospective employer to throw out your résumé without further ado. They may not even trigger a conscious response; sometimes an interviewer with a surplus of applicants will decide to put your résumé in the "maybe" or "reject" pile without really stopping to think why.

Listings that reveal your race, religion, or politics are often throw-out factors, but sports, social organizations, and marital status can also be equally dangerous. We have already discussed a few activities that could be a negative to employers. Serving in a fundamentalist Christian community outreach organization might be important to you as a person, but for you as a candidate it could be job-search poison. Your too-extensive list of sports might raise the suspicion that you won't be happy working long desk hours. Your citation of various self-help and enlightenment seminars could cause many employers to ignore your real job qualifications. Even a listing that unintentionally reveals where you grew up can be a throw-out factor, so watch what extra messages may creep in with listings such as your permanent address, high school, or early summer jobs.

Examine your résumé from top to bottom for throw-out factors. In particular, read your ACTIVITIES or other special listings especially carefully as they often include throw-out factors. Since most throw-out factors are extraneous in the first place, removing them is no loss.

Remove Excess Verbiage and Statements of the Obvious

The next step is to edit your entire presentation for circumlocutions, passive constructions, statements of the obvious, unsubstantiated boasting, arrogance, excess adjectives and adverbs, and boring phrases that could be made more active and colorful. First, see what you can throw out without damaging your overall presentation. The more routine duties you omit, the more room you have for special projects and accomplishments.

Then, review each sentence as if you were a prospective employer. You want to be wowed. Rewrite anything that does not wow you, using a more active voice or more compelling language. As any witness to a crime or historical incident will tell you, there are thousands of different ways to describe the same event. You want to use the one that will most effectively sell your skills cluster to a prospective employer.

Do not remove credentials. It may seem obvious that in order to practice law or medicine you must have the credentials to do so, but your résumé or c.v. absolutely must list your basic qualifying credentials.

Consistency, Consistency, Consistency

Next, audit your draft for consistency. If you include months in some dates, it may be prudent to list the rest of the dates the same way. If you use bold type for one company name, use bold for all the company names. If you use bullets, use them in the same way every time. If you give the annual sales for the first three companies you worked for, be sure to do so for the fourth and fifth as well. Inconsistency in a résumé is the sign of a disorganized and unsystematic mind. Employers are more forgiving of a typo or an occasional misspelling than they are of inconsistencies in layout and design.

Balance and "Look"

Finally, your résumé has to have an easy-to-read look to it. You can accomplish this by leaving a good deal of white space and by careful use of bold lettering. Important information should jump out at the reader. The résumé should look balanced from top to bottom, and all four margins should be about equal.

Careful manipulation of font size, margins, line spacing, and design can make any presentation look balanced, easy to read, and professional—unless you have too much information. If you still have so much information that it cannot be printed attractively on a single sheet of paper, go back to Occam's razor and cut some more, or decide to abandon the "one-page" rule in favor of a more attractive two-page presentation.

E-Search Versions

Once you have a good, paper-based version of your résumé, you can convert it easily into the most common e-search version. The most common electronic résumé is simply your paper version—same words in the same order—submitted electronically as a plain text file. Make the first word of the résumé "Resume," with no accents, and the last words should be "End resume." Remove secondary page headings. Otherwise, everything remains the same.

You can also add a keywords list, either at the top or the bottom of your regular paper-based version, where you throw in every noun you think anybody would ever search for. The more obscure the keyword the better. Nobody is going to search for soft skills, such as "well organized," but if you speak Farsi or have expertise in fractals AND chaos theory, sooner or later someone in the world will call you about it.

The other form of e-résumé is the HTML version. This is a more interesting style, allowing you to create a multilevel document using hypertext. For example, you can sprinkle your document with phrases like this: "For other examples of economic analysis, press here," or "Want to see the complete bibliography?" and so on. Most word processing programs can convert your résumé into and out of HTML rather easily. The rules for writing such sections are the same as for a regular résumé.

Be sure to submit your e-résumé in exactly the format requested. Most automated résumé banks will automatically dump nonstandard submissions, usually without notifying you about the problem. If an employer requests an e-résumé, find out whether they want it in ascii, or Word, or WordPerfect, or HTML, or something else. If they can't open your file, they won't. One good idea is to call your résumé up into the body of the e-mail message, and attach it in the format requested. Follow the subject line instructions or you lose.

While it is true that e-résumés are the latest thing, here are two points to keep in mind: First, you develop a good e-résumé exactly the same way you develop a good paper résumé—by anticipating your employer's needs and presenting your background relative to those needs. Second, you shouldn't rely on the Internet to find a job. It's a job search tool, like many others. It doesn't replace a good search plan and a well-thought-out candidacy.

Well, enough about that. On to the samples!

Example

The following two résumés are for the same person. The first one was the student's unguided first attempt, the second was written using the principles espoused in this book. May you see as much improvement in your own efforts!

Peter Golyn
2332 Carole Way
Berkeley, California 94704
Phone (510) 555-4020

Education

High School: The Branson School, Marin County California
College: The University of California at Berkeley. Currently a senior majoring in political science.

Employment Experience

From January 1998 through September 2000 I was an employee of the Occidental Housing Company of Oakland. My duties included screening and negotiating with clients over the phone, negotiating with clients personally and initial appraisals of multi-residential housing complexes throughout the East Bay. I also performed many clerical/filing tasks in which I became proficient at computer programs such as Excel, MS Word, and Damar. I worked directly under the president of the company, Nickel Geronimas.

References

Nickel Geronimas, President, Occidental Housing, Phone (415) 555-1134.
Paul Solis, Phone (415) 555-1556.

Peter Golyn
Pgolyn@alumni.Berkeley.edu
2332 Carole Way
Berkeley, California 94704
Phone (510) 555-4020

PROFILE

Real Estate Analyst – Sales Assistant – Research Assistant/Intern
- Earned 100% of college expenses while working in real estate field. Basic experience in acquisitions analysis, cash flow projections, pro forma analysis, appraisal, due diligence, sales and marketing.

- Computer skills: Damar, MS Word, Excel. Can learn new programs easily (self-teach, no training necessary).

EDUCATION

University of California Berkeley, California
B.A., Political Science   6/2000
- Social Science degree, including advanced training in statistical analysis and quantitative reasoning.

EXPERIENCE

Occidental Housing Company Oakland, California
Lead Prospector (Acquisitions)   (part-time and full-time) 1/1998–9/2000
- One of the first people hired by this rapid growth, entrepreneurial real estate management company. Report directly to the President. Company now has approximately 75 employees on payroll, and hundreds of units under management.

- Team Leader over a staff of four Junior Prospectors, surveying and assessing investment potential of apartment buildings/complexes throughout the Greater East Bay.

- Represented OHC in initial negotiations with sellers. Prepared detailed acquisition reports complete with profiles on comparable properties. Delivered detailed briefs to acquisition team and to top management.

- Located and profiled over 20 viable acquisitions in East Bay. Over 100 units were purchased by the company.

- Also knowledgeable on property management issues, including accurate pro forma projections for properties under management.

Terra-Hydro, Inc.   San Ramon, California
Senior Executive   (part-time and full-time) 12/1994–1/1998
- Provided land acquisitions throughout Central California for this small, entrepreneurial group: research, analysis, initial negotiations, appraisal and comparable profiles. Located 12 parcels for further consideration (several were purchased).

Boxer Elking Garrison, Attorneys-at-Law   Oakland, California
Clerk   (part-time and full-time) 1/1992–12/1994
- Handled legal filing, phones, document control, general office support.

REFERENCES **Excellent references available from all former employers.**

97

CHAPTER 11

Samples, Samples, Samples: From Accounting to Zoology

Clark Kent
CK@phonebooth.net

2001 Outer Limits Circle
Metropolis, U.S.A. 00101
Telephone: (123) 456-7890

CAREER OBJECTIVE
Seeking a challenging position in the field of criminal justice that makes the best possible use of my unique skills, abilities, talents, and enthusiasm.

SUMMARY OF QUALIFICATIONS
- Able to leap tall buildings in a single bound.
- Faster than a speeding bullet.
- Can stop a speeding locomotive with bare hands.
- Licensed private pilot (I love to fly).
- Possess natural bullet deflection talents.
- Unique skill to see through anything (except lead).
- Able to turn back time.

PROFESSIONAL EXPERIENCE
Daily Planet, 1948 to Present
Metropolis, U.S.A.

MILD MANNERED REPORTER
Responsibilities include day-to-day news investigation and reporting. Special periodic column on **Truth, Justice, and the American Way.** Work on a media team with L. Lane and J. Olsen. Routine news work, including traffic, weather, obituaries, and other duties assigned.

SPECIAL ACCOMPLISHMENTS
- Charter Member, **Justice League of America.**
- Employment Longevity Award, Daily Planet, 40 years.
- Member, **Screen Actors Guild.**

EDUCATIONAL BACKGROUND
Special education in **All the Knowledge of the Universe** completed in infancy.
Smallville High School, Smallville, Iowa
GED, 1947

REFERENCES
Mr. Perry White   Mr. Bruce Wayne
Editor-in-chief   Noted Millionaire
Daily Planet   Gotham City, U.S.A.

JOSEPH JUDDLEY
JJuddley@alumni.UCSB.edu

199 Minna Street
San Francisco, California 94105

Telephone / Message:
(415) 555-7730

> A strong résumé from a student who has never held a full-time job.

INTERESTS

Financial Analysis / Investment Analysis
High technical/analytical aptitude. Demonstrated skill for quantitative analysis in both scientific and business applications. Advanced user of spreadsheet applications, including pro forma development and "what if" modeling (Mac or PC environments). Proven communication skills as demonstrated in teaching and leadership roles in extracurricular and employment settings. Conversational Spanish.

EDUCATION

UNIVERSITY OF CALIFORNIA, Santa Barbara, California

degrees

B.A., Accounting, minor in **Economics**, 2000
B.A., Chemistry, 2000

activities

Captain, UCSB Sailing Team
Captain, UCB Sailing Team (UCB, 1997–98)
• Planned and coordinated weekly regattas involving up to 40 competing students and an official race committee of 10.

projects

• Conducted short- and long-range investment analyses on NYSE stocks using Excel. Tested company valuation principles in relation to actual stock values. Tested market trend theories.
• Studied LBOs of eight companies from origination in the 90s. Developed methodologies to forecast their progress and potential for success or failure into the 00s.
• Completed a business valuation study on a $270 million subsidiary of a Fortune 100 company as part of potential offering memorandum.

EMPLOYMENT

UCSB CHEMISTRY DEPARTMENT, Santa Barbara, California
Research Associate, 1996–1997, 1999
• Conducted experiments in strict accordance with written methodologies to originate data used in Prof. Pritchard's articles published in the Journal of the American Chemical Society (JACS).

SAN DIEGO YACHT CLUB, San Diego, California
Lead Instructor, Summer 1997
• Organized and managed summer Junior Sailing Program serving 180 students, aged 8 to 18. Trained and supervised 10 instructors. Reported to the SDYC Board of Directors.

PACIFIC COAST INTERCOLLEGIATE YACHT RACING ASSOCIATION
Vice President, 1998   Irvine, California
• Served on the Board of Directors. As a team, the Board sets collegiate regattas for the West Coast. Our goal during this time was to strengthen and centralize the association, which we did.

100

Note the personal interest created in this candidate via unusual educational background and activities.

MICHAEL SANDOVAL-JOHNSON
MSJohnson@USFCA.edu

574 Third Street, #237
Sunnyvale, California 94089

EDUCATION

UNIVERSITY OF SAN FRANCISCO (USF)   San Francisco, California
Bachelor of Liberal Arts   2001
Certificate of Saint Ignatius Institute: A Great Books Program   2001
   Psi Chi Society, National Honor Society
   National Hispanic Scholarship Fund, Academic Scholarship
   Wilbur-Brayton Scholarship Award, Recipient

OXFORD UNIVERSITY   Oxford, England
Blackfriars Stadium (initiated by invitation)   1999–2000
   Oxford Union Society (Internationally Renowned Debating Club), Lifetime Member

EMPLOYMENT

MADSEN PERSONNEL SERVICES   San Francisco, California
General Office   (full-time/part-time/holidays) 1994–Present
   Gained reputation for competence and reliability, earning first choice on challenging
   assignments. Proved ability to walk into any office environment and be productive immediately.
   Served many major corporations and key accounts for Madsen, including law, public relations,
   insurance, oil, information, banking and finance companies. Skilled in all common PC-based
   business applications (word processing, spreadsheet, database, presentation graphics).

UNIVERSITY OF SAN FRANCISCO   San Francisco, California
Night Operations Manager, Lone Mountain Dormitories   1998–1999
   Supervised and delegated assignments to three student assistants. Responsible for safety and
   wellbeing of 500 students.

LA BAGUETTE BAKERY   San Francisco, California
Assistant Manager   summer–fall 1997
   Worked full-time while attending school full-time while earning top grades. Opened, closed, bal-
   anced daily receipts, hired and trained staff, ensured customer service.

WELLS FARGO BANK   San Francisco, CA
Senior Retail Banking Clerk   1996–1997
Teller Trainee   1996
   Selected to be first person to hold Employee Loan Processing position. Cross-trained in
   numerous positions and functions, including collections and consumer lending.

SHIRTIQUE, INC.   San Francisco, California
Cashier (Assistant Manager)   1995

ACTIVITIES / COMMUNITY SERVICE
Oxford University Choir, Oxford Aularium Chorus, Baritone-Tenor.
Oxford K.E.E.N., Counselor to the physical handicapped (Kids Enjoy Exercise Now).
Oxford Jacari, Tutor.
Youth Homes Inc., Counselor to troubled teens.
USF Society of Theology Students, Co-Vice President.
USF College Players, Board Member and Publicity Director.
Located and corresponded with birth family after 25-year separation.
U.S. Olympic Trials (swimming), 2000.

101

Lawrence Pottsdam
pottsdaml@mba.duke.edu/alumni

237 Ashley Avenue
Raleigh, North Carolina 29403

Office: (919) 555-4430
Residence: (919) 555-6018

PROFILE
Honors MBA graduate with academic achievements complementing over ten years of management experience. Strengths include marketing, operations analysis, and administrative management. Effective combination of financial, accounting, organizational and leadership skills. Proven track record of success including start-ups and increases to gross, share and margin.

EDUCATION
MBA, International Business, Duke University, 2000
Special Projects:
- Marketing Audit for Raleigh Ballet. Completed competitive analysis of performing arts in the area (ballet, symphony, opera, theater). Evaluated sources of earned income and contributions, as well as marketing mix of programs, promotions and pricing policy relative to audience demand. Extensive data analysis, with recommendations for implementation.
- Prototype Study for Bargetto Winery. Responsible for research methodology, implementation, data acquisition, analysis, report to management.

Certificate, Marketing, Duke University, 1997
BA, Psychology, *with honors,* Lewis University, Lockport, Illinois, 1989

EXPERIENCE
Delicacies, Raleigh, North Carolina, 1994–1999
General Manager
Full charge manager of this international food import business, $1.5 gross revenues, 30 employees. Prepared monthly financial statements through P&L. Hired and motivated an intelligent sales staff. Administered employee relations, customer relations, insurance, banking, purchasing, accounts receivable and payable, payroll, and daily cash and inventory control. Improved control of business throughout period of rapid expansion. Identified and successfully implemented three growth areas for the business. Achieved growth rate in excess of 20% per annum on average.
Special Projects:
- Designed and implemented all internal business systems in collaboration with CPA. This includes IT and accounting for three profit centers.
- Built new revenue stream by identification of market need for premium corporate gifts. Initiated business relationships, set pricing, negotiated contracts, coordinated events. Grew gifts business at 42% average annual rate between 1995 and 1998.
- Applied expertise on Italian wine and food products. Conducted educational wine seminars and training sessions on wine selling for sales staff. Taught wine appreciation at local university.
- Wrote complete catalogue for wines including descriptions and food pairings.
- Panelist for the Wine Page, Raleigh Examiner newspaper.

Hinsdale Golf Club, Clarendon Hills, Illinois, 1989–1994
Assistant Manager, 1991–1994
Supervisor, 1989–1991
Operations manager for this exclusive private club near Chicago. Applied financial and staff management skills. Dealt directly with the clientele and the Board. Reported to the General Manager. P&L responsibility for food and beverage operations.
Special Projects:
- Researched, designed and implemented new food items and menus for special events.
- Hired staff. Wrote training manuals, established standard procedures, improved quality and quantity of staff performance.
- Participated in preparation of $2 million annual budget. Provided pricing and cost analysis on special services. Prepared profit reports on private parties and club functions.

HEATHER PEARL CROMIE
hpcdoll@yankee.net

399 Beacon Terrace
Boston, Massachusetts 02143

Telephone / Message:
(617) 555-3444

INTEREST	**Children's Theatre**	
EDUCATION	<u>Boston University,</u> Boston Massachusetts	
	Bachelor of Arts, *magna cum laude*	2000

    Major: Interdisciplinary Arts
    Activities:
      "The Wedding" (wrote/directed/performed)
      "Cry Once" (lighting designed)
      "Five Roads" (stage managed)
      "What's Going On?" (wrote/directed play about children w/ AIDS)
      Theatre Action Group (street theatre)
      Whiptail Women's Art Collective
      Dance-a-bility (disabled dance workshop)
      Other Theatre, Puppetry, Clowning
      Organizer, Regional Ultimate Frisbee Tournaments

<u>Brandeis University</u>, Waltham, Massachusetts	1992–1993

Major: Mathematics
Activities: Varsity Basketball
               Varsity Soccer

<u>Make-A-Circus</u>, Boston, Massachusetts	Spring 2000

Course: Clown Training

<u>Dynamics of Color Conference</u>, Boston, Massachusetts	Fall 1999

Course: Leading workshops for Children on the Topic of Racism

<u>Rainbow Theatre Group</u>, London, England	Fall 1998

Course: Theatre for the Developmentally Disabled

EXPERIENCE   <u>Children's Center for Movement Therapy</u>, Boston, Massachusetts 1999, 2000–Present
Theatre / Puppetry Instructor / Dance Teacher
    Created and implemented teaching and activity lesson plans for students with
    cerebral palsy. Incorporated stretching and muscle building into theatrical fun.
    Created Halloween show with John Berns. Performed at Halloween carnival
    and five area nursery schools.

<u>Hole-in-the-Wall Gang Camp</u>, Ashford, Connecticut	Summers 1999, 2000

Theatre Director
    Created theatre programs for campers (5- to 17-year-old children with
    life-threatening illnesses). Every single camper participated in a skit, song
    or dance each season. Also active in swimming and overnight camping,
    including story-telling.

prior   **Art Teacher,** St. James School
          Teacher's Aide, Happy Times Nursery School
          Program Leader, Kennebunkport Department of Parks and Recreation
          Photographer's Assistant, Olde Time Photos
          Swim Instructor, Times Farm Camp

TRAVEL	Bicycled in Scandinavia, U.K., Western Europe.	1998–1999
	Lived and worked in London.	1998
	Lived and studied in Guatemala.	1997

103

Sheila Madeleine Lent

maddylent1@aol.com

7391 Leary Avenue NE
Seattle, Washington 98707

Telephone:
(206) 555-4594

INTERESTS   **Economics, International Development, International Trade**

STRENGTHS
- Advanced knowledge of Latin American issues. Fluent in Spanish; some proficiency with German.
- Self-motivated, creative, energetic. Background in project development and management.
- Computer skilled, including financial analysis and economic modeling.

EDUCATION

B.A., Economics   May 2000
Whitman College, Walla Walla, Washington

Institute of European Studies, Vienna, Austria   Spring 1999

EXPERIENCE

Community Development, Peace Corps, Rio Verde, Ecuador   2000–2003
- Developed and delivered seminars on poultry production to groups of up to 120 adults. Co-wrote proposals with the Ecuadoran farmers. Obtained loan awards from the Trickle Up Foundation based in New York City.

- Built a new Peace Corps school. Wrote proposal for the Peace Corps Partnership Foundation that resulted in funding from Chase Manhattan Bank. Organized community matching efforts.

- Organized and managed Dental Hygiene Project, Women's Education Group, and several cottage industry development projects.

Bank Teller, Bank of America, Seattle, Washington   2000
- Gained understanding of banking at the retail operations and customer service level. Provided fast, friendly and accurate retail banking services.

Ranch Hand and **Manager**   Summers, 1992–1999
Amery Simmental Ranch, Lyle, Washington
- Hired, trained and supervised ranch hands. Purchased and sold herd of cattle in competitive markets. Researched genetic history; made breeding recommendations. Compiled and entered financial data on computer.

ACTIVITIES

Treasurer, Kappa Alpha Theta Sorority, Whitman College   1997–1998
- Maintained $16,080 budget through trial balance on computer.

Special Activities Committee, Whitman College   1997–1998
- Coordinated major public events, including Vienna Boys' Choir and San Francisco Ballet. Co-managed $50,000 budget.

Women's Coalition, Whitman College   1998–2000
- Charter Member. Organized Women's Resource Center.

Secretary, Economics Department, Whitman College   1998–1999
- Organized and coordinated Search Committee for new faculty members.

Host and Driver, Admissions Department, Whitman College   1998–2000

104

Note how the profile section of this résumé adds a power it would certainly lack without it.

Jennifer Cuzak
surfrgrl@earthspan.com

1699 Winthrop Street
Cambridge, Massachusetts 02138   (617) 555-6219

OBJECTIVE

A position with **Club Med** as a **Mini Club Med Gentile Organizateur.**

Strengths
- Consistent commitment to young adults and children combined with career in finance. Result: ability to relate successfully to Club Med parents, as well as their children.
- Ability to generate a large volume of activity ideas. Commended for creative activities in every position dealing with children.
- Experience with emotionally disturbed and behaviorally challenged children. Trained to deal compassionately and effectively with a wide range of behaviors.
- Club Med patron and true believer.

EDUCATION

Boston College   Chestnut Hill, Massachusetts
B.A., Human Development (emphasis on **Child Psychology**)   June 2001
- Dean's List (GPA: 3.5)
- Alumni Admissions Organizations

RELATED EXPERIENCE

The Children's Hospital   Boston, Massachusetts
Counselor (Intern), Judge Baker Child Guidance Center   1999–2000
- Planned and led weekly activities and field trips. Supervised meal times (breakfast, lunch, snacks). Consulted with psychiatrists and social workers on treatment programs. Gained ability to assist disturbed children in understanding their emotions and expressing themselves in non-violent and socially acceptable ways.
- Teacher's Aide for marine biology unit, reading groups, behavior modification sessions. Leader for expressive art therapy: paint, clay, decoupage, anything and everything.

Newton-Weston-Wellesley-Needham Multi-Service Center   Newton, Mass.
Counselor (Adolescents)   1998–1999
- Helped students to write in their journals, prepare dinner, and discuss whatever was of interest to them (school, sexuality, peer pressure, drug abuse, family problems, divorce). This is a drop-in and residential facility with an affiliated health clinic.

ADDITIONAL

- Currently babysit a newborn and a two-year-old several times per week for a highly successful investment broker.
- Big Brother/Big Sister, Boston.
- Boston Ballet Auxiliary Association.

BUSINESS EXPERIENCE

Morgan Stanley Dean Witter & Co.   Boston, Massachusetts
Sales Assistant   Summers, 1998, 1999

105

This student has never worked for pay a day in her life, but note that she has more than enough information to fill a résumé.

JUDE NOSSADAY

nossadayj@nsuva.edu
3721 Homestead Place, Cleveland, Ohio 44121
(216) 555-0913

STRENGTHS

- **Finance:** Finance emphasis in both graduate and undergraduate studies. Broad base of knowledge and skills in corporate finance, including entrepreneurial capitalization issues. Strong desire to apply education to real-world situations.
- **Analytical Skills:** Analytical by nature. Solid problem-solving abilities. Research and investigation skills, including international sourcing and fact-checking.
- **Personal Attributes:** Strong leadership skills. Decisive and goal-oriented. Effective in both individual and team competitive situations.
- **Communications:** Articulate, persuasive and quick thinking. Trilingual English/Mandarin/Indonesian.
- **Computers:** Mac and PC, all common business applications.

EDUCATION

Norfolk State University, Norfolk, Virginia   1998–2001
M.S.B.A., Finance Emphasis (GPA: 3.9/4.0)

Coursework included:
- **Finance:** Financial Management; Financial Reporting and Analysis; Financial Markets and Institutions; International Corporate Finance.
- **Banking:** Bank and Thrift Management; International Banking.
- **Investments:** Portfolio Management; Investments.
- **Management:** Business Development; Managerial Analysis and Communication; Business Policy and Strategy.

Accomplishments/Affiliations:
- **Treasurer, Minority Student Association.** Managed revenues and funds. Developed and implemented programs to promote cooperation and friendship between MSA members, the university, and the community.
- **Member,** Asian Business Association.
- **Member,** Finance Student Association.
- **Member,** Phi Alpha Delta.
- **Member,** American Management Association.

Oregon State University, Corvallis, Oregon   1996–1998
B.A., Finance. Emphasis in Banking and Investment. Minor in Chinese. (GPA: 3.8/4.0)

Coursework included:
- **Finance:** International Financial Management; Management of Financial Institutions.
- **Banking:** Monetary and Banking Theory.
- **Investments:** Security Analysis & Portfolio Management; Real Estate Investments.
- **Management:** Business & Its Environment; Business Policy; Management Information Systems.

Accomplishments/Affiliations:
- **Vice President, Permias** (Indonesian Student Association). Member of team to unite Indonesian students. Helped create/implement programs to introduce Permias to the University Community.

DANIEL KUMI
dan.kumi@swarthmore.edu

Temporary Address:
Box 1901
Swarthmore College
Swarthmore, Pennsylvania 19081
(215) 555-8388

Permanent Address:
c/o D.J.K. Kumi
#1995 Plaza Tower
New York, New York 10003
Message: (212) 555-1995

EDUCATION

Swarthmore College, Swarthmore, Pennsylvania
Candidate for degrees of **Bachelor of Science in Engineering** and **Bachelor of Arts in Economics,** with a concentration in **Public Policy,** expected May 2002 Recipient, Stephen G. Lax Scholarship for "academic distinction, leadership qualities, and a definite interest in business."
Harvey Mudd College, Claremont, California
Exchange student, Spring 2001.

EXPERIENCE

Office of Technology Assessment, U.S. Congress, Washington, D.C., *Summer Intern.*
Developed a model using mathematical and computer modeling techniques to determine developing countries with a potential for sustainable biomass energy system. Examined the role of U.S. policy in encouraging the adoption of improved technologies for economically and environmentally sound energy development in developing countries. June–Aug. 2001.

Southern California Gas Company, Claremont, California, *Co-Consultant.*
Assessed the economic, environmental, and the engineering design implications of biotechnology and its intersections with the natural gas industry. Jan-May 2001.

Public Computer Center, Swarthmore College, *Computer Consultant* and *Technician.*
Coordinated scheduling of repairs, upgrading and preventive maintenance (including campus computer network). Provided technical support, error analysis, consulting, and guidance to students in the use of all computer hardware, software and documentation supported by the Computing Center. Assisted professional staff in the development and implementation of computer workshops. Aug. 1999–Dec. 2000.

American Red Cross Society, Media, Pennsylvania, *Volunteer.*
Designed a format for computerizing the financial information of the Delaware County Branch, using SEROL R/IV. June–Aug. 1999.

Swarthmore African Studies Group, Swarthmore College, *President.*
Organized club meetings and public functions to broaden campus perspectives on African and African-American issues. Jan.–Dec. 2000.

Athletics Department, Swarthmore College, *Security.*
Supervised activities at college gymnasium, control of entrance/egress and property. Sept. 1998–Dec. 2000.

National Service Secretariat, Ghana, *Extension Officer, Fish Farming.*
Led a team of volunteers to educate the community on the advantages of fish farming, and on daily pond management as part of the community improvement program of the National Service Scheme. Nov. 1996–Aug. 1997.

TECHNICAL SKILLS

Solid experience in the use of spreadsheet programs (MS Excel, Quattro Pro), statistical packages (SAS, Jump), word processing applications (MS Word, WordPerfect, Xywrite, FreeWord), graphics programs (QuarkXPress, Harvard Graphics, PresentationsPro), mainframe computing (VAX, Sun, Apollo), and networks (Internet, Bitnet). Also: GEN IV, GEN V, and Hyper GEN.

EXTRACURRICULAR

Disc Jockey, college FM radio station; Captain, International Club Soccer. Active in the African Studies Group and the International Club.

107

Note the division of experience into functional categories.

Bruce Folkerth

zineman@uaoh.edu/radio

3721 Sweeney Avenue
Cleveland, Ohio 44138
(216) 555-9872

INTERESTS

Content – Writing – Editing – Publicity – Promotions – Public Relations
- Experienced music critic, conducting interviews with artists, coordinating with artists' management and recording companies.
- Highly reliable, deadline trained, strong general administrative and organizational skills.
- Ambitious, professional, committed to excellence.

EDUCATION

B.A., English, University of Akron, Ohio, 2001

EXPERIENCE
writing

The Patrol, www.musicpatrol.com, Cleveland Heights, Ohio, 2000–Present
Zine Staff Writer
- Review concerts and records, with a specialty in identifying and showcasing non-mainstream bands. Research musical events. Coordinate with talent, management, and recording companies. Regularly solicited by the editor for story ideas and for advice on strategic direction of the zine. Staff-writer, fall 2000–Present, New York stringer, summer 2000.

The Akron Buchtelite, Akron, Ohio, 1998–2001
Staff Writer
- Developed story ideas, researched and wrote articles, entered stories into the computer, assisted with paper layout and design, and other areas of operating a small newspaper.

Alternative Press, Cleveland, Ohio, 1999–2000
Contributing Writer
- Reviewed the national underground music scene. Stressed the uniqueness and importance of non-mainstream bands.

additional

Doubleday Books, Cleveland, Ohio, 1999–2001
Cashier
- Served as information source for customers regarding author, title and publisher. Wrote up special orders for books that were not in stock. Kept shelves full of latest releases as well as older titles.

Spitting Up Elvis, Akron, Ohio, 1998–1999
Drummer
- Punk rock/new wave band playing the Kent State circuit.

WRITING SAMPLES

References, additional information, review clippings, promotional writing samples provided on request.

108

Johanna Bell

jaybell@rain.net

427 – 80th Avenue NE
Seattle, WA 98134 ·

Telephone:
(206) 555-8517

OBJECTIVE: To find meaningful employment in **Environmental Sciences** or **Ecology**. Qualified for field or office assignments.

STRENGTHS:
- Strong education combined with office and administrative experience. Additional experience as field biologist.
- Bookkeeping, accounting, invoicing and records management skills, including MS Office.
- Professional telephone/public relations skill. Good detail person. Comfortable with volume of simultaneous responsibilities.
- Research and investigation skills, including library research, sourcing, purchasing/procurement, and similar functions.

EDUCATION:

B.S., Environmental Studies,   2001
B.A., Soviet Studies,   2001
The Evergreen State College, Olympia, WA

- Earned double degree with wide range of electives.
- Conversational in Russian language; studied Russian language and Soviet and Russian culture.
- Advanced knowledge of fisheries issues, including three contracts as a U.S. observer on foreign-flag fishing vessels (Soviet and Japanese).

EXPERIENCE:
(while student)

Joint-Venture Representative,   2001
Marine Resources Company International, Seattle, WA

- Worked on bridge of an 82-meter Soviet fish processing ship in the Pacific and Bering Seas. Coordinated incoming tonnage from U.S. ships. Spoke and interpreted Russian and English.
- Invited to work with two other boats due to reputation for working hard (sometimes over 36 hours at a stretch) and efficiently.

Observer,   1999, 2000
National Marine Fisheries Service (NOAA), Seattle, WA
- Served as official representative of the United States government aboard foreign-flag fishing vessels in U.S. territorial waters. Indirectly in charge of crews of several hundred fishermen. Inspected and documented fishing tonnage. Spoke and interpreted Russian.

Research Assistant,   2001
Sentencing Guidelines Commission, Olympia, WA
- Performed research on the Washington state information bank, SCOMIS. Compiled data and entered into computer. Gained informal understanding of sentencing guidelines and judicial methodologies.

Research Assistant,   2001
Merlyn M. Bell, Consultant, Seattle, WA
- Collected primary data from county jail files on felony inmates' real time-in-jail for comparison to state sentencing guidelines and to actual sentences rendered. Traveled to county jails in Washington.
- Filled out standard data forms and entered study data onto computer.

Assembler,   1997
Symetrix, Inc., Seattle, WA

109

Susannah Mamada Lujan

lujansm@syracuse.edu
11305 Long Branch Road
Bath, New York 13205
(607) 555-1452

PROFESSION: **Teacher (French, Spanish, ESL, Language Arts)**

CREDENTIAL: **Teaching Certificate,** State of New York, pending

EDUCATION: Syracuse University, Syracuse, New York
B.A., Education, with **Romance Languages Endorsement,** June 2000

University of Guadalajara, Guadalajara, Mexico
Spanish Language, Literature & Culture, January–June 1998
Additional Studies:
  SUNY-Binghamton, 1993–1995

EXPERIENCE: Independence Elementary School, Syracuse, New York, Spring 2000
teaching **Language Teaching Practicum, French & Spanish**
Developed and taught language curriculum for students in third-grade enrichment classes. Created exciting lesson plans without textbook or collateral materials. Allowed to be in full charge of class.

Remsen High School, Remsen, New York, Spring 2000
Student Teacher, Spanish & ESL
  Planned and taught Spanish I & II to two classes of students from grades 9–12. Also developed and taught ESL class for non-English-speaking students from Mexico, Central America, Haiti, and Vietnam. Created successful learning atmosphere to reach students from very divergent backgrounds. Allowed to be in full charge.

Central High School, Syracuse, New York, Spring 1999
Junior Block Teacher
  Developed new and interesting curriculum for two Spanish I classes. Allowed to be in full charge.

Syracuse University, Syracuse, New York, Spring 1999
Language Teaching Practicum (College Level)
  Led two classes in weekly Spanish conversation group. Developed techniques to encourage confidence and get students to take risks.

additional Onandaga County Literacy Program, Syracuse, New York, 1999–Present
Tutor (volunteer)

Onandaga County rural fire District 31, Syracuse, New York, 1994–1997
Engineer (only woman engineer)

Malone's Apple Orchard, Elmira, New York, seasonal, 1996–1998
Dryer Tender (supervised Hispanic assistants)

Holiday Tree Farm, Wanakena, New York, 1995–1996
Supervisor (organized, delegated to, supervised and translated for Spanish-speaking crews)

ACTIVITIES: Gardening, food preservation, photography, travel, Spanish literature.

REFERENCES: Credentials file with transcripts and recommendations provided on request through Career Development Center, Syracuse University, Syracuse, New York, 13205.

> Here is another student who doesn't follow a strict chronology—to her benefit.

Margaret Knobloch

Office: (415) 555-9700, ext. 823
Residence: (510) 555-1728

OBJECTIVE: **Sales / Marketing / Account Relations**

STRENGTHS:
- Demonstrated self-starter with effective combination of organizational and communication skills.
- Strong liberal arts education combined with public relations, promotions, office, administrative and customer service experience.
- Professional appearance. Advanced telephone and customer interaction skills.
- Demonstrated leadership aptitude; strong work ethic; computer literate.

EDUCATION:

B.A., Spanish / English Literature   expected Dec. 2001
American University
- Fluent in Spanish: read, write, translate, interpret.
- Dean's List (with up to 17 units per semester)
- Founder of Kappa Gamma, a new, campus-based philanthropy group. Later aligned Kappa Gamma with Alpha Phi to become first campus chapter of this national sorority, and the first new sorority in many years.

Year Abroad, University of Seville, Spain   1999–2000
- Studied Spanish Language, Literature & Culture.
- Traveled extensively in Spain and the rest of Europe.

Diploma, Grassmount High School, Bethesda, Maryland   1998
- Sophomore Class President, Student Council President, Student Body Vice President.

EXPERIENCE:
career experience

Promotions Intern, Winterland Productions, San Francisco, California
                              Summer 2000, Winter Holidays 2000–2001
- Originally recruited to coordinate launch of a national "J.C. Penney Rock & Roll Program." Served as key contact, representative, motivator and problem solver for over 500 accounts in the program. Supervised clerical staff.
- Solved 1001 problems daily. Worked overtime as needed. Repeatedly commended for service above and beyond management expectations.
- Helped build a $30 million business from scratch!

additional

Visa Courier, Capitol Visa Service, Washington, D.C.   Part-time 1998
- Prepared and processed visa applications as liaison between customer and foreign embassies. Demonstrated a talent for "negotiating" with consular staffs who had a habit of disapproving applications for no reason.
- Got many visas approved that had been denied to the applicants themselves.

Front Office, Betty Walton, M.D., Washington, D.C.   1997–1998
- Provided front office management. Maintained calendars. Processed payments. Handled incoming phones. Screened all calls and visitors.

Bar Staff, T.G.I.F.'s, Washington, D.C.   Part-time 2000
- Completed professional waitstaff training program (64 classroom hours). Passed comprehensive exam with one of the highest scores.

Assistant Manager, Karl's Eidelweiss Inn, Libertyville, Illinois
                                                  Summers 1997, 1996

- Opened, closed, inspected work on each shift. Lived directly above the restaurant. Worked 12-hour shifts, 6 days/week.

111

Stanford Rappaport
multilingual@lonestar.net
Curriculum Vitae

> This résumé could be considered a curriculum vitae except for the profile, which makes it more of a résumé even though it is titled 'curriculum vitae.'

Mailing Address:
392 Bonaventura Drive
Austin, Texas 78741
(512) 555-5633

PROFESSION:
Technical Translator / Technical Writer

EXPERTISE:
- **Languages: English, French, German** (completely fluent: speak, read, write, translate, interpret into, out of, or between any of these three languages, including technical, scientific and business manuscripts and documents). Conversational proficiency in **Russian, Spanish, Chinese.** Translating experience with approximately 30 languages and dialects, with emphasis on the major and minor Romance and Germanic languages.

- **Technical Writing:** Experienced technical and academic writer, editor, proofreader. Programming experience and understanding of software development process.

- **Additional:** Nationally rated chess player (ranking: Expert). Symphony musician.

EDUCATION:
M.A. (ABT), French Linguistics, University of Texas, Austin, 2001
B.A., French and **German** (double major), Tulane University, New Orleans, Louisiana, 1996

EXPERIENCE HIGHLIGHTS:
Texas Energy Research Associates, Inc., Austin, Texas, fall 1998, 2001–Present
Technical Translator
- Translate technical and business documents into English from French, German, Spanish, Italian, Portuguese, Danish, Norwegian, Swedish and Dutch. Major ongoing assignment: Translate technical materials on computer software, computer hardware, physics, nuclear engineering, and agriculture from French and German into English.

Database Programmer
- Performed programming and systems maintenance functions on both Windows NT and Unix-based systems.

Tipton Cole & Company, Austin, Texas, spring 1998
Database Manager
- Developed, tested and documented relational database management system software for industrial hygiene applications for a major oil company.

Technical Writer
- Selected to develop documentation for numerous projects, including working directly with the company's best programmers and analysts.

Holt Reinhardt & Winston, Austin, Texas, 1997
Academic Writer
- Wrote selected passages in French textbooks for this publisher. Developed French pronunciation and grammar exercises for textbook and supplementary materials.

continued

STANFORD RAPPAPORT C.V./ **PAGE 2**

EXPERIENCE HIGHLIGHTS:
(continued)

Linguistics Research Center, University of Texas, Austin, Texas, 1996–1997
Research Assistant
- Proofread material in over 30 foreign languages. Compiled bibliography for etymological dictionary of the Gothic language. Handled related database on unix-based system.

University of Arkansas, Fayetteville, Arkansas, fall 1994
Translator
- Translated material on physics and astrophysics from German into English.

ACADEMIA:
University of Nice, Nice, France, 1996
Instructor, English Department

University of Texas, Austin, Texas, 1994–1995
Instructor, French Department

Keimyung University, Daegu, South Korea, 1990
Instructor, English Department

ADDITIONAL EDUCATION:
Russian, University of Arkansas, Fayetteville

Mandarin Chinese, University of Texas, Austin

Korean, Keimyung University, Daegu, South Korea

German, University of Heidelberg, West Germany

ADDITIONAL:
Highly committed. Seeking long-term career position involving ongoing challenge and opportunity for growth. Open to contract and short-term special project assignments. Excellent references from all former employers.

113

MARK O'CONNEL ROGET

marksetgo@windy.com

Local Address:
15237 Ashbury Way
Evanston, IL 60202
(815) 555-3782

This student's background clearly demonstrates the value of getting a head start on your career through related internships and work experience.

INTEREST

Financial Operations

• Solid technical understanding of financial instruments, trading, and operations. Excellent memory for policies, procedures and details. Effective training and supervisory skills. Efficient and accurate.

EDUCATION

Loyola University of Chicago, Chicago, Illinois
B.A., Finance, 2000

EXPERIENCE

Pershing 7 Company, Chicago, Illinois, and New York, New York
Floor Broker, NYSE, 2000–Present

• Hand-picked for this position by officer in the Chicago branch. Execute orders on the floor of the NYSE. Relay information on market conditions to clients, solve problems as they arise. Supervise Floor Manager, Wire Operators, and Runners.

Order Desk Clerk, Chicago, summers/holidays/breaks, 1998–1999

• Coordinated between floor brokers and international clients on options transactions. Also cross-trained as an Assistant on the Currency Desk, interacting with Canadian and U.S.-based currency traders. Worked full time while completing degree in night school.

Prudential-Bache, Inc., Chicago, Illinois
Stock Options Clerk (Intern), summer 1997

• Coordinated between brokers and traders to ensure accurate trading on accounts. Verified margin accounts stayed within credit limits. Communicated directly with clients as necessary. Balanced and posted trades to accounts daily.

Francis Manzo & Company, Mount Prospect, Illinois
Sales Assistant (Intern), winter break 1997

• Sales assistant to a major equities broker. Handled customer inquiries and request for quotes, prioritized and qualified incoming calls, gained knowledge of investment instruments. Also did some cold-calling on behalf of the broker.

Chesley & Dunn, Investment Bankers, Tampa, Florida
Sales Trainee (Intern), fall 1996

• Gained understanding of sales and equities, options, fixed-income products.

LICENSURE

Credentials presented upon interview.

114

Note how this candidate features classroom design experience convincingly.

Patricia L. Tuori

Telephone: (408) 555-53034
E-mail: gooddesign@aesthete.com

EMPHASIS: **Commercial Interior Design**

EDUCATION: **B.F.A., Interior Design**   2000
Academy of Art College, San Francisco, CA
• Awarded Merit Scholarship in Open Competition
• Special Projects:
   Clayton Restaurant. Senior Commercial Project. Designed 3500 sq. ft. building adjacent to existing structure in historical "Western Town" style, including interior and space plan for indoor/patio restaurant. Plans, presentation materials, model.
   International Shipping Company. (IBD Award.) Developed design for 9th floor of Shell Building (100 Bush, San Francisco). Provided design concept, space plan, finishes, presentation boards, floor/ceiling plans, reception desk, model.

Liberal Studies   1996–1997
Dominican College of San Rafael, San Rafael, CA
• Awarded Scholarship for the Oxford Summer Program

EXPERIENCE: **Laura Ashley, Interior Design Services,** San Francisco, CA   1998–2000
Assistant Designer
• Worked directly with clients. Provided on-site design services. Prepared financial contract bids. Initiated, conducted and completed interior design engagement.
• *Significant Projects:*
   American River Hospital, Sacramento. Prepared bid and presentation materials for $150,000 project (custom-design birthing rooms). Met with hospital medical personnel for design research. Presented proposal to hospital executives.
   Private Residences of Dave Hartley of Channel 3 News. All bedrooms.
   Other Private Residences, Bay Area. Completed interior design of homes of up to 7000 sq. ft. Space planning, colors, finishes, furnishings, treatments.

Omega Designs, San Francisco, CA   1998
Designer
• Provided residential interior design consultation.
• *Significant Project:*
   Arlington family. $160,000 redesign of luxury residence, including close interaction with every family member and historical research of existing furniture and rugs.

SKILLS: Strengths include model building, space planning, color and texture specifications, perspective drawings, drafting, rendering, and creation of presentation materials.

ADDITIONAL: Counselor and Coach, international track competitions trip through Europe, Sir Francis Drake High School. Resident Counselor, San Domenico School. Manager, Tres Chic Boutique.
• Office, administrative and business management skills. Articulate and professional; qualified for client interaction.
• Full range of commercial and residential interior design skills, including development and drafting of complete design plans.

PORTFOLIO: Letters of recommendation and portfolio provided on request.

115

MAXINE G. COHEN
artscience@eastlink.net

66 West 82nd Street
New York, New York 10003

This student's background also demonstrates the value of getting a head start on your career through related internships and work experience.

EDUCATION

degrees
STANFORD UNIVERSITY, Stanford, California
M.A., East Asian Studies   2001
   Emphases: Mandarin Chinese Language; History of Chinese Art & Culture
HARVARD UNIVERSITY, Cambridge, Massachusetts
B.A., Art History (minor in Economics)   1999
   Studio Arts Program, Florence, Italy   Fall 1997
   Socioculture of Australia, Sydney, Australia   Winter 1997

post-graduate
SOTHEBY'S HOUSE, London, England
Sotheby's Educational Studies   Fall 2001
   Attended course of study covering identification of Asian art and artifacts through
   analysis of form, decoration, and knowledge of historical development of styles.
   Also studied hagiography and iconography in private tutorial. Conducted, presented
   and defended original research. Previewed and attended Sotheby's sales.

leadership
NATIONAL OUTDOOR LEADERSHIP SCHOOL (NOLS)
Kenya Environmental Trip   Fall 1999
   Three-month mountain trek and jungle safari featuring Mt. Kenya, Nyuraman,
   and coastal areas. Trained in group decision-making, survival, and team building.
UNIVERSITY OF PITTSBURGH, Pennsylvania
Semester at Sea   Fall 1998
   Traveled around the world on the U.S.S. Universe.

EXPERIENCE
MONTAGUE GALLERY, New York, New York   Winter 2001
Intern
   Researched "Young Couple at a Springtime Meadow," a painting by the French
   Impressionist Henri Martin. Researched artist's life, milieu and painting's history.
   Wrote marketing material to accompany sale of the painting.
TIANJIN FOREIGN LANGUAGES INSTITUTE, P.R.C   Fall 2000
Instructor
   Developed syllabus and taught courses in English, American culture, and
   American business protocol.
STANFORD PROJECT ON INTERNATIONAL CROSS-CULTURAL EXCHANGE
(SPICE), Stanford, California   2000–2001
Research Assistant
   Researched and wrote background material for secondary school curriculum on
   China, including units on Chinese art and artisans.
IBM, White Plans, New York   Summer 1999
Assistant Producer
   Produced executive and product-training videotapes. Coordinated and moderated
   a series of roundtable discussions for quality assessment program.
PITKIN COUNTY DRY GOODS, Aspen, Colorado   Winter Holidays, 1993–1996
Assistant Manager, The Ski Shop
Head, special Orders Department
Sales Associate
   Involved in most areas of this well known sport clothing store. Participated in
   special events: Aspen Music Festival, Salute to the Southwest, Aspen CARES
   (benefit). Consistently averaged $3000+ for personal daily sales.

ACTIVITIES
List on request.

116

Sometimes enthusiasm
and availability are
a student's best assets.

Richard P. Adcock
morphen@criticalmass.org

Telephone:
(213) 555-7469

SKILLS:
- **Cinematographer**
- **Videographer**
- **Grip**
- **Production Assistant**
- **Film/Tape Editor**

Available as needed, 25 hours per day, 366 days in each and every year.

EXPERIENCE:
KPSX TV, Canoga Park, California, September 1998–May 2001
Camera Operator, Production Assistant, Grip

Camera Operator for studio production, live coverage of sporting events, and breaking news. Grip for motorized and manual dollies. Technician for electronic and manual film edit, 3/4 to 1/2 transfer, and 1/4 sound to full coat and edit.

Designed and built sets, backdrops, and some props. Purchased film stocks, consulted with film labs for developmental procedures, designed large-scale interior and exterior, day and night lighting projects. Participated in student film projects.

CREDITS:
Director, Director of Photography, Casting, Director, Camera Operator
The Game
Ruth
Godzilla
Option II
The Grand Evasion
Circle R
A Crowd of One
The Magic Elevator
The Collision
The Streets of Bellefonte

ADDITIONAL
EXPERIENCE:
Dennis, Guy & Hirsh, New York, New York, July 2001
Production Assistant
"Olympic Commercial" for Budweiser.

AFFILIATIONS: American Film Institute

EDUCATION:
California State University, Northridge, California
Bachelor of Arts in Film, 2000

AVAILABILITY: See above.

117

REBECCA LEMOV
R.Lemov@alumni.Yale.edu

503 Cortez Circle
Miami, Florida 33133

Telephone / Message:
(305) 555-8331

STRENGTHS: **Editing, Writing, Proofreading, Research, Design**
- Technical command of the English language: grammar, syntax, semantics, spelling, punctuation. Detailed knowledge of *The Chicago Manual of Style* and *The Associated Press Stylebook.*
- Experience in copywriting, copyediting, proofreading, and production.
- Studio artist with illustration and production design experience. Exposure to magazine art direction, soliciting artwork, and working with artists.

EDUCATION: **YALE UNIVERSITY,** New Haven, Connecticut
B.A., English   2001
- Graduated *magna cum laude,* with Distinction in the Major
- Nominated for Rhodes Scholarship
- National Merit Scholar

Additional Studies:
- Art Institute of Chicago, Chicago, Illinois
- Leo Marchutz School of Art, Aix-en-Provence, France

EXPERIENCE: **TIKKUN MAGAZINE,** Oakland, California   Summer 2000, 2001–Present
Editorial Assistant
- Provide editorial, artwork, and production assistance for the largest-circulation Jewish magazine in the United States, a bi-monthly critique of politics, culture and society.
- Work directly with the editor-in-chief, proofreading, copyediting, and evaluating manuscript submissions.
- Provide illustration and editorial design for articles.
- Direct office and administrative management.

Special Projects:
- Researched and summarized articles by women in Tikkun, to recruit more women writers.
- Staffed two conferences sponsored by the magazine.

SMITH & WATTS, Miami, Florida   Summer 1999
General Office
- Member of the drafting team and an administrative assistant for landscape architecture and environmental planning firm.
- Drafted site plans, prepared scale illustrations.
- Contributed to development of formal bids, proposals, presentations.

PUBLIC CITIZEN, Washington, D.C.   Fall 2000
Research Assistant
- Worked with the director on study of government regulatory agencies (EPA, NHTSA) under the Reagan-Bush administration, 1989–1997.
- Analyzed government and legislative documents, drafted position papers, proofread and copyedited sections of the report.

OTHER:
- Editor for *Graduate Admissions Essays: What Works, What Doesn't, and Why,* by D. Asher, 10 Speed Press, August 1999.
- Long-distance bike treks in California and New England; backpacking in Sierras; touring in Europe.
- Varsity Sports (Swimming, Cross-Country, Track).

PORTFOLIO: Work samples provided on request.

118

This résumé is too long, but full of great data. I wouldn't cut a word of it. It's a perfect example of the exception that makes the rule.

K. W. D. CHRYSLER (Mr.)

Connecticut College Box 1177
New London, Connecticut 06320-2213
(203) 555-4882
(203) 555-2343 (fax)
kwdc@swarthmore.edu

Education

Connecticut College, New London, Connecticut **Bachelor of Arts,** expected May 2002
  • Major: Economics; minors: Applied Music, German
  • Dean's List every semester (GPA: 3.73)
  • Buttenwieser Scholar (highest undergraduate award)
  • Founding Member, Center for International Studies and the Liberal Arts
  • Other Activities: Choir, German Club (treasurer), German and Economics Advisory Boards, College Republicans, Campus Tour Guide, Racquetball, Tennis

Institut für Europäische Studien, Freiburg, Germany Fall 2000
  • Studied Politics, Economics, and Law of the EC (GPA: 3.85)
  • Visited all major EC institutions/discussed integration issues with EC leaders

Universitat Regensburg, Regensburg, Germany Summer 2000
  • Studied German Language, Philosophy, and Economics in Bavarian city.
  • Selected as one of only 48 students from North America

Yale University, New Haven, Connecticut Summer 1999
  • Completed 1 year's curriculum in 8 weeks in Summer Language Institute
  • Awarded Zertifikat Deutsch als Fremdsprache for proficiency in German

Warwick High School, Lititz, Pennsylvania Diploma, 1998
  • Graduated with Distinguished Honors (GPA: 3.82)
  • Presidential Academic Fitness, Best Mallet, and Chorus Awards

Work Experience

Corporate Finance Intern, Salomon Smith Barney, Frankfurt, Germany Summer 2001
  • Researched and identified acquisition and divestiture targets for presentations
  • Translated and compiled factual information on German companies
  • Initiated coverage on Austrian beverage manufacturers
  • Wrote debt/equity offering memoranda for real estate deals

Institutional Equity Intern, Bear, Stearns & Co. Inc., New York, New York January 2001
  • Studied profitability of ADR and convertible business with institutional clients
  • Determined relative market position among other competing firms
  • Identified and investigated incorrect charges to departmental budget

Equity Analyst/OTC Trading Intern, Lehman Brothers, New York, NY January 2000
  • Exposed to equity research by meetings with middle and senior level analysts
  • Assisted Vice President of OTC Institutional Equity Trading
  • Entrusted with advertising equities over the autex network
  • Helped perform large block program trades

Broker's Assistant, Lehman Brothers, New Haven, Connecticut Summer 1999
  • Attracted over 40 new clients to the firm
  • Prospected Municipal Bonds, Annuities, Stock, and Commodity Funds
  • Improved client relations through phone calls/mailings and prompt response to inquiries
  • Wrote and implemented a highly successful cold-calling script

Research Assistant, Diversity Strategic Planning Team, Connecticut College Year 1998–99
  • Helped identify ways to define and increase racial and socio-economic diversity on campus
  • Lauded for 70-page white paper on incorporating diversity issues into the liberal arts curriculum
  • Created informational network that cut across bureaucratic lines

119

Organizational Involvement

Associate Publisher (CFO), <u>College Voice Publishing Group</u>,
Connecticut College   January 2000–Present
- Compiled, audited, and managed $42,000 budget
- Increased ad revenue by approximately 25% through aggressive marketing
- Increased fundraising 163% from $7000 to $18,000 in one year
- Developed cold-calling system; raised $1000+/week
- Lobbied school administration, trustees, and SGA on newspaper-related issues
- Recruited and managed advertising staff
- Improved contact with parents and alumni; increased subscription sales
- Formulated editorial policy through voting Executive Board seat

Presidential Associate, <u>Student Government Association</u> (SGA)   Year 1999–00
- Advised Executive Board on policy management issues as a full voting member
- Expanded role of this position to include strategy/policy planning
- Budgeted, audited, allocated funds (achieved $500 surplus through fundraising)
- Influenced college-wide decision-making through frequent meetings with Trustees, College President, Vice-Presidents, Faculty, Deans, and other student leaders
- Initiated movement to include students on key administration committees
- Envisioned, planned and chaired first SGA intra-school conference on leadership

Committee Experience

<u>Priority Planning and Budget Committee</u> (PPBC)   Year 2001–02
- Elected to the most powerful college-wide representative committee
- Participated in developing annual budget for the college
- Implemented and refined five-year strategic plan; prioritized strategic goals of the college

Founder and Chair, <u>Student Development Committee</u>   January 2000–Present
- Conceived of initiative to use students in college's development tasks
- Managed student phone-a-thon, raising $186,000 (86% above goal)
- Traveled with President for presentations to alumni in New York, Connecticut, Florida
- Increased visibility and responsibility of student component of development efforts

Co-Chair, <u>Ad-Hoc Committee on Student Governance</u>   Year 1999–00
- Elected to review governance structure of SGA
- Heightened efficiency through restructured Executive Board and Committees
- Slashed bureaucracy; improved working effectiveness of SGA

<u>Student Response to the Strategic Plan Committee</u> (SRSP)   Year 1999–00
- Coordinated and compiled student input on five-year strategic plan
- Lauded by President and Trustees for 90-page analysis
- Headed movement to implement January academic term

<u>Trustee Student Liaison Committee</u>   Year 1999–00
- Presented student concerns on strategic planning, divestment, and endowment to college trustees at quarterly meeting

<u>Trustee Committee on Shareholder Responsibility</u>   Year 1999–00
- Elected to debate issues surrounding the college's investment policy
- Coordinated student responses on divestment issues
- Served on divestment policy sub-committee

<u>Advisory Council to the V.P. of Finance</u>   January 2001–Present
- Elected to represent student viewpoints on financial, safety and staffing issues
- Learned about college's financial and accounting functions

Note this technique of putting functional headings down the left margin and dividing experience into BUSINESS and OTHER.

Margo Winters
winters99@landline.com

permanent address:
511 Gary Road
Cheyenne, WY 82001
(307) 555-9871

EDUCATION

Swarthmore College
Candidate for **Bachelor of Arts** in the **Honors Program** ongoing
Major in **Economics,** minors in **Mathematics** and **Computer Science**

Richardson High School
Graduated May 1997 **with honors,** 13th/650, Richardson, Texas
National Merit Scholar, National Honor Society
President/Math Club, Vice President/German Club

BUSINESS EXPERIENCE

Market Research
Intern, Semiconductor Industry Service, Dataquest, Inc., San Jose, California. Interfaced with research staff, industry experts, and clients. Wrote and helped publish six 15- to 30-page research profiles on major U.S. semiconductor manufacturers. Summer 2000.

Sales Support
Sales Assistant, Electronic Systems, Siemens Aktien Gesellschaft, Erlangen, Germany. Supported sales department for electronic systems to the food and paper industries. Formulated planning models and graphs on personal computer. Summer 1999.

Financial Planning
Intern, Annual Planning Department, Frito-Lay, Inc., Dallas, Texas. Participated in the corporate financial planning process. Generated profit and loss income statements under numerous scenarios of sales mix and production allocation. Summer 1998.

Communications
Office Assistant, Marketing Communications Dept., Mostek Corporation (a division of United Technologies), Carrollton, Texas. Assisted marketing professionals in varied daily tasks and special fifteenth anniversary activities. Summer 1997.

Advertising
Intern, Communication Plus – Advertising/Public Relations, Richardson, Texas. Selected in open competition from school district-wide pool of recommended applicants for pre-professional internship in advertising. Fall semester 1996.

OTHER EXPERIENCE

Counseling
Resident Assistant, Swarthmore College. Liaison between students, deans, housekeeping and maintenance staff. Fall 1999 to present.
Co-Coordinator and **Facilitator, Swarthmore College Race Relations Workshop.** Helped plan and conduct Racism Awareness workshops. Presented a controversial video tape and effectively led discussions on racial issues. Fall 1999 to present.

Organizational
Budget Committee, Swarthmore College. Served on executive committee which allocates and manages $200,000 Student Activities Fund. Served on sub-committees for hiring paid treasurer and staff, purchasing student body vehicles, and implementing a new computer accounting system. Fall 1996 to fall 1998.

Academic
Consultant, Swarthmore College Computing Center. Assist student users in word processing, programming and computing problems on PRIME 9950 mini-computer, SUN workstations, and APPLE Macintoshes. Spring 1996 to present.

121

Tierney Britz
Tierney997@aol.com

430 Gaslight Parkway, #8
Indianapolis, Indiana 46217 (USA)
Telephone: (317) 555-0729

Here is yet another
example of abandoning
chronological order to
concentrate on strengths.

EDUCATION	Indiana University, Indianapolis, Indiana **M.A. Candidate, English Language Studies,** 2002 • Concentration: **Teaching English as a Second Language** University of Indianapolis, Indiana **B.A., Psychology,** 1998 Belmont High School, Elkhart, Indiana **Diploma,** 1994 I.E.S., Vienna, Austria **Studies Abroad,** Fall 1996 • Concentration: **English Literature** **German Language and Literature**
LANGUAGES	**Italian, German, French**
COURSEWORK	• **Seminar on the Structure of English** (graduate) • **Graduate Study—TEFL*** (graduate) • **Grammar and Rhetoric of the Sentence** (graduate) • **Phonology and Morphology** • **Transformational Grammar** • **Second Language Acquisition*** • **Advanced Composition**
RELATED EXPERIENCE	Indiana University, Indianapolis, Indiana **English Tutor,** Spring 2001 • One-on-one instruction and tutoring of college-age non-native speakers of English. Includes coaching with academic writing as well as addressing issues at basic levels (sentence structure, subject-verb agreement, etc.). • In full charge of the tutoring sessions. Develop lesson plans addressing issues specific to each student. Delegate outside assignments reflecting each student's needs. • Teach students to incorporate specific English lessons into well-structured essays and compositions. Recreation Center for the handicapped, Indianapolis, Indiana **Teaching Assistant,** Fall-Winter 1997–98 • Led classes for mentally and physically handicapped children and adults. Taught spelling and mathematics. Created games to convey concepts and to make learning fun. • Structured and chaperoned group outings, dinners, exercise sessions, and other activities.
ADDITIONAL EXPERIENCE	Abbe's Clothing Store, Indianapolis, Indiana **Retail Sales** and **Bookkeeping,** 1998–Present

Scheduled for summer 2001.

122

PAUL COUCH
couchp@uscca.edu/alumni

726 West Street, Apt. D
Costa Mesa, California 92627

Telephone/Message:
(714) 555-0137

STRENGTHS

Financial analysis and all mathematical/statistical based analysis. Skilled in Excel and Quattro Pro.

Background in project planning and assessment of profit potential of proposed business activities.

Demonstrated ability to be successful with a wide range of individuals, from men and women business executives to non-English-speaking construction laborers.

Strongly career-oriented. Available for travel and relocation as needed for continued career advancement.

EDUCATION

<u>University of Southern California</u>, Los Angeles, California
B.S., Business Administration, expected may 2001

Emphasis:
• Entrepreneurial Studies

Selected Coursework;
• Corporate Finance
• Organizational Behavior
• Applied Economics
• Information Systems
• Analytical Decision Models & Operations Management Theory

• Accounting & Financial Reporting
• Applied Managerial Statistics
• Strategic & Competitive Analysis
• Marketing & Sales

Activities:
• Delta Chi Fraternity (Treasurer)
• Real Estate Association
• Entrepreneur Association

EXPERIENCE

<u>HCV Pacific Partners</u>, Los Angeles, California
Financial Analyst, winter 1999–2000, fall 2000
• Analyzed potential development options for a 14-story financial district highrise. Developed "best and highest use" analysis, including scenario modeling on multiple variables.
• Developed $26 million redevelopment business plan including seismic retrofit, with five years of pro formas for the property.
• Also reviewed acquisition proposals at the rate of three or four per week, analyzing potential of investment properties.

<u>Dorét Construction</u>, Los Angeles, California
Construction Laborer, summer 2000
• Assisted in construction of a Kaiser Hospital. Developed basic knowledge of large-scale construction techniques and practices.

<u>Brinks, Inc.</u>, Los Angeles, California
Air Courier Supervisor, 1998–1999
• Received incoming high value air shipments (usually jewelry, currency or financial instruments). Routed and dispatched to three carriers.

<u>Adalante Group Enterprises</u>, Costa Mesa, California
Assistant Manager, 1993–1998
• Co-manager of $750,000 business with ten employees, a "saladeria" in a mall food court. Achieved gross profits as high as 32%.

123

DANIELLE S. PEATTIE
DSPeattie@ISPI.net

130 Hickory Drive
Nashville, Tennessee 37214

Office: (615) 555-2028
Residence: (615) 555-0922

PROFILE
Human Performance Technologies / Training & Instruction / Human Resources

- Experienced instructor. Energetic, enthusiastic, able to create atmosphere of learning and attention to detail. Experience in all phases: pre-training assessment, training and performance/knowledge testing, quality assurance, follow-up.

- Strengths include customer service training, entry-level management skills, PC applications, standard operating procedures (SOP), high-accuracy bookkeeping, all aspects of retail operations.

- Available for business travel as needed. Capable of prolonged performance at fast pace. PC skilled. Some exposure to multi-media. Good business writer.

- Member, Society of Human Resources Managers.

EDUCATION

VANDERBUILT UNIVERSITY, Nashville, TN   expected 2001
B.S.B.A. (Bachelor of Science in Business Administration)
Concentration in **Human Resources Management**

EXPERIENCE

KROGER INC., Memphis, TN   summers and some holidays, 1998, 1999, 2000
Training Instructor

- Full-time instructor, 8 hours/day, 5 days/week. Instructed new hires, promotions, and management trainees. Coordinated training function with store managers. Wrote official memos to all stores concerning changes in training or SOP. Reported to the Training & Development Supervisor.

- Trained management personnel on bookkeeping, computer procedures, personnel policies, store policies, and related.

- Trained store staff on SOP, customer service, and position integration. Trained trainers on presentation skills for OJT to other staff.

- Modified and/or developed training materials as needed.

Sample Project:

- Train-the-Trainer for 35 Debit/Credit Coordinators and File Maintenance Clerks from stores. Recruited specific students from Division. Organized and implemented training manual and program. Trained personnel to load and update software. Scheduled and coordinated these trainers' mission throughout 235 stores in Division. Troubleshooter and key contact for the whole process.

JACKSON LOCK COMPANY, Nashville, TN   part-time, spring 2000
Intern (Human Resources)

- Analyzed jobs and work flow. Redesigned job descriptions for all Product Engineers. Developed Salary Surveys to determine competitive practices. Developed benchmarks for seniority and experience levels.

WORK SAMPLES ON REQUEST

Terese Lawler
TL76@fans.wired.com

c/o Wallace Stubenski
449 South Cloverdale Avenue, Apt. 302
West Hollywood, California 90036

Telephone:
(213) 555-9766

INTERESTS   Television, Film, Media

SKILLS   **Research, Production, Post-Production**
- Very strong research and fact-checking skills. Effective copywriter for press releases and PSAs. Good phone. Light accounting and financial experience. Available overtime, nights, weekends, you name it. You hire me, your worries are over.
- Wide ranging knowledge of liberal arts, film, broadcast and print media, other arts, culture, sports, history.
- Fluent in Lithuanian (very handy!).

EDUCATION   <u>**University of California,**</u> San Diego
B.A., Visual Arts / Media and **B.A., Communications**   2000
- Provost's Honors with Double Bachelors
<u>**University of London,**</u> England
Certificate, British Media & Culture   1998

EXPERIENCE   <u>**Entertainment Tonight**</u> **(Paramount),** Hollywood   Summer 1999
Research Assistant / Media Clearance / Production Assistant
- Researched and evaluated stories, provided fact-checking, organized research library, filed stories.
- Promoted to Media Clearance Department, working with attorneys on legal matters for Phantom Menace.
- Selected for many production and post-production duties, working with segment directors.
- Promoted again to work as P.A. for segment producer for "The Insider," researching story material and file footage.
<u>**Hard Core Film Productions,**</u> San Diego   1998–1999
Producer / Publicist / Assistant Director / Accountant
- Co-Founder of Hard Core Film Productions, a student film production company organizing groups of up to 100 students on "full-scale" student film projects (16 MM format). Member, Executive Council.
- Designed and set up the accounting system for this program.
- Producer, "Bloodfall." Raised $6,784 in production funds. Recruited and supervised cast and crew of 52.
- Publicist/Fundraiser, "Bugs in Our Hair." A.D. for "Nuclear Wasted."
<u>**Times Mirror – Dimension Cable Vision,**</u> Vista   1998–1999
Production Assistant / Camera Operator
- Assisted in writing scripts and shootings scripts. Assisted in post-production. Camera Operator for City Council meetings.
- Selected by producers to be assistant director on some commercial shoots.
<u>**20/20 Television,**</u> London, England   Summer 1998
Production Assistant / Research Assistant
- Wrote 20/20 proposal for "The Effects of Technology on Children," submitted to B.B.C. and Channel 4.
<u>**KSDT FM Radio,**</u> San Diego   1996–2000
Public Affairs Director / Assistant News Director
- Producer for weekly UCSD public affairs program airing on KSDO AM, a commercial station. Member, Steering Committee, KSDT.

125

Lee Sifani
itsallgood@lake.web

2828 Sylvan Street, #2
Ann Arbor, Michigan 48112

Telephone:
(313) 555-5654

PROFILE: **Management . . . Marketing . . . Sales**
- Eager to contribute to the rapid growth of a progressive, entrepreneurial company with a quality product.
- Qualified by business education, successful sales and customer service management experience, and entrepreneurial nature.
- All general office and computer skills.
- Highly motivated. Available as needed for travel, overtime, special projects, etc.

EDUCATION   **B.S., Management**   2001
Purdue University, Lafayette, Indiana
- Dean's List and Distinguished Student Award (GPA: 5.3/6.0)
- Alpha Lambda Delta Scholastic Honor Society
- Purdue Women's Soccer Club and Intramural Volleyball Team
- Member, Treasurer & Newsletter Chair, Association of Collegiate Entrepreneurs (A.C.E., Purdue Branch)
- Member, National Creative Thinking Association

National Conference   2000
National Association of Collegiate Entrepreneurs

Turkish Language & Culture Intensive Program   1998
Bougizici University, Istanbul, Turkey

EXPERIENCE: *Sales Manager*   2000–Present
Scentura Creations / Exclusive Creations, Chicago, Illinois
- Created and implemented aggressive direct sales campaigns for men's and women's fragrance products.
- Interviewed, hired, trained and motivated a sales team of 15 direct sales associates.
- Led sales meetings, wrote scripts, demonstrated technique, established individual sales goals and incentive plans.
- Managed all sales administration and daily accounting.

Sales Associate   1999
Lutterloh's Garden Shop, Lafayette, Indiana
- Sold flowers, plants and nursery items in large "wholesale to the public" store. Trained as Assistant Manager. Supervised gardening crew.
- Offered position of Manager but declined to continue with business degree program.

Office Assistant   1995–1998
Evansville Metal Products, Inc., Evansville, Indiana
- Gained experience and skill in all back-office management functions, including preparing spreadsheets on Lotus 1-2-3, handling client relations by telephone and correspondence, routine accounting (A/P & A/R).
- Managed personal business for the President, including serving as the liaison between the President and his stockbroker.

TODD SIRIMONGKOLVIT

3dmon@design.com

2547 Sutter Street
San Francisco, California 94115

Telephone:
(415) 555-8611

INTERESTS **Architecture & Design**

- Fine arts background spanning art history, studio arts, and criticism. Seeking exposure to architecture and design in anticipation of pursuing master of architecture program.

- Skills include mechanical drafting, perspectives, model building, design details.

EDUCATION UNIVERSITY OF CALIFORNIA EXTENSION, Berkeley, California
Construction Documents, Spring 2001

UNIVERSITY OF CALIFORNIA, Berkeley, California
A.B., Arts, 2000

CHABOT COLLEGE, Hayward, California
Pre-Architecture, 1996–1998

SUNSET HIGH SCHOOL, Hayward, California
Diploma, College Preparatory Studies with emphasis in **Art**, 1996

SELECTED PROJECTS
- Design According to Human Needs—A Study of Rincon Centre.

- Post-Design Evaluation—Walter Haas Park, San Francisco.

- Historical Study of City Planning—Thomas Jefferson Plan, Jeffersonville.

- Art Installation—Wurster Hall, U.C. Berkeley.

EMPLOYMENT THAI BURIN, Bangkok, Thailand
Designer, Summer 1999

- Designed residential projects, consulting directly with the client. Prepared construction documents subject to review by senior architects. Coordinated with the Project Director.

- Designed in modern Eastern architectural styles, incorporating Western design theories and Eastern construction practices. Used foreign language skills: Fluent in Thai; knowledge of two dialects of Chinese, including Mandarin.

REFERENCES Portfolio with work samples provided on request.

127

TANIA FICONA PAZERI
TFPEsq@legal.net

40 East 9th Street, Apt. 308
New York, NY 10003

Telephone/Message:
(212) 555-1316

INTERESTS
- **International, Environmental, Constitutional, Medical Law**
- **Corporate Law, General Litigation**

LANGUAGES
Fluent in French, Italian
Proficient in Arabic

EDUCATION
COLUMBIA UNIVERSITY SCHOOL OF LAW, New York, NY
J.D. Candidate, expected 6/2002
  Dean's List
  Vice President, Student Bar Association
  Phi Alpha Delta Legal Fraternity
  International Law Society
  Women's Association
  Westlaw and Lexis

NEW YORK UNIVERSITY, New York, NY
B.A., History-Legal Studies, 6/1998
  Honor Students' Society
  President, International House Council
  Events Organizer, International House Program Office

EXPERIENCE
legal

COLUMBIA CONSTITUTIONAL LAW CLINIC, New York, NY
Externship, 8/2000–Present
  Selected to serve on a litigation team of three students and Professor Mort Cohen. Provide legal and factual research in preparation of a lawsuit asserting the constitutional rights of poor and clinically incompetent people in need of medical treatment who are denied the right of a surrogate decision maker. Research and summarize points of law, draft memorandums, interview potential plaintiffs, contribute to ongoing development of case strategy.

BRONX OWN RECOGNIZANCE PROJECT, Bronx, NY
Internship, 6/1997–6/1998
  Interviewed defendants, researched and verified strength of community ties, prepared reports on findings with recommendations. Attended arraignments for felony and misdemeanor defendants. Followed up on defendants after release, to remind them of court dates and to ensure their compliance with the terms of their release.

non-legal

COLUMBIA SCHOOL OF LAW, New York, NY
Fundraiser, Development Office, 2–7/2000

OAKLAND COMMUNITY COLLEGE, Auburn Hills, MI
Student Assistant, Science Department, 2/1995–4/1996

PUBLIC MENTAL HEALTH HOSPITAL, Pontiac, MI
Intern, 2–4/1995

SPEAKING
"Findings from the 'Decade for Women': Approaching a New Millennium," given before the NYU International House Lecture Series, Fall 1998.

AFFILIATIONS
Member, New York Women Lawyers

CALIDA L. COLEMAN

7320 Shorepointe Drive
Detroit, Michigan 48220
(313) 555-6120

Objective   To continue achieving excellence in educational pursuits through high school, and to graduate from a university while continuing singing, acting, and theatrical interests.

Education   **Clinton Elementary School,** Detroit, Michigan, 1997 to present
GPA: 3.75/4.0

Study / learn complicated 5th-grade materials:
- math
- science
- reading
- English
- social studies

Maintain outstanding attendance and conduct.
Photo selected to appear in current school promotional literature.

Plymouth Day Care School, Detroit, Michigan, 1997
Completed rigorous program of kindergarten studies. Mastered phonics foundations and socialization skills. Performed in Christmas and Easter programs.

Activities   **Clinton School Players**

- You're A Good Man Charlie Brown—May 2002—Snoopy
    Performed two solo songs and significant dialogue

- Hello Dolly —May 2001—Judge
    Speaking and tap dancing role

- 42nd Street—May 1999—Cast
    Cast and chorus member, significant tap dancing.

- Peter Pan—May 1998—Cast
    Dancing and singing roles.

Music

- Piano lessons since 1998, with continuing progress to more complex pieces by Bach, Beethoven, Chopin, Czerny, Liszt, Mozart, and others.

Interests   Mathematics, reading, writing stories, singing, dancing, performing, and my continuing research of American amusement parks.

129

Annie S. Prinkle

Asprinkle@zool/ahl/michigan.edu
121 Valentine Circle
Lansdale, PA 19446
(215) 555-0827

INTEREST   A position as **Nutritionist** or **Veterinary Assistant** with the Bronx Zoo.

STRENGTHS
- Knowledge of rodent, canine, feline, equine and primate nutrition, including pathologies.
- Knowledge of clinical/microbiology laboratory techniques.
- Read, write, speak, translate German.

EDUCATION   **The University Of Michigan,** Ann Arbor, Michigan
B.S., Zoology, *summa cum laude,* 2000

Emphases: • Microbiology • Parasitology • Biochemistry • Evolution
Skills: Recombinant DNA technology, protein synthesis and regulation, plasmids and cloning, restriction endonucleases, organic chemistry, spectrophotometer, autoclave, chromatography, titration, dissection, nutrient plate preparation, analysis of blood and fecal samples.

RESEARCH   **Prof. R. Heihnricht, The University of Michigan**
Only undergraduate selected for trip to Kenya to investigate ecosystem coefficients to an outbreak of equine fever among Grevy's zebra, *Equus grevyi*. Laboratory manager, in charge of microscopes and field lab equipment, sterilization, integrity of specimens. Sponsored in part by the Government of Kenya.
Prof. W. Derr, The University of Michigan
Laboratory assistant in insect-insect parasitology research that served as the foundation for Prof. Derr's paper, "A micro-model of co-evolution," which won the NSF Lamarck Award for best paper on evolution, 1999.
Prof. Y. Yang, The University of Michigan
Performed literature survey to catalog abstracts and articles on all known water-producing fauna for a period of the last twenty years.

MAJOR PAPERS   "A Surprising Analysis of the Nutritional Properties of Major Brands of Rat Block: The Sum of the Parts ≠ Effect of the Whole," presented to the Regional Meeting of Research Animal Husbandry Professionals, Madison, Wisconsin, 1999.
"Toward a New Taxonomy: Some Logical Challenges as a Result of Recent Advances in Genetic Engineering," selected by the *Michigan Undergraduate Science Journal* as best undergraduate paper of 1998–1999 (Summer 1999, pp. 128–136).
"Metabolism and Exercise, or Why Laboratory Nutrition Data Don't Work Out," honors thesis presented to the Zoology Department, U. Mich., May 15, 2000.

EMPLOYMENT   **The University of Michigan,** Ann Arbor, Michigan, 1999–2000
Teaching Assistant / Laboratory Instructor, Dept. of Zoology
- Prepared and presented undergraduate laboratory teaching assignments for Prof. Y. Yang.

The University of Michigan, Ann Arbor, Michigan, 1996–2000
Husbandry Caretaker
- Cared for rats, mice, cats, and monkeys for the Depts. of Psychology, Biology, and Zoology. Also occasionally served as relief husbandry caretaker for the School of Agriculture and the School of Veterinary Medicine, including experience with large animals.
- Initiated and managed the "Rats on Loan" program with three local school districts.
- Earned 50% of educational expenses through employment.

130

CHAPTER 12

How to Write a Technical Résumé

YOU JUST LEARNED HOW TO WRITE A TECHNICAL RÉSUMÉ

Technical résumés are not really any different from standard business résumés. As a matter of fact they are structurally identical: heading, profile, education, and experience. The main difference is that a technical résumé almost always includes a profile of technical skills (whereas profiles are otherwise optional in an entry-level business résumé). Also, at the risk of stating the obvious, the information can be presented in much more technical language. While a standard business résumé should make sense to any mailroom clerk, a technical résumé may be totally unintelligible to anyone outside the targeted discipline.

In a technical résumé you will put even less emphasis on any education or experience that is not directly related to the technical skills cluster you are presenting. Any career you may have had before gaining the targeted technical expertise will be mentioned only briefly. If you have experience with an obsolete computer programming language, omit it or put it in a KEYWORDS or ADDITIONAL list at the bottom of your presentation. In general, a technical résumé is even more focused than the typical business résumé; if an item doesn't support your candidacy, leave it out.

Technical recruiters, headhunters, human resources professionals, and principals in entrepreneurial, high-tech firms tell me that they look especially for these three things:

> Qualifying technical skills
> Evidence of intelligence
> Neatness and consistency

Qualifying technical skills are usually presented in a profile. If a recruiter is looking for a C++ programmer or a UNIX systems administrator, they will look no further than the profile to see if you have these skills to offer. Remember to list your qualifications in order of interest to the employer, not the order of interest to you. You might choose to rank your skills like this:

"Expertise in ___, ___, ___. Knowledge of ___, ___, ___. Some exposure to ___, ___."
Note that it is common to list technical skills that you may need to brush up on, or may
need a few days to become fully proficient with. Even if it has been a year since you
programmed in AUTOBAHN or used an autoclave, don't be afraid to list it. Remember
that employers are buying your technical aptitude as well as your proficiency.

On the other hand, you should resist the urge to make any false claims. If you never
mastered a skill, or you just walked by the room where once you think maybe they
were discussing gas chromatography or wireless LANs, do everybody a favor and leave
it off your résumé entirely.

It may be essential to list specific classes you have taken if they indicate skills that would
not be evident from your degree title and experience. List class projects that indicate
you have gained a particular technical skill. And, of course, use every trick and technique you learned from the chapters on business résumés. The final document must
indicate that you have the necessary technical skills to perform in the position you
have targeted.

Here is one classic presentation of a technical skills cluster:

EXPERTISE   **CADD Systems Administration**
- **H/W:** Macs and PCs w/ all peripherals in all configurations.
  XOBEX parallel AI workstations.
- **O/S:** Windows NT, DOS thru ∞, OS/n, UNIX System IX,
  CLIX for KIGDS.
- **Languages:** 3D/TIME gen5, Bentley/Intergraph
  (user-programmable macro files created in text editor).
  Microstation Development Language (MDL—a version
  of CYRIL).
- **S/W:** AutoCAD R22, PC/320 Microstation R3.3/R4.0, EDG,
  Z Soft, Object Stor, Visual Bank, and all common office apps.

◉ ◉ ◉

Evidence of intelligence is more difficult to establish. In fact, you shouldn't address
the issue directly at all. Putting "IQ: 145" on your résumé might be considered gauche,
or even worse, might intimidate a boss with an IQ of 140. Putting "quick learner" on
your résumé is such a cliché that you'll be lucky if they don't count it against you. You
can list your GPA, but unless it is 3.5 or higher, I wouldn't recommend it.

One middle manager who is responsible for hiring young engineers told me that he assesses a candidate's intelligence by how the résumé is constructed. "I can tell by how well they are able to anticipate my criteria, and how efficient they are at presenting their data relative to those criteria." In other words, anticipate your employer's needs and present your data in the most efficient format. Obviously, mind readers have a distinct advantage in this process.

Employers are impressed by students who have been appointed by faculty to positions that demand intelligence. If you were a TA or a test grader or a personal research assistant, it is almost guaranteed that you are smarter than the average plebe. Honors and awards can also be good indicators. Even the briefest mention of this type of data can strengthen a technical résumé considerably.

Here is an EDUCATION section that effectively conveys this candidate's intelligence:

SAN JOSE STATE UNIVERSITY, San Jose, California
Bachelor of Science, Electrical Engineering, May 2000
Grade Point Average: 4.0 in major, 3.9 overall
President's and Dean's Scholar
Derick Morgan Scholarship
Chinese American Engineers & Scientists Scholarship (1st place nationwide)
Senior Design Project:
• Designed and constructed a solar detector which enabled device to position itself for maximum exposure to sunlight. Successfully applied digital, analog, and electromechanical concepts. Achieved 0.03% variance from ideal.

⊙ ⊙ ⊙

Neatness and consistency, important to any résumé, are crucial in technical résumés. I sat next to a rather famous scientist/entrepreneur on a plane once, and from San Francisco to Chicago we discussed his theories on hiring scientists and engineers. "I don't read the résumé at all at first. I hold it out at arm's length and ask myself, 'Is this work that I would want to represent my company?' If the answer to that is no, I don't even read it," he said. "If it looks okay, next I look for inconsistencies. Consistency is like logic, and if a person can't be consistent, he can't be logical. How can I entrust the simplest project to someone who can't even construct an internally consistent résumé?"

I once wrote a résumé for a product development engineer who developed key components used in commercial sound systems worldwide. He was an expert in applied physics and electronics, but his résumé was a disaster. He had typed it out on onionskin paper, smeared it, copied it, and then copied the copies and the whole thing was poorly organized to begin with. He couldn't understand why no one was calling him, and yet his true skills were entirely hidden by his presentation.

Neatness and consistency are good indicators of a person's attention to detail. Nobody wants a junior engineer whose slovenly work habits are going to screw up a project or department. No matter how smart you are, you still need to appear well organized, especially at the entry level.

Technical Résumés Are Often Project-based

Special projects are often highlighted on technical résumés. Much of the work done in engineering and science can be broken down into discrete projects—little stories, in effect, that are interesting to read and effectively convey a candidate's experience and abilities. Although entry-level applicants may not have a string of projects to report, you should know about this technique for use later in your career. Here are two examples from senior professionals, a turbine engineer and a structural engineer, to give you an idea of the preferred construction:

Sample Projects:

> **Field Service Engineer / Project Manager,** Humboldt Bay Unit 2. Provided technical direction for turbine generator inspection and rotor bore exam through start up and turbine vibration analysis.

> **Job Safety Coordinator,** Helms Hydrogeneration Storage Project, Shaver Lake. Developed safety and evacuation plans, wrote work procedures, contracted for standby paramedic and emergency medicine procedures, investigated safety problems.

> **Lead Engineer, Planning & Scheduling,** Diablo Canyon Power Plant. Prepared work packages to identify what components and parts needed to be inspected, and wrote procedures, work plans, and check-off lists.

> **Field Engineer,** Life Extension Study, Pittsburg Unit 5. Investigated unit condition and obtained data for life extension study. Co-planned the study; coordinated with project engineer.

◉ ◉ ◉

134

Sample Projects:

> **Field Engineer** on Jolliet TLWP floating platform for Conoco, installed in 1712 feet of water in the Gulf of Mexico. This was a first-of-its-kind installation. Supervised and coordinated 60 welders, riggers, divers, surveyors, tugboat captains and marine crane operators. Developed classes and trained field crews (foremen, engineers, winch drivers, mates, etc.) every day for two weeks. Successfully applied engineering plans never tried before.

> **Field Engineer** and **Construction Supervisor** on upgrade and refit of Crane Vessel Hermod from 5000 tons to 9000 tons lift capacity, Port of Rotterdam. Kept project on schedule. Up to 1000 personnel per day contributed to project. Ensured build-out to plans. Made inspections with Certifier from Lloyds. Controlled material flow. Completed project in just six months. (Bidding shipyards had estimated in excess of 1 year). Total project cost US $80,000,000.

> **Company Representative** at the fabrication facility, Gulf Marine Fabricators, Aransas Pass, Texas. Verified compliance to design provided by our engineering department. Updated scheduling and filed progress reports with home office. Modified rigging layout, reducing costs by improving over one mile of heavy installation. Supervised during jacket load out 924,000 tons.

⊙ ⊙ ⊙

Whether you were the guiding force behind the project or the third assistant to the second shift engineering support assistant, listing projects will give your résumé more heft.

When you read over the samples in the next chapter, look for concise profiles of technical skills, effective presentations of coursework and class projects, evidence of intelligence, neatness and consistency, project-based experience reports, and all the other aspects of a good résumé. Whether your area of expertise is analytical chemistry or microwave telecommunications, these examples can guide your efforts and help you craft a better résumé.

CHAPTER 13

Samples, Samples, Samples: Technical Résumés

Patrick Olis Reyes
reyesp@AI.umass.edu

permanent address
Route 1, Box 231
Ocean View, DE 19970
(302) 781-8388

school address
Engineering MS 37818
University of Massachusetts
Amherst, MA 01003

SKILLS

Computing Infrastructure Management / Release Engineering
- Unix and NT Systems Administration: Emphasis on Security and Laptops
- Release Engineering of large C/C++/Java packages

EDUCATION

University of Massachusetts, Amherst
B.S.E.E., with emphasis on Operating Systems, Compilers,
Software Engineering, 2000

Senior project:

Release Engineer for a major internal application consisting of 150+ binaries and libraries. Built scripts to automate testing, configuration and RCS. Designed and released TCL/SQL interface. Developed software to interface with semi-conductor equipment.

SPECIAL PROJECT

Research Assistant to Prof. Weisen
S/W Release Coordinator
- Coordinated release of Galileo Project software (300K lines of C/C++, 130K lines of Java, 6+ Unix Platforms and NT). Communication point for on-site and off-site developers. Planned, built, and tested releases. Ported to Unix and NT systems. Set coding standards, reviewed and integrated student designs.

EXPERIENCE

University of Massachusetts, Amherst
UNIX Systems Administrator, Engineering Systems Department, 1999–2000
- Managed all aspects of 4060 Unix Workstations (Mostly Sun, but also HP, SGI, DEC). Upgraded hardware, performed backups, tightened departmental security. Managed FTP site, WWW site. Supervised student employees (Programmer/Analysts).

NT Systems Administrator, Electrical Engineering Department, 1998–1999
- Packaged CVS/SSH for internal use. Setup video and PowerPoint capture pilot project with GSRC.

Help Desk, Undergraduate Computing, 1997–1998
- Wrote user guides using FrameMaker. Source code manager for Documentation Group. Assisted customers with problems via e-mail, telephone, and counter service.

PERSONAL

Have traveled to five major American deserts for lightweight, long-distance trekking. Amateur desert botanist.

KEYWORD LIST

Unix, NT System Administration, e-commerce, e-business, online transactions, security systems, encryption, firewall design, C+, C++, Java, HTML, TCL, SQL, RCS, Sun, HP, Hewlett-Packard, SGI, DEC, FTP, CVS, SSH, GSRC, help desk, technical support, online support systems, FAQ compilations, documentation, technical writer, grant proposals, Software Release Engineering, Scientific Computing.

137

MINDY DARROW
darrow3@bostoncollege.edu /alumni

> This student had experience at a top biotech company, and decided to list it before education.

permanent address
174 Post Street
San Francisco, California 94113

KNOWLEDGE

Biochemical Manufacturing / Protein Purification
Small- and large-scale Amicon chromatography columns. Romicon and Millipore ultrafiltration cartridges. Continuous feed Alfa Laval centrifuges. Gaulins homogenizers. Various centrifugal and displacement pumps. Waters Millipore HPLC. Small-scale lyophilizing equipment. Hewlett-Packard spectrophotometers. Large-scale in place stainless steel tanks. Large- and small-scale glycol heat exchangers. Amsco glassware washers and driers. Finn Aqua and Amsco autoclaves. MS Office Suite. Claris Works.

EXPERIENCE

Genentech, Inc., South San Francisco, California
Product Recovery Operations
Senior Technician (Intern)
Summers 1999, 2000

Conducted the large- and small-scale recovery and purification of proteins utilizing various ultrafiltration and chromatography processes in a GMP environment. Coordinated day-to-day purification activities for marketed products. Oriented new staff. Wrote and revised GMP tickets and SOPs for specific manufacturing processes, e.g., wrote the SOPs for steam sterilizing of in place and portable stainless steel tanks and associated filters used in the final purification facility.

Also provided technical support on purification processes to R&D labs working with HPLC and lyophilizing equipment. Assisted in scaling up projects from R&D into clinical trials, including revision GMP documents and SOPs to facilitate transition.

Only undergraduate intern ever promoted to this level of responsibility.

Lab Services Technician   Summer 1998
Acid washing of organic chemistry glassware used in production and R&D. Maintained sufficient supplies of sterile lab equipment to meet production and R&D requirements.

Biology Department, Boston College, Chestnut Hill, Massachusetts
Research Assistant   1999–2000
Research assistant for Dr. Y.C. Ting in Cytogenetics laboratory, experimenting with Maize tissue. Prepared culture media and maintained records of experimental media compositions. Analyzed tissue culture response. Directed own pilot experiment with Teosinte tissue culture. Ordered supplies and equipment.

ADDITIONAL SKILLS

Genetics: Electrophoretic determination of DNA molecules. Preparation and observations of mammalian chromosomes. Identification of regions of DNA using Southern Blotting. Study of inheritance patterns of mutant traits in Drosophila.

Chemistry: Qualitative and quantitative analysis, pH titrations, spectrophotometry, column and thin layer chromatography, chemical extractions, recrystallization, distillation.

EDUCATION

Boston College, Chestnut Hill, Massachusetts
B.S., Biology and **B.A., Philosophy,** 2001

138

Note this student's project-
based experience listings.

Geneva M. Heller, E.I.T.
helleronit@aol.com

Telephone:
(510) 555-6139

EXPERTISE: **Mechanical Engineering**
HVAC Design

KNOWLEDGE: Heating, ventilating and air conditioning systems, cooling and heating load calculations, hydronic system calculations, and domestic/industrial plumbing systems. Proficient in use of TRACE computer program for energy budget analysis and comparison of HVAC system types.
Engineer-in-Training, State of California.

EDUCATION: University of California, Berkeley, CA
B.S., Mechanical/Environmental Engineering, December 2001
ASHRAE Technical Seminars, San Francisco, CA
Accoustics, Indoor Air Quality, Summer 1999
Santa Clara University, San Jose, CA
Temperature Controls for HVAC Systems, Spring 1999

EXPERIENCE: Keller & Gannon, San Francisco, CA
HVAC Engineer (Junior), 1999–Present
Provide engineering calculations and design drawings under supervision of senior mechanical engineer; collaborative and team projects.

Domestic:
• **Lawrence Berkeley Laboratory,** Berkeley, CA
Designed layout of low conductivity water system and heating/ventilating system for Advanced Light Source Building.
• **Mare Island Naval Shipyard,** Vallejo, CA
Prepared energy budget analysis for use in selecting most energy-efficient HVAC system. Designed complete HVAC and plumbing systems.
• **Kunia Field Station,** Oahu, HI
Modified existing HVAC system to accommodate new computer facilities.
• **Department of Energy,** Washington, D.C.
Design of ventilation system for sixty-mile-diameter Superconducting Super Collider Tunnel.

International:
• **Army Corps of Engineers,** European Division
Investigated, analyzed and charted underground utility lines for Master Planning Project of U.S. military community in Frankfurt, Germany.
• **Army Corps of Engineers,** European Division
Prepared domestic technical models and calculations for Energy Analysis Program based in Ankara, Turkey.

ARAMCO, Houston, TX
Junior Engineer (Intern), Summer 1999
Reviewed piping and instrumentation diagrams of onshore and offshore drilling platforms.

AFFILIATION: **Student Associate,** American Society of Heating, Refrigeration, and Air Conditioning Engineers (ASHRAE), Golden Gate Chapter, San Francisco

Note lack of strict chronology.

Sergei Bismarjian

SB187@EECS/UCBerkeley.edu
372 Lenten Street
Pinole, California 94564
(510) 555-8119

EDUCATION
University of California, Berkeley
B.S., Electrical Engineering, Bioelectronics, 2000
B.S., Biochemistry, 2000

	With concentrations in **Hazards – Safety – Bioengineering**
honors	Graduated *magna cum laude*
	Dean's Honors, 1996–2000
	Cumulative GPA: 3.84
merit scholarships	U.C. Berkeley Briggs Scholarship, 1997–2000
	U.C. Berkeley Torossian Scholarship, 1997–2000
	U.C. Berkeley Mangasarian Scholarship, 1996–1999
memberships	U.C. Berkeley Honor Students' Society, since 1999
	Golden Key National Honor Society, since 1999
	Outstanding College Students of America, since 1998
	Eta Kappa Nu Engineering Society, since 1997

EXPERIENCE

Baker, Wright, Dean, DeOme Law Offices, Oakland, 12/1996–11/1997
Investigating Engineer
- Investigated chemical, biological, biochemical, and electrical accidents in research, medical and industrial facilities throughout the nation on an on-call/as-needed basis.
- Performed experiments and calculations to determine source(s)/cause(s) of accidents. Prepared case reports detailing system/procedural flaws.
- Researched handling, storage, transportation and disposal of genetic and infectious materials. Kept abreast of changing regulatory requirements.

Neurobiology Lab, University of California, Berkeley, 1/1998–5/1999
Research Assistant
- Prepared and handled set-up of equipment and apparatus for neurobiological experiments involving effects of recombinant DNA.
- Inserted electrode with microdrive into frog's cochlear nucleus to capture the electrical discharge of neurons caused by artificially induced sound.
- Used oscilloscope and audio system. Entered and analyzed data using various software programs on RT-11.

Smith-Kettlewell Medical Research Institute, San Francisco, Summer 1999
Research Assistant
- Assisted with measuring electrical impulses resulting from eye movements of a macaque monkey. Prepared and cared for monkey. Performed careful insertion of electrode into the uvula using microdrive. Utilized oscilloscope and speaker to capture Purkinje cells.
- Gathered, entered and analyzed results using DAT computer, Fortran program, RT-11 for saccadic and pursuit analysis. Created, combined and averaged files, and produced histograms.
- Designed special circuits for different experiments and made specialized tools using electromechanical equipment.

LANGUAGES   Armenian and Russian.

140

Sylvia Chevrier

SC2001@biology.stanford.edu

1930 Waverly Place
Palo Alto, California 94301

Office: (510) 555-5395
Residence: (408) 555-5026

PROFILE
Clinical Research Associate
- Proven ability to independently manage Phase I and Phase III clinical trials, including all relations with physicians, study coordinators, administrators, and others. Knowledge of FDA regulations. Skilled on Mac and PC platforms (office and analytical programs, including MedTest and TrialTracker).

EDUCATION
Stanford University
Stanford, California
B.S., Biological Sciences
5/2001
- Knowledge of neurobiology, signal transduction in cells, human physiology, immunology, nutrition, genetics, psychology, and numerous other areas.

EXPERIENCE
Bartax Laboratories
HQ: Alameda, California
Clinical Research Associate Intern
6/2000–1/2001

Hired to coordinate Phase I trials in the treatment of multiple sclerosis. Verified data from four study sites nationwide, approximately 100 patients total (traveled). Ensured compliance to FDA regulations and trial protocols. Monitored budget administration; initiated requests-for-payment. Selected accomplishments:
- Collaborated with CRAs, physicians, and company managers to write amendments to trial protocols.
- Negotiated details of new contracts with investigators and hospital administrators.
- Solved logistical problems with timely delivery of drugs (refined the drug demand projections to improve planning and eliminate supply bottlenecks).
- Resolved data discrepancies for period 1999–2000, eliminating two-year backlog.
- Sponsored company training: Effective Study Monitoring (GCPs, FDA Regulations, Adverse Event Reporting), Effective Business Writing.

V.A. Medical Center
Palo Alto, California
Senior Hemodialysis Technician
8/1997–9/1998

Acted as manager of Technical Department, in charge of 18 dialysis machines and the training and technical development of four new Hemodialysis Technicians. Documented and logged use, testing and maintenance of dialyzers, in compliance with hospital and departmental procedures. Ordered supplies as needed. Represented hospital to vendor technicians. Contributions:
- Revised the Technician Training Manual
- Under the direction of the Chief, Dialysis Technology, researched effects of varying dialysate sodium concentration during patient treatment; provided nursing in-service and wrote technical procedure incorporating results.
- Also trained as Patient Care Technician, three months of intensive training leading to assignments in direct patient care.

Department of Neurology, Stanford Medical Center
Stanford, California
Research Assistant
10/1996–6/1997

Co-designed and conducted a laboratory experiment for S. Peroutka, M.D., Ph.D. Collaborated on writing protocols. Surveyed literature on receptor binding techniques and chloride channels. Investigated binding of 3H verapamil and 3H strychnine to a receptor in the intestine. Analyzed and plotted data (Scatchard analysis).

prior

Office Assistant, Financial Services, Stanford University
Administrative Assistant, Primary Care Network
Office Assistant, Department of Nuclear Medicine, Stanford Hospital
Laboratory Assistant, Department of Genetics, Stanford Medical Center

This applicant is selling military experience and puts it ahead of his education

Cyrus R. Rosenberg

geeksrule@jobshop.net

c/o 9710 Lower Buckeye Road
Phoenix, Arizona 85012   (602) 555-5558

EXPERTISE: **Electronics Technician**
- Seeking bench or field technician position using strong diagnostic and troubleshooting skills.

SKILLS:
- Can construct, diagnose, repair, and maintain a very wide range of electronic and microchip-based equipment, to the individual component level.
- Strengths include (1) radio and communications gear, including microwave and radar, (2) television, VCR, consumer electronics, and cable transmission equipment, and (3) a range of microchip-based equipment, including dedicated computers built into other equipment.
- Can read and utilize any tech manual, shop manual or schematic diagram.
- Some experience running computerized diagnostic programs. Extensive experience with full electronics shop tools.

EXPERIENCE: **U.S. Navy**   February 1998 to February 2000
Electronics Technician
- Part of a team of electronics technicians responsible for every electric and electronic device onboard ship. Trained in creative problem solving (there are no parts suppliers at sea).
- Maintained, calibrated, and troubleshot analog and digital radar equipment, communications equipment, Tacan, IFF, and cryptographic equipment. Also maintained and repaired onboard entertainment systems.
- Planned and completed two comprehensive overhauls of Air Search Radar System.
- Demonstrated leadership and reliability. Earned advancement in rate in shortest possible time-in-service.
- "Secret" Security Clearance.

Underwriters Laboratory   Summer 1997
Laboratory Technician (Intern)
- Hands-on electrical/electronic testing and component-level troubleshooting on consumer products: transient voltage surge suppressors, electromagnetic interference filters, computer keyboards, monitors, audio amplifiers, electronic medical equipment, lighting ballasts, transformers, CB radios, adaptors, and others.
- Experience with oscilloscopes, multimeters, logic analyzers, frequency counters, signal generators, signal conditioners, printed circuits, wire wrap tools, chart recorders, and other bench tools.
- Disassembled products, conducted testing, recorded data, wrote summaries of findings.
- Trained new technicians in how to do tests, how to operate equipment, and computer logging system.

PRIOR: Electrician's Helper in residential and commercial construction.

EDUCATION: **Basic Electricity/Electronics School**
Electronics Technician "A" School
Synchro/Servo Principles Training
Three Maintenance Schools on Classified Equipment
Petty Officer Indoctrination School
B.S., Astronomy, Arizona State University   December 1997

142

Loretta Royston

LR22@UT.EDU
Telephone:
(512) 555-0372

Mailing Address:
2130-B Kensington Drive
Austin, Texas 78740

PROFILE

Originality and resourcefulness in developing innovative analytical models and solutions using interdisciplinary approach of **physics, statistics, and mathematics.** Dedication and drive reflected in strong academic and employment records; balanced course load of 15–17 units per semester with 40+ hours per week employment.

EDUCATION

University of Texas, Austin
Bachelor of Science in Physics, minor in Mathematics, March 2000
• Dean's Honors
• JFK National Honor Society
• National Physics Society

EXPERIENCE

International Business Machines, Inc.   Austin, Texas
Reliability Engineer/Statistician   June–September 1999
  Devised method of statistical analysis to interpret results of process testing for newly developed engineering practice. Worked directly with engineers in charge of designing and developing cutting-edge engineering process which significantly enhanced product quality and reliability.
  • Devised original approach to this revolutionary technology, statistical model of the process itself, and working interpretation of test results.
  • Authored chapter on statistical methodology for inclusion in book to be released in conjunction with this product.
  • Wrote technical paper detailing statistical data of new engineering process.
  • Received offer of permanent position with IBM based on contributions.

Department of Defense, Engineering Division   San Diego, California
Engineering Technician, Product Support Systems June 1997–June 1999
  Created tests, charts and engineering presentations related to procurement and support systems. Reviewed engineering drawings and maintenance plans.
  • Civilian member of Quality Assurance team responsible for testing and inspection of Mobile Facilities to determine potential problems and ensure integrity of automated test equipment.
  • Actively contributed to writing, formatting and design of government manual entitles "Handbook for Dealing with Contractors and Processing Delivery Orders," which was distributed to all DOD contractors.
  • Wrote database program to track delivery orders and status of active contracts for capital equipment.
  • Received cash award for outstanding performance.

University of Texas, Austin, Memorial Union   Austin, Texas
Night Manager and Team Leader   December 1996–January 2000
  Co-supervised operations and scheduling of five-story Memorial Union building serving student population of 18,000. Oversaw 15 night managers.

COMPUTERS

Skills include: Windows NT, Windows ∞, MS DOS ∞, Linux, MS Word, WordPerfect, Unix/VMX, Auto-CAD, Grafstat, Floating Point Planner, DataMine, and numerous other software packages for charting, tracking, analysis, and reporting. Programming abilities.

143

> Sometimes a student's major can serve the same function as an objective or profile statement.

Sean Padraic Condon
SeanCondon@business.rensselaer.edu

present address
19 Nassau Street
Troy, New York 12173
(518) 555-2437

Education	**B.S., Management** expected December 2002 Concentrations: **Business Information Systems** and **Finance** Rensselaer Polytechnic Institute, Troy, New York GPA in IT/Computer Science: 3.7 GPA in Business/Economics: 3.23
Experience	**System Programmer/Analyst** 5–9/2002 Power Generation Division, Gas Turbine Operations General Electric Co., Schenectady, New York *Team member on the following projects:* • Integrated database entry programs with existing operating system for design modifications of gas turbine uprates. • Standardized input forms. • Developed sales proposals for all CM&U options for existing GE gas turbines. • Organized and compiled a handbook used for generating standardized performance data on GE gas turbines.
	Co-Op Analyst/Project Engineer 1–8/2001 Power Generation Division, Gas Turbine Operations General Electric Co., Schenectady, New York *Team member on the following projects:* • Prepared components of multimillion dollar proposals. • Analyzed and generated emissions data for gas turbines. • Calculated and guaranteed performance levels for turbine uprates. • Updated and created programs for existing operating system. • Created and assembled a handbook of gas turbine uprates and their effect on performance and emissions. • Trained and assisted new co-op engineering students.
	Foreman 5–8/2000 Fairwinds Landscaping Company, Eastham, Massachusetts • Supervised crews. Scheduled work flow in logical, efficient manner.
Honors	Frank R. Fuller Scholar Dean's List of Distinguished Students Rensselaer Academic Scholarship Phi Kappa Tau Academic Scholarship
Leadership and Other Activities	Tour Guide/Student Host Admissions Programs (appointed) Finance Chair, Phi Kappa Tau (elected) Interfraternity Council Alcohol Monitor (appointed) Varsity Baseball plus Intramural/Interfraternal Sports
Keyword List	BIS, MIS, IT, CIO, C/C++, Visual C++, HTML, SQL, Perl, Ada, Pascal, Office 2000, Windows 98, Windows 95, Windows NT, MS-SQL, Excel, Word, Unix, Java, Adobe PhotoShop, OOA/OOD, CAD/CAM/CAE, CPT, SPICE, MAT LAB, Firewall, Security, e-commerce, online transactions, Internet, intranets, Auto CAD, Turbo CAD, Microsoft PROJECT, Corel, Quattro Pro, Object Programming

CHAPTER 14

How to Write a Curriculum Vitae

CURRICULA VITAE ARE STILL RÉSUMÉS

Despite their venerable name, curricula vitae are simply a specific sort of résumé, the style preferred by candidates for medical, academic, teaching, and research positions. Most of these candidates have an educational background directly related to the positions they seek, so education is always featured first. Even after 20 years of research, your degrees and the schools where you earned them will overshadow your experience.

The main differences between general résumés and c.v.'s are:

C.v.'s almost never list an objective, and seldom have a long narrative profile. They are sometimes diagrammatic, giving exceptionally brief listings for each experience. Your credentials and preparation will have to speak for themselves. If you want to make a more elaborate argument for your candidacy, you must do it in your cover letter.

C.v.'s are properly more understated than business résumés, and any hint of braggadocio or other self-congratulation is likely to backfire on the author. Similarly, c.v.'s should look rather plain. Even if your computer is full of little pointing hands, fancy page borders, bullets, bells, and whistles, save them for another time. When they are nondiagrammatic, c.v.'s can contain blocky job descriptions of some great length—but the emphasis is always on content, not form. (Of course, if you follow the guidelines in this book, you should be able to construct a c.v. that is beautiful in both form and content.)

Name dropping is more common in c.v.'s than in résumés. Let's say that you performed research under a certain professor. While you would probably list only her title in a business résumé, a c.v. would most likely include her name. Science and academe are small worlds, and it is likely that a prospective employer will have heard of a given specialist in her own field. Similarly, if you went on clinical rotations at a given hospital, name it; your future employer might have hospital privileges there. I think you get the idea.

Unlike résumés, c.v.'s can run on for pages and pages. They should, however, be very neatly organized, with clear headings and distinct conceptual divisions, so that they can be skimmed as easily as a two-page résumé.

In addition to the usual catalog of degrees and job histories, c.v.'s often contain many more categories of information. Experience may be divided between headings for TEACHING and RESEARCH; education may be divided between DEGREES and CONTINUING EDUCATION or ADVANCED TRAINING; publications may be divided into subcategories of BOOKS, ARTICLES, CONFERENCE PRESENTATIONS, ABSTRACTS, BOOK REVIEWS, and UNPUBLISHED PAPERS. How you organize this material determines its impact on your reader.

Scour Your Background for Evidence to Present

As with technical résumés, employers get clues about your intelligence and focus from the way you organize and present your c.v. data.

Your presentation will be judged largely on the number and nature of listings. Material that you may think of as irrelevant may end up cinching your presentation. If you gave fourteen lectures in the last year, don't say, "but that's obvious"—list them! Make them interesting!

When you have published dozens of books and journal articles you can afford to skip the obvious; when you are fresh out of school (if anyone can ever be said to be "fresh" out of a rigorous program) it is better to let the search committee know exactly what you have done and, by inference, what you can do.

For example, citing your doctorate in nonverbal communication establishes your basic credentials, but listing lectures like the following is a much more effective way to give the search committee a feeling for who you are as a person and an intellectual:

Outside Lectures & Courses
Portland Bar Association
    "The Total Argument"
    "Choosing Jurors: Consider the Nonverbal Evidence"
    "Nonverbal Communication in the Courtroom: Whose Side Are You on, Anyway?"
    "The Defense Attorney and Nonverbal Communication"
    "Prepping Your Client for Courtroom Appearances: You Never Get a Second
       Chance . . ."

University of California, Long Beach
Department of Industrial Design
    "Proxemics"
    "Use of Space to Communicate"

University of California, Berkeley
School of Architecture
    "Space and Power in Corporate America"

University of California, Los Angeles
Film School/Broadcast Communication Arts (joint presentation)
    "Nonverbal Communication in Film and Television: Mastering the Total Message"

Southern Conference of Law Enforcement Officers
    "Nonverbal Communication in American Subgroups"

Portland Art Museum
    "Communication & Aesthetic Consciousness"
    "A New Interpretation of Spatial Relations in Renaissance Group Portraiture"

As with any other résumé, review your total universe of material before deciding what to include, what to feature, and what to omit. Review all potential data in the following categories:

Degrees	Study abroad	Volunteer experience	Appointments
Dissertations	Teaching	Service	Consulting
Theses	Workshops	Languages	Practica
Pro bono	Clinics	Laboratory skills	Activities
Continuing education	Seminars	Technical skills	Sports
Training	Conferences	Computer skills	Travel
Specialization	Symposia	Licenses	Bibliography
Expertise	Publications	Credentials	Addenda
Profession	Translations	Honors	Assistanceships
Interests	Presentations	Scholarships	Keywords
Employment	Papers	Fellowships	Lectures
Research	Exhibitions	Grants	Committees
Additional class projects	Academic/service/ performance awards	Honorary/professional/ social affiliations	*All* other college studies

After compiling this raw data, use the **Résumé Ingredients Rule** and every trick and technique you have learned in this book to present your background in the most compelling order and format for your targeted reader.

One last note: Bibliographies longer than two pages, or any other category with more than two pages of information, should be separated out from the main body of the c.v. Of course, different disciplines have different protocols for bibliographic data and you will need to learn and follow those for your profession. Bibliographies used to be assembled in chronological order, so that the author could add new data to the bottom with a typewriter, but with the advent of computers, bibliographies should run in reverse chronological order like everything else (as a general rule).

The samples in the next chapter run the gamut from diagrammatical c.v.'s to c.v.'s that are virtually indistinguishable from business résumés. In general, the more compelling your credentials (or at least your presentation of them), the briefer your narrative discussion of qualifications and experience can be. Conversely, the more you need to establish what you have to offer, the more closely your curriculum vitae should resemble the résumés presented earlier in this book. There is nothing wrong with this. In fact, many documents with "curriculum vitae" written on them are really straightforward résumés, like Mr. Rappaport's sample in Chapter 11 (p. 98). There is a seamless continuum between these two styles, and where your presentation falls is up to you and the nature of your background. Do note the last sample c.v. in the next chapter. It is in a rather conservative European style, a little different from what we are used to seeing in North America.

CHAPTER 15

Samples, Samples, Samples: Curricula Vitae

LAUREN A. PEABODY
Curriculum Vitae

peabody@esquire.net
18 Pacific Palisades
San Francisco, California 94131

Offices: (801) 555-8900 or (415) 555-1600
Residence: (415) 555-7366

EDUCATION	**UNIVERSITY OF CALIFORNIA, HASTINGS COLLEGE OF THE LAW:** **J.D.,** 1986 **Member,** Hastings Constitutional Law Quarterly, 1985–1986

UNIVERSITY OF ARIZONA:
Ph.D., Government, 1980
    Dissertation: *Influence Relationships among State Supreme Courts*

UNIVERSITY OF UTAH:
M.S., Political Science, 1977
B.S., Political Science, 1976

AMERICAN SOCIETY FOR PUBLIC ADMINISTRATION, Washington, D.C.:
Fellowship, 1981–1982

TEACHING

UNIVERSITY OF CALIFORNIA, Berkeley, California
Lecturer, (Boalt Hall) School of Law, 2000–Present
    "Federal Criminal Law."

GOLDEN GATE UNIVERSITY, San Francisco, California
Lecturer, School of Law, 1999
    "White Collar Crime."

HASTINGS CENTER FOR TRIAL AND APPELLATE ADVOCACY,
San Francisco, California
Instructor, 1994–1999
    "Trial Practice Workshop."

UNITED STATES DEPARTMENT OF JUSTICE, Washington, D.C.
Instructor, Attorney General's Advocacy Institute, 1992–1999
    "Trial Practice Workshop."

WESTMINSTER COLLEGE, Salt Lake City, Utah
Lecturer, Division of Social Sciences, 1990
    "Constitutional Law."

GOLDEN GATE UNIVERSITY, San Francisco, California
Lecturer, Graduate School of Public Administration, 1984–1985
    "Criminal Justice Information Systems."

WEBER STATE COLLEGE, Ogden, Utah
Lecturer (full-time), Department of Political Science, 1980–1981
    "American Government" and "Constitutional Law."

UNIVERSITY OF ARIZONA, Tucson, Arizona
Teaching Assistant, Department of Government, 1977–1979
    "American Government."

PRACTICE

UNITED STATES DEPARTMENT OF JUSTICE, San Francisco, California
Assistant Chief, Organized Crime Strike Force, 1/1999–8/2001
Attorney, Organized Crime Strike Force, 1/1996–1/1999
    Prosecution of organized crime cases, with emphasis on white-collar
    prosecution of union and corporate officials under RICO and various
    theft, fraud, and internal revenue statutes. Recent reported cases:

Lauren A. Peabody

C.V./Page 2

United States v. Tham, 884 F.2d 1262 (9th Cir. 1999)
United States v. Holland, 880 F.2d 1091 (9th Cir. 1999)
  (Co-trial counsel)
Special Achievement Award, 1998.

UNITED STATES DEPARTMENT OF JUSTICE, Salt Lake City, Utah
Assistant U.S. Attorney, 3/1990–1/1996
  Criminal and civil litigation including trials of the following cases: bribery
  of public official, perjury, obstruction of justice, murder, rape, mail and
  wire fraud, bank robbery, extortion, assault, stolen property, employment
  discrimination, medical malpractice, national environmental policy act,
  quiet title, et al.
  Special Achievement Award, 1992.

FABIAN & CLENDENIN, Salt Lake City, Utah
Associate Attorney, 6/1986–2/1990
  Civil litigation, with emphasis on trial of commercial cases; some defense
  of criminal and juvenile justice defendants.

FIRST APPELLATE DISTRICT COURT OF APPEAL, San Francisco, California
Clerk (Extern), 8–12/1985

OFFICE OF THE DISTRICT ATTORNEY, Alameda County, California
Summer Legal Assistant, 7–8/1985

**CONSULTING &
POLICY
DEVELOPMENT**
UNITED STATES DEPARTMENT OF JUSTICE, Washington, D.C.
Consultant, 8/1983–6/1986
  In association with U.S. Dept. of Justice and Public Systems, Inc., of Sunnyvale,
  California, drafted federal privacy regulations related to criminal history
  information: 28 C.FR 20.1-20.38

INSTITUTE OF JUDICIAL ADMINISTRATION—AMERICAN BAR
ASSOCIATION JUVENILE JUSTICE STANDARDS PROJECT, Washington, D.C.
Member, Drafting Committee on Administration, 1/1983–1/1986
  Reviewed proposed juvenile justice privacy and management standards.
  See IJA-ABA, Standards Relating to: Juvenile Records and Information
  Systems (1985); Planning for Juvenile Justice (1985); Monitoring (1986).

UNITED STATES DEPARTMENT OF JUSTICE, Washington, D.C.
National Advisory Commission on Criminal Justice Standards 7 Goals
Deputy Staff Director, 7/1981–7/1983
  Directed staff of commission which produced standards for crime reduction
  and system improvement at state and local levels nationally. Contributed
  materially to sections on criminal information systems and planning.
  Special Achievement Award, 1983.

SERVICE
UTAH EQUAL RIGHTS LEGAL DEFENSE FUND, Salt Lake City, Utah
Member, Board of Directors, 1988–1992

SECOND DISTRICT JUVENILE COURT, STATE OF UTAH
Member, Citizens Advisory Committee, 1988–1990

FIFTH CIRCUIT COURT, SMALL CLAIMS DIVISION, STATE OF UTAH
Judge Pro Tempore (pro bono), 1990

AMERICAN CIVIL LIBERTIES UNION, Salt Lake City, Utah
Member, Legal Panel, 1988–1990

Lauren A. Peabody

**PAPERS &
PUBLICATIONS**
"Political Scientists as Expert Witnesses," 24 PS: *Political Science & Politics* 521 (September, 2001).
"A Theory of Jury Trial Advocacy," 1994 *Utah L. Rev.* 763.

Note, "Informational Privacy: Constitutional Challenges to the Collection and Dissemination of Personal Information by Government Agencies," 3 *Hastings Const. L. Q.* 229 (1986).

Contributing Editor, National Advisory Commission on Criminal Justice Standards 7 Goals, *A National Strategy to Reduce Crime & Report on the Criminal Justice System,* U.S. Dept. Just. (1983).

"Crime Specific Goal Setting," paper presented to the National Conference of the American Society for Public Administration (March 21–25, 1982).

ADMISSIONS
United States Supreme Court
United States Court of Appeals (Ninth and Tenth Circuits)
United States District Courts (Utah and Northern District of California)
Supreme Court, State of California
Supreme Court, State of Utah

additional information provided on request

KEETER T. KOWLANASKI

keeter@aol.com
2209 Funston Street
San Francisco, California 94118
(415) 555-6020

CURRICULUM VITAE

EDUCATION	University of California, School of Dentistry, San Francisco, California **D.D.S.,** expected June 2002 Hampden-Sydney College, Hampden-Sydney, Virginia **B.S.,** Chemistry Major, May 1997
COMPETITIVE SCHOLARSHIPS	Research Fellowship, National Institute of Health (NIH), Bethesda, Maryland, Summer 1999. St. John's Scholarship, The College of William and Mary, Williamsburg, Virginia, 1995–1996. Research Fellowship, Loma Linda University Medical Center, Loma Linda, California, 1996. Research Fellowship, The Associated Western Universities, Salt Lake City, Utah, Summer 1995. Academic Scholarship, Kate Sterling Bunnell Foundation, Stratford, Connecticut, 1993–1994.
TABLE CLINICS & PRESENTATIONS	"A Second-Generation Pulpal Cooling Device," H.E. Goodis, K. Kowlanaski, J. Robinson, J.M. White, an abstract and poster presentation accepted for the IADR meeting in Acapulco, Mexico, April 2001. "Pain Management: C-FOS Initiates Endogenous Opiates in the CNS," K. T. Kowlanaski, Blair A. Kirk, M.A. Ruda, presented at the CDA Scientific Session, Anaheim, California, April 2000. "Pain Management: Co-Localization of the Endogenous Opiate, Dynorphin, in the CNS with C-FOS, a Marker of Cellular Activity," Keeter T. Kowlanaski, Blair A. Kirk, M. A. Ruda, presented at the UCSF Dental School Alumni Meeting, San Francisco, California, November 1999.

PROFESSIONAL SERVICE	UCSF Dental School, San Francisco, California, 1998–Present
	CDA Student Representative (elected position)
	    Arrange speakers on special topics, recently with an emphasis on practice management. Have arranged lectures by accountants, bankers, certified financial planners, practice management consultants, practice brokers for dental students.
	    Special project: In concert with the CDA representatives from the other four California dental schools, lobbied for passage of California AB2956, which would allow dental students to work as dental hygienists.
	    Also sit on the Board of Student Government at UCSF Dental School, and sit with full voting rights in the CDA House of Delegates.
	
	UCSF Dental School, San Francisco, California, 2000–2001
	Assistant Coordinator, Associate Resource Program
	    Assisted in creating this innovative program under the auspices of the California Dental Association Task Force on the Young Professional. The program places area dentists who are interested in obtaining an associate in contact with juniors, seniors and recent graduates of these dental schools.

153

Health Careers Club, College of William and Mary, Williamsburg, Virginia
President, 1996–1997
Vice President, 1995-1996
Coordinated and promoted speaking events for this pre-medical/pre-dental club with 330 members. Co-creator of the club's mentor program, pairing club members with area dentists and physicians for frank discussions and observation of practice. Also directed community service functions, including fundraising for children's health organizations.

Medical-Dental Explorer Post, Stratford, Connecticut, 1990–1992
Secretary
Coordinated and promoted guest speaker series, arranged one-on-one career guidance counseling, and coordinated tours of area medical-dental offices.

RESEARCH
1999

National Institute of Dental Research (NIH), Bethesda, Maryland, Summer

Research Fellow
Researched literature and prepared the research plan. Investigated the basic mechanisms of pain and endogenous opiates, how they are initiated and how they affect the control of pain in the CNS, involving small animal surgery, histology and immunocytochemistry, and design of statistical methodologies on computer.
Also attended lectures on all aspects of research, public health, future of dentistry, future of healthcare in the United States, grant development and grant-writing techniques.

University of California, Los Angeles, 1997–1998
Research Assistant
Conducted research in neuroendocrinology on the effect of hormones on the maturation of the central nervous system in Sprague-Dawley rats and the common finch involving histology, immunocytochemistry, and radioimmuno-assay. Prepared papers for publishing, provided computer modeling and statistical analysis, performed literature search and review.

Loma Linda University Medical Center, Loma Linda, California, 1996
Research Intern in Radiation Oncology
Assisted J. O. Archambeau, M.D., F.A.C.R., on research project undertaken in conjunction with Beckman Research Institute, City of Hope. Conducted literature search and review. Designed computer model to demonstrate three-dimensional structure of dermal capillaries. Developed original proce-dures to model radiation damage using resin castings of microvasculature. Resulted in the manuscript, "Three-Dimensional Dermal Vessel Configuration: A Radiation Parameter," by R. Shymko and J. O. Archambeau. Also designed and installed an on-line tutorial for medical residents to learn to use Med-Line to access the National Library of Medicine.

Crocker Nuclear Laboratory, Davis, California, 1995
Student Research Fellow
Assisted nuclear medical research project undertaken in conjunction with the University of California, Irvine, Medical Center. Derived theoretical framework from literature search and review. Performed calculations and laboratory tests on radioisotopes. Devised original chemical procedures to isolate Cobalt-55 isotope. Resulted in the manuscript, "Cyclotron Production of PET Radionuclides I: Cobalt-55 from High Energy Protons on 58-Nickel Targets," by M. C. Lagunas-Solar and O. F. Carvacho.

Keeter T. Kowlanaski   C.V./Page 3

EMPLOYMENT   Offices of Jon Bauer D.D.S., Hollwood, California, 1997–1998
                    Dental Office Assistant
                       Had direct patient interaction and assisted with procedures. Gained
                       overview of office administration, including scheduling, billing, solving
                       problems with insurance companies, and review of overhead figures.

                    Williamsburg Community Hospital, Williamsburg, Virginia, 1995–1997
                    EKG Monitor Technician
                       Interpreted EKG test results and reported abnormalities to staff of ICU.

ACTIVITIES   UCSF Dental School
                       American Society of Dentistry for Children
                       Student Research Group (IADR)
                       Student Member, ADA
                       Student Member, CDA
                       UCSF Dental School Representative to the CDA
                       Xi Psi Phi Professional Dental Fraternity
                       American Association of Dental Schools

                    Hampden-Sydney College
                       Health Careers Club (330 members)
                       President, 1996–1997
                       Vice President, 1995–1996
                       Alpha Chi Sigma Professional Chemistry Fraternity
                       Chemistry Club
                       Psychology Club

                    High School
                       Junior Achievement, Chairman
                       Medical-Dental Explorer Post, Secretary
                       Chemistry Explorer Post

COMMUNITY   Special Olympics, San Francisco, California, 1999
SERVICE   **Founder & Coordinator, Dental Students & Youth Bowling Program**

                    Special Olympics, Fairfield, Connecticut, Summer 1996
                    Coach, One-on-One, Track & Field

                    Citizenship Award, Greenwich Association of Retarded Citizens, 1996

                    Stratford Organization to Aid the Retarded (SOAR), 1989–1992
                    Instructor of Elementary Reading and Mathematics

                    Audubon Society, Fairfield, Connecticut, 1986–1992
                    Wildlife Veterinary Aide

                    Sheehan Center for the Elderly, Bridgeport, Connecticut, 1991
                    Recreation & Ambulatory Aide

ADDITIONAL   Additional information and clarification provided on request.
INFORMATION

155

Margaret S. Blair, M.D.
Curriculum Vitae

290 Green Street, #4
Memphis, Tennessee 37205
(615) 555-0778

dr.blair@medline.com (clinical use only)
margaret77@loftis.com (all other uses)

TRAINING

Memphis Medical Center, Memphis, Tennessee
Residency, General Surgery
2001–Present

Memphis Medical Center, Memphis, Tennessee
Internship
2000–2001

EDUCATION

Rush Medical College, Chicago, Illinois
M.D.
2000
  Junior Member, Alpha Omega Alpha.
  Dean's Office Summer Research Fellowship, 1997.
  Preservation Technician, Department of Organ and Tissue Recovery.

Brandeis University, Waltham, Massachusetts
M.A., Chemistry
1996
  Independent Research, Organic Chemistry/Natural Product Synthesis.
  Faigl-Berger Teaching Fellowship.

Dartmouth College, Hanover, New Hampshire
B.A., Chemistry
1994
  Undergraduate Thesis, Biochemistry.
  Sphinx Senior Honor Society.
  Dartmouth Women's Rugby Club (Captain).
  Alpha Delta Sigma Sorority (President).

L'Universite de Toulouse-Le Mirail, Toulouse, France
Foreign Study Program
Spring 1992

University of Notre Dame, South Bend, Indiana
National Science Foundation Program
Summer 1989

RESEARCH & WORK EXPERIENCE

Pfizer Central Research, Groton, Connecticut
Jan–Sep 1996
Assistant Scientist
  Completed numerous projects as a member of a team seeking to develop new
  protocols to speed clinical trials.

Department of Therapeutic Radiology, Rush Medical Center, Chicago, IL
Summer 1997
Research Fellow
  Investigated prostaglandin induced protection of tumor cells from ionizing radiation.
  Awarded the Dean's Office Summer Research Fellowship based on research proposal.

Rush-Presbyterian-St. Luke's Medical Center, Chicago, Illinois
Aug 1997–Jan 1999
Preservation Technician
  Assisted in procurement and preservation of donor organs. Also on call ten nights per month.

156

Margaret S. Blair, M.D.   C.V./Page 2

Undergraduate Research Program
Dartmouth College, Hanover, New Hampshire   Summer 1993
Research Associate
  Awarded grant to pursue independent research topics in biochemistry, one of which became my
  senior honors project (thesis available).

Dartmouth College Department of Chemistry, Hanover, New Hampshire   Fall 1992
Laboratory Technician
  Instructed students in the use of UV-VIS and IR spectrophotometers.

Harvard University, Cambridge, Massachusetts   Fall 1989–Spring 1990
Research Assistant
  Conducted a research project in biochemistry at Harvard's Radioisotope Laboratory. The project
  received second prize at the Massachusetts State Science Fair.

PUBLICATIONS

1. W. R. Hanson, M. S. Blair, K. DeLaurentis and F. D. Malkinson, "Modification of Radiation Injury
of Murine Intestinal Clonogenic Cells and B-16 Melanoma by PGI2 or Flurbiprofen," in
Prostaglandin and Lipid Metabolism in Radiation Injury (T. L. Waldin and H. M. Hughes,
editors), Plenum Press, New York, 1996.

2. W. R. Hanson, M. S. Blair, K. DeLaurentis and F. D. Malkinson, "Radioprotection of B-16 Murine
Melanoma in vivo by Exogenous Prostaglandin I2 and the Cyclo-oxygenase inhibitor, Flurbiprofen."
Abstract presented to the Joint International Meeting of the European Society for Dermatologic
Research and the Society for Investigative Dermatology, June 22–26, 1995, Geneva, Switzerland, and
to the International Conference on Prostaglandin and Lipid Metabolism in Radiation Injury,
October 2–3, 1995, Rockville, Maryland.

Wallace O. Windemeir

halfnote@aol.com

2418 Turquoise Drive
Hercules, California 94547

Telephone:
(510) 555-6096

PROFILE
Violinist, Concertmaster.

EDUCATION
M.M. (Master of Music), **Violin,** with honors, 1983
Yale University School of Music, New Haven, Connecticut
Student of Broadus Erle, Syoko Aki, Aldot Parisot, Walter Trampler

B.A. Music, 1978
San Francisco State University, San Francisco, California
Student of Ferenc Molnar

Special Student, Violin, 1979–1981
Peabody Conservatory of Music, Baltimore, Maryland
Student of Bert Senofsky

J.D. (Juris Doctor, Law), San Francisco Law School, 1988
Member, State Bar of California

PERFORMANCE HIGHLIGHTS

San Francisco Opera Center, Western Opera Theatre, Spring Opera,
San Francisco, California, 1999–Present
Concertmaster
 Completed two national tours, in charge of 13 violinists. Concertmaster, 2000–Present.
 Principal 2nd, 1999. "Madam Butterfly," "Aida," "The Barber of Seville," "La Boheme," "Magic
 Flute," "The Marriage of Figaro," "Don Giovanni," "Boris Gudenov," and dozens of others.

Midsummer Mozart Festival, San Francisco, California, 1986–Present
Violinist, Assistant Concertmaster
 Performed more works of Mozart than any other orchestra in the Western Hemisphere.
 Honored by the Austrian government in 2001. Six recordings on Sonic Arts.

San Jose Symphony, San Jose, California, 1988–Present
Violinist, Assistant Concertmaster
 Intermittent.

Shorenstein-Nederlander Productions, San Francisco, California, 1988–Present
Violinist
 Perform violin parts for Broadway shows showing in San Francisco's Theatre District. "Kismet,"
 "Sound of Music," "Camelot," "My Fair Lady," "The Music Man," "Peter Pan," "Oklahoma,"
 "The King & I," "Sweeney Todd," and dozens of others.

California Symphony, Contra Costa and Alameda Counties, 1999–Present
Violinist

Oakland – East Bay Symphony, Oakland, California, 1977, 1994–Present
Violinist

Studio Work, 1978–Present
Violinist
 Violinist for recordings and stage performance, including work with Linda Ronstadt, Frank
 Sinatra, Johnny Mathis, Tony Bennett, Frankie Lane, Aretha Franklin, and TV work such as the
 upcoming NBC movie "Mississippi."

San Francisco String Quartet, San Francisco, California, 1995–Present
Violinist
  Regular performances.

American Conservatory Theatre (ACT), San Francisco, California, 1998–1999
Violinist
  String Quartet. "Sunday in the Park with George," and "Annie Get Your Gun."

Cabrillo Music Festival, Santa Cruz, California, 1991–1993 1995–1997
Violinist
  Emphasizing contemporary music, including working directly with Elliot Carter,
  Aaron Copland, Hans Werner Hense, Ralph Towner, and others.

New Haven Symphony, New Haven, Connecticut, 1981–1984
Violinist

Richmond Symphony, Richmond, Virginia, 1978–1981
Violinist

MAJOR RECITALS

Gold Coast Chamber Players Recital, San Francisco, California, 1999
Violinist
  Trio and quartet.

Old First Church Recitals, San Francisco, California, 1988–1991
Violinist
  Two solo recitals, piano quartet, Malcomb Arnold concerto for two violins.

CREDENTIAL

Music Instruction, Junior College, State of California, life

TEACHING EXPERIENCE

Private Teaching, 1977–Present
Performance Instructor
  Have instructed private students for over twenty years.

San Francisco Community Music Center, San Francisco, California, 1996–1998
Violin Teacher
  Taught violin to students of all ages. This position was very important to me because
  I had a chance to teach beginning students for the first time in many years.

MILITARY

U.S. Army, 1978–1981
Specialist E-5
  Military Listed Occupational Specialty: Violinist. Played for the White House.

RACHEL WARD SIMON
Curriculum Vitae
hagit@justmail.com

304 – 14th Street, #2
Berkeley, California 94560

Telephone/Message:
(510) 555-2467

EDUCATION

Pacific Graduate School of Psychology
Ph.D. Candidate, Clinical Psychology

Palo Alto, California
expected 2002

Emphases: Clinical, Developmental Psychology
Recipient: Israeli Student Scholarship (Academic)

San Francisco State University
M.A., Developmental Psychology

San Francisco, California
1999

Thesis: *Self-esteem, Parenting Styles, Communication: Determining a Developmental Link*
Emphases: Counseling Electives, Practicum

University of California Irvine, California
B.A., Psychology

1995

PRACTICA

Berkeley Center for Child Study
Counselor (designate)

Berkeley, California
9/1999–9/2000

Will be observing and assisting with individual child and adolescent therapy, including testing, diagnosis, and case presentation.

U.S. Behavioral Health (USBH)
Intake Coordinator

Emeryville, California
2/1999–Present

Provide telephone crisis intervention, intake assessment, advocacy and referral to local inpatient and outpatient services for clients from all over the United States. USBH is a managed mental health care corporation. Deal with a complete range of psychoses and chemical dependency issues. Allowed to take on the responsibilities of an Assistant Case Manager, under supervision of senior clinical staff member: provide triage, arrange hospitalization, prepare initial treatment plans with therapists and hospitals, review and approve long-term treatment plans, monitor after-care programs, maintain ongoing client case files, serve as liaison between client, local hospitals and clinicians, and USBH. Selected to train incoming staff. Selected to demonstrate/present before potential clients (corporate HR officers).

T.A.L.K. Line
Counselor

San Francisco, California
12/1998–Present

Telephone counselor for 24-hour child abuse hotline. Provide crisis intervention, education and counseling to parents. Requires ability to assess nature and intensity of the client's problem quickly, and to develop a therapeutic response in one confidential telephone contact. Maintain knowledge of related referral network (entire Bay Area).

Private Practice of Haim Helprin, Ph.D.
Intern

Los Angeles, California
7–10/1998

Obtained psycho-medical histories, observed therapy sessions, discussed treatment plans and therapeutic techniques with the doctor.

Haight-Ashbury Psychological Services
Intake Counselor

San Francisco, California
9/1996–6/1997

Conducted intake interviews, provided triage and initial assessment, escalated cases as needed, participated in patient evaluation sessions with clinical interns. Also managed the referral system; this clinic sees patients with a very wide range of problems, and referral was an important aspect of the intake counselor's position. Trained new counselors.

Rachel Ward Simon **C.V./Page 2**

Topanga West Canoga Park, California
Psychological Intern 3–9/1996
Participated in psychotherapy of patients in an unlocked inpatient ward, group and one-on-one sessions. Provided talk therapy, crisis intervention, and training/coaching in daily living skills.

RESEARCH Childhood Development Center, S.F.S.U. San Francisco, California
Observer 1–6/1997
As part of experimental methodologies class, observed and recorded the activities of pre-school children for one semester. Designed recording system related to issues of social competence and attachment. Recorded data and performed statistical analysis. Interviewed parents and compared parental perception with actual performance of child.

Haight-Ashbury Psychological Services San Francisco, California
Research Assistant 9/1996–6/1997
Assisted Dr. Peter Poses with an anger research project. Served as an actor-facilitator, creating angry response behaviors in research subjects during videotaped session.

The Farm School, University of California Irvine, California
Researcher 9/1992–6/1993
Worked under the direction of Dr. Michael Butler, dean of Social Sciences for U.C., Irvine, founder and executive director of this well-known experimental education program. Was the only undergraduate selected to organize and teach an experimental class at The Farm School: "Testing Models of Self-esteem Training in an Elementary Class of Girls and Boys: Toward Developing Applied Techniques for Teachers," using a gymnastics class as a medium. Organized and taught the class, conducted pre- and post-class testing and follow-up research. Was invited by Managing Director of the school to write the class into future curriculum planning. This class was highly popular, and became the strongest extra-curricular activity at the school.

TEACHING Challenge to Learning School San Francisco, California
Teaching Assistant / Substitute Teacher 9/1997–7/1998 (currently on-call)
Assisted in teaching classes of S.E.D. and L.D. students, 14 to 18 years of age. Taught the pre-college library and study skills unit. Provided one-on-one and group psycho-educational counseling.

College of San Mateo San Mateo, California
Instructor, Psychology Department 2–6/1998
Developed and taught seminar-style psychology course, one of the core requirements for the California Higher Education Teaching Credential. Integrated experiential exercises into the curriculum (play therapy, concentration enhancement, memory games, relaxation games).

San Francisco State University San Francisco, California
Teaching Assistant, Developmental Psychology 9–12/1997
Co-developed lesson plans, lectured, wrote/administered/graded tests for class with 65 students. Was entirely responsible for this class during professor's illness.

Rachel Ward Simon   C.V./Page 3

San Francisco Jewish Community Center   San Francisco, California
Unit Head / Supervisor   5–9/1997
Organized activities for summer day camp for school-age children. Coached and supervised eight camp counselors. Planned and orchestrated three two-night camping trips involving 150 campers.

The Farm School, University of California   Irvine, California
Teaching Assistant   9/1992–6/1993
Assisted an elementary school teacher, then was selected to organize and teach a gymnastics class as mentioned above. This is a developmentally graded program. Participated in research, assisted in staff meetings, oriented and trained new assistants. Producer/director for the end-of-year program.

Camp Huggy Bear   Woodland Hills, California
Camp Director / Head Teacher   Summers, 1990–1992
Owned and operated an innovative summer day camp serving up to 20 children, ages 8 to 12. Hired and trained four camp counselors. Organized activities such as "Pizza Making & Water Balloon Fight Day" and "Disneyland Day."

BUSINESS Executive Caterers (John Wayne Tennis Club)   Newport Beach, Cal.
Full Charge Manager   8/1995–7/1996
During year off from college, had full profit-and-loss responsibility for a catering business. Hired and trained staff, set policies and procedures, developed menu, analyzed pricing and profitability, established bookkeeping and administrative systems. Developed bids and proposals for events; organized private parties. Ran café, managed two dining rooms and outdoor seating area.

Camp Huggy Bear   Woodland Hills, California
Owner / Operator   Summers, 1990–1992
Designed this business as mentioned above, including forms, waivers, child/parent database, and all policies and procedures.

AFFILIATIONS American Psychological Association (APA)
Western Psychological Association (WPA)

FOREIGN LANGUAGE Hebrew (fluent: speak, read, write, translate).

162

CURRICULUM VITAE

This is a European-style c.v.
Note the understatement.

Name:	Merideth Martin LAUER
Address:	17 Rosemond Avenue Scarborough North Yorkshire England
Telephone:	370 883
Nationality:	British
Marital Status:	Single
Dependents:	None
Date of Birth:	28th March 1967
Driving License:	Full

EDUCATION

1978–1983	**The Convent of The Ladies of Mary** Queen Street Scarborough North Yorkshire
O'levels	English Language (3), Human Biology (4), Domestic Science (5)
C.S.E.	Mathematics (2)
1983–1985	**Scarborough Technical College** Catering Department Lady Edith's Drive Scarborough North Yorkshire
City & Builds of London	Housekeeping (Distinction), Reception (Credit), Food Service (Credit)
Other Courses Attended:	First Line Management Selection and Interviewing Techniques Management Budgeting Industrial Relations Middle Management
Affiliate Membership	Hotel and Catering Institutional Management Association

WORK EXPERIENCE

October 1998– December 2000	Executive Housekeeper Shk. Hamad Bid Isa Al.Khalifa **The Crown Prince of Bahrain** Crown Prince Court P.O. Box 28788 Riffa Bahrain Duties: Responsible for the organisation of housekeeping needs in two Palaces. I liaised with contractors in refurbishment projects, recruited household staff and served as purchasing officer for any household needs.

163

November 1993– September 1998	College Housemistress **Norland Nursery Training College** Denford Park Hungerford Berkshire Duties: Responsible to the Principal for organising the cleaning of the College with a domestic staff of 14 whom I appointed, trained and supervised. I prepared and managed my department budget, ordered all domestic stores and chose and purchased all College furnishings and furniture. I deputised in the absence of the Administrator and Catering Manager and had pastoral care of 150 students.
November 1992– November 1993	Housekeeper/Dresser **T.R.H. Prince and Princess Michael of Kent** Kensington Palace London W8 Duties: Supervision of the cleaner. Organised any special cleaning of furniture and furnishings. Purchased all foodstuffs, prepared and served breakfast for their Royal Highnesses. Prepared and served lunch if either Prince or Princess Michael were entertaining. Arranged extra staff for dinner parties. As dresser, I was responsible for all aspects of Princess Michael's wardrobe—cleaning, pressing, mending and arranging fittings. I was responsible directly to their Royal Highnesses.
November 1990– November 1992	Assistant Domestic Services Manager (November 1990–February 1991) Domestic Services Manager (February 1991–November 1992) King's Health District **Dulwich Hospital** East Dulwich Grove London SE22 Duties (Assistant Domestic Services Manager): Responsible for the supervision and training of the cleaning staff. I assisted in the staff record keeping and the organisation of the duty rotas. When the manager left I was offered the post of Manager. Duties (Domestic Services Manager): I was responsible for the organizing of the cleaning of the Hospital, staff accommodation and outside clinics. I had a staff of 128 Domestic assistants and orderlies and five supervisors. I was responsible for the department budget. I interviewed and appointed the domestic staff, completed their clockcards and was involved in any disciplining of the staff.
December 1986– November 1990	Housemaid/Ladies Maid—Senior Housemaid **H.M. The Queen** Buckingham Palace London W1 Duties: Responsible for the cleaning of a specific area and as a ladies maid I was responsible for the unpacking, washing, pressing and repacking of visiting lady guest's clothes. After two years I was promoted to Senior Housemaid and was responsible for the training of new housemaids in cleaning skills, ladies maid duties and their conduct in the presence of Royalty and visiting foreign dignitaries. This job, although based at Buckingham Palace, took me to all the Royal Residences within Britain.

164

March–October 1986	General Assistant
	Newburn House Hotel
	Alma Square
	Scarborough, North Yorkshire

Duties: Assisted in all the different areas of the Hotel Kitchen, Dining Room, Bar, Housekeeping. I was responsible directly to the manager. This was a small family run Hotel. The owners I had known for some time. Upon my return to Scarborough, they asked me to join them. I was able to gain more widespread knowledge of a Hotel rather than working within the confines of a specialist department.

July 1985–March 1986	Floor Housekeeper
	Trust House Forte
	Excelsior Hotel
	Glasgow Airport
	Paisley, Strathclyde

Duties: Responsible for the supervision and training of the cleaning staff. Reported to reception on room availability. Liaised with the maintenance department about any repairs or replacement. Responsible to the Executive Housekeeper. Housekeeping had always been the subject which I enjoyed most at College and so it was the natural choice when deciding upon a career direction. I chose to go to the Excelsior Hotel as I knew it to be a busy commercial establishment with high standards, allowing a good grounding in the correct operation of the Housekeeping Department.

PERSONAL INTERESTS

Snow skiing, reading (particularly biographies), travel, needlecrafts.

REFERENCES

The Chief Housekeeper
Buckingham Palace
London
W1

Her Royal Highness Princess Michael of Kent
Kensington Palace
London
W8

Mrs. L. E. Davis M.Phil, S.R.N. F.R.S.H.
(Principal)
Norland N.T.C.
Denford Park
Hungerford
Berkshire

Shaikha Sabeka Bint Ebrahim Al Khalifa
P.O. Box 25575
Awali
Bahrain
Arabian Gulf

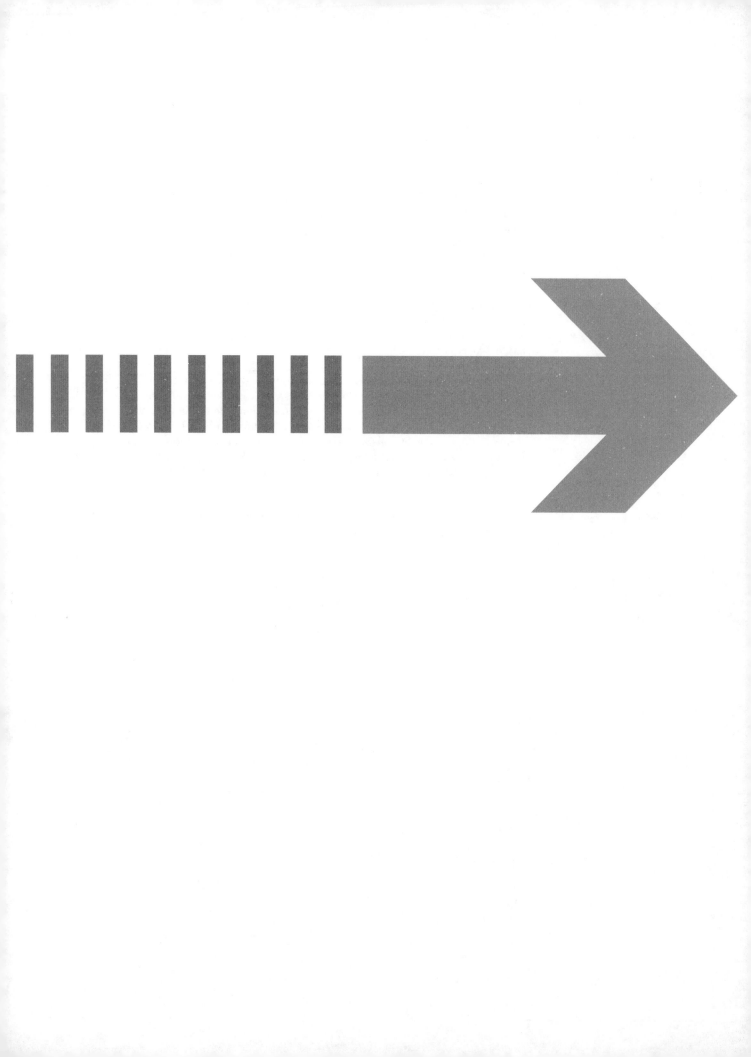

part

③

**Cover Letters, Interviews, & Job Search
Tips & Techniques**

A QUICK OVERVIEW

No matter how good your résumé or curriculum vitae is, it won't do you much good if it is used incorrectly. For example, you should not send your résumé to anyone without calling to follow up. In one recent employee search performed by a small company, the hiring manager received over 60 applications but only four phone calls. Three of those who called were interviewed and two of them were hired. By making that simple telephone call, candidates improved their odds from roughly three percent to 50 percent!

How you target, deliver, and follow-up on your résumé is extremely important—even more important than your résumé itself in many cases. An undue reliance on newspaper help-wanted ads can create unbelievable competition for yourself, while the feature articles and business section of that same newspaper can serve as an encyclopedia of good, easy-to-approach leads for a savvy jobseeker.

Part III of this book is a quick overview of effective job-search practices, using a sales and marketing model for search techniques.

CHAPTER 16

Planning and Organizing a Search

JOB SEARCH CYCLES

The ideal job search would begin with an appropriate internship in the summer between freshman and sophomore years. Then, it would progress through more challenging internship and job experiences until the candidate's experience is a balanced complement to her education. Upon graduation, the ideal candidate would have industry exposure, a clearly defined job target based upon her knowledge of that industry, and a diverse but related education.

Not everybody is so focused or prescient about her career goals, however. In fact, most students aren't. This can be a positive thing—you should allow ongoing investigations to influence your ultimate career goals. You may discover that you don't enjoy some job functions you once imagined that you would, or learn that the industry you have targeted is poised for a long, precipitous decline. You must be flexible in your approach.

Nevertheless, the earlier you pursue your career interests the better, and internships are a valuable way to demonstrate interest and gain critical industry exposure. By January of your junior year, you should have targeted a job, internship, or volunteer experience for the summer between your junior and senior years. The most competitive internships will be locked up as early as March. (If you are a second-semester senior with no industry experience, do not despair. It is never too late to seek volunteer, unpaid, or postgrad internship experience. If your job search stalls, you must consider these options.)

From the beginning of senior year, every student should participate in the career events sponsored by her college office of career planning and placement. In addition to the on-campus recruiting program, most universities offer interest and aptitude testing, as well as seminars on how to research companies, write a résumé, interview, and plan and

169

manage a career. Pay particular attention to the interview coaching classes. Honest feedback on your appearance, grooming, posture, and demeanor is invaluable. Your closest friends may not be able (or willing) to help you in this area.

If you have even the remotest interest in the employers recruiting on your campus, participate in the on-campus recruiting cycle. These programs vary, with offers usually not firming up until the spring semester. Remember, however, that the overwhelming majority of your peers will find a job on their own. You should not rely on on-campus recruiting as your only job-search strategy; by winter of your senior year you should have a list of companies that you would like to contact on your own. Early in the spring, you should begin serious off-campus interviewing for positions that would begin immediately after graduation.

If you graduate without a firm offer, be prepared to launch a full-court press for a position. If you need to take a part-time or evening job to support yourself during the remainder of your search, do so, but don't let that job interfere with your efforts to land a career-track job. You should be ready to devote yourself to your job search full-time, from Sunday evening through Friday afternoon.

Hiring Cycles
Many companies have established hiring cycles, or patterns of hiring. This may mean that they hire only at certain times of the year, and/or that they have an established formula for hiring, either out of habit or policy.

Any company with a management training program is likely to hire only a few times a year. This includes major retailers, accounting and consulting firms, almost all law firms, and many banking and financial institutions. Some companies' hiring cycles are completed months before any new hires actually start work. Even if you are an outstanding candidate, if you approach these companies out of their cycle, you stand a great chance of being forgotten long before the next cycle begins.

Similarly, most companies have established hiring practices. Knowing where you are in their standard hiring process will make you a more effective candidate. Some companies require a certain number of interviews. Some require a certain number of qualified applicants before they can start interviewing. Some companies can make a hiring decision in less than a week, while others are known for routinely taking over 60 days to hire the lowliest clerk.

For example, I had a client who became frustrated with an application. "They're jerking me around," she said. "I've been over there five times for interviews, and they still haven't made a decision." By the fourth interview, she let it be known that she was irritated with the process. Too bad. I found out later that she had been their first choice, but someone else got the job, someone who asked them about their hiring practices and was told that he would have a series of five interviews followed by a reference check before a decision could be made. He kept selling himself in all five interviews and won the prize.

In order to guard against nepotism and other forms of favoritism, and to ensure that they hire the best workers they can, even small companies may have policies like the following: all jobs shall be advertised or placed with headhunters, minimum qualified applicant pool of five, minimum interview pool of three, minimum interview series of three, résumé verification and reference check for the top applicant, no applicants rejected until final negotiations with the new hire are completed.

The interesting thing about hiring cycles is that they are no big secret. If you ask a company about its hiring practices, they will almost always tell you.

Consider Your Job Search Project as a Whole
You are about to launch a full-scale sales and marketing campaign, with market research, direct mail, telemarketing, networking, and personal sales work. These aspects are complementary and synergistic, and your ability to orchestrate them will determine your success.

Candidates tend to view the search process as a series of applications and rejections. A job search is not a series of discrete events, but an organic whole. It is only as a whole that a job search can be properly understood, fine tuned, and managed. No one application or rejection should define or dominate your job search.

Your goal is not just to get a job offer. If you do half the things in this book, you will get job offers. As a matter of fact, it is critical that you not get distracted by early offers for jobs that will not support your overall career goals.

Your goal is to get the right job to launch your career.

171

If you have been following the book, you have one or more career directions in mind to serve as guiding principles for your search. You already have clearly defined job targets ready to drive your initial efforts. Your goal now is to:

> Identify a large volume of raw leads
> Develop raw leads into specific, targeted individuals
> Approach and sell to these individuals
> Follow through on the loose ends and details that your search will generate in volume

When you first launch your job search, you will perform these functions in strict order. As the search builds up a full head of steam, however, you will be doing all of these things at once. You need some organizational tools to control this project. If you have a notebook computer, you can database the whole project with sort keys for dates, names, companies, interview summaries, and so on. If you don't have a computer permanently welded to your fingertips, you can use mechanical devices to the same end.

I prefer 5 x 8 cards to record leads and job search activities. We'll discuss how to use them in greater detail in just a moment. You will also need a good datebook or a personal organizer with enough room to enter several appointments per hour, a postal scale, plenty of stationery, standard business-size envelopes for letters, 9 x 12 envelopes for letters with résumés, postage stamps, the ability to generate letters and customize résumés quickly, a reliable ISP and business-like e-mail address, and a fault-free answering system on your telephone. It is also a good idea to acquaint yourself with priority mail, local same-day, and overnight courier services. You will need to be able to fax your résumé, but remember, every time you fax it, follow up with a printed copy by mail. Try to avoid folding up your résumé—the print will flake off (if it is laser printed) and it won't look as good when it arrives. You should know that a 9 x 12 envelope takes extra postage even if it is under one ounce; you want to make sure your application materials do not arrive marked "Postage Due."

Once you have these raw materials in place to support your search, you're ready to begin.

Identify a Large Volume of Raw Leads

Raw leads are companies you might be interested in investigating, and specific people you might be interested in discussing your job search with. Record raw leads on 5 x 8 cards at the earliest opportunity. Be sure to list the name, title, and daytime phone of your targeted contact, if you have one (if you don't, the next section will teach you how to generate them). Note the exact source of the lead (the precise person, magazine article, or dream that gave you that lead). Note the date each card was created. Finally, note any helpful inside information such as, "Jane said he's always at his desk by 6 a.m.," or "*Business Week* article said they are expanding market share in Florida."

Work like a journalist! Get the exact spelling of names and titles. Record exactly which issue of *Business Week* the article was in. Verify the obvious, "Is that Glen with one 'n' or two?" "Is that S-M-I-T-H or S-M-Y-T-H-E?" Be sure to find out whether Leslie, Chris, or Gene is a Mr. or a Ms. Obtain full addresses and phone numbers at the earliest possible opportunity. Your careful attention to detail will save you time and trouble later.

You want to take careful, precise, accurate notes on your lead cards, because you will be making many hundreds of these.

○ ○ ○

You must be creative and prolific in generating raw leads for your job search. Relying on the on-campus interview program and help-wanted ads for job leads makes about as much sense as playing the lottery to achieve financial security. Of course poor strategies will work for some, just as some people do win the lottery, but the overwhelming majority of good leads will not appear in the newspaper or on the interview schedule at the career office. You need a more complete universe of lead sources.

Here are the main sources of job-search leads:

> Networking via existing personal and professional relationships
> College alumni and leads provided by your office of career planning and placement
> Company names generated from media research and other resource materials
> Online job sites and the online recruiting sites of companies
> Newspaper and trade press want ads and other sources for announced job openings
> Headhunters and agencies

Networking leads are everybody you know and everybody that you have some type of direct connection with. Make lists in the following categories:

> Family
> Friends and old friends
> Parents of friends
> Friends of parents
> Old employers
> Professional acquaintances, including anyone you ever met at a professional convention or meeting
> All members of any church, synagogue, ashram, mosque, or the like to which you have ever belonged
> All members of any club, committee or organization to which you have ever belonged

The interesting thing about networking leads is that they can be delightfully unpredictable. Resist the temptation to say, "How could Aunt Grace know anything about Wall Street?" Aunt Grace's stockbroker may owe her a favor, and you could be it. Anybody in employment counseling can recite dozens of unlikely connections that resulted in a job offer.

College alumni and other leads from the career office can be gold mines of information, especially during the early stages of your search when you are still trying to decide exactly which industries and jobs to target. Make friends with the staff of the career planning and placement office. They can help you find alumni who are webmasters, art directors, television producers, investment bankers, resort managers, or astronauts. Most colleges and universities publish alumni directories that you can use. Also, most colleges have many more companies that favor graduates of that institution beyond the ones that actively recruit on campus. To get leads at those companies, make an appointment with the most seasoned career counselor at the career planning and placement office.

Here are some common questions to use when informational interviewing with alumni:
   (1) How did you get into this industry?
   (2) What would you do differently if you could start over in this industry?
   (3) What education or other credentials are most critical to break into this industry?
   (4) What advice would you have for a young person like me?
   (5) What are some typical starting salaries in this field?

Be sure to be very nice to alumni career contacts. Other students need these contacts, too, and alumni will only be willing to continue as a career contact if you are nice, polite, and considerate.

Company names can be generated by plain, old-fashioned research. If your college library is weak on business reference books, venture into the nearest city library one or two afternoons a month. There are hundreds of specific job guides which you will only discover by looking for them.

Company names can also be found in broadcast and print media. Newscasts on business events are full of company names and relevant information. Print media, including the business press, the trade press, and the popular press, are great sources of timely information on companies. Incidentally, every industry from carnivals to mechanical engineering to motion pictures has trade press. If you are serious about an industry, employers will expect you to be a current reader. Look in the *Encyclopedia of Associations*, call the national headquarters of the association most directly related to your future career interest, and ask the receptionist the names of relevant periodicals.

Be sure to fill your lists with small and obscure companies as well as industry leaders. Most of the job growth on this continent is provided by small companies. The general trend among very large corporations is contraction, so if you are smart you will give a lot of consideration to working for a company with $100 million to $10 million annual

174

sales (middle-market), $10 million to $1 million (small business), or even smaller entrepreneurial and start-up companies.

Online resources can help you in three very important ways: (1) They can provide you with names of companies, information on industries, and other leads to pursue further online and offline. (2) They can provide you with exposure by listing your résumé on job boards and databanks. This can be useful especially if you have unusual skills such as speaking Arabic or possessing a pilot's license, but may be less so if you are a generalist. And (3) you can apply to employers directly on their recruiting sites, which are usually sub-sites of companies' human resources pages. Shy students and those willing to move anywhere can take particular advantage of online job searching, but in general, students should not rely too much on online tactics. You get jobs by talking to people, and most surfers use online media to avoid talking to people.

Here are some of the sites that you should check out:
1. www.aol.com (click on Business and Careers in Web Center)
2. www.careerpath.com
3. www.careermosaic.com
4. www.headhunter.net
5. www.jobsearch.org
6. www.hotjobs.com
7. www.dice.com
8. www.careerbuilder.com
9. www.nationjob.com
10. www.jobsmart.org
11. www.careers.wsj.com
12. www.occ.com
13. www.excite.com/careers
14. www.careermag.com
15. www.monster.com
16. www.jobtrak.com
17. www.intellimatch.com
18. www.statejobs.com
19. www.hire-ed.org
20. www.jobweb.org
21. www.careerxroads.com
22. www.job-hunt.org
23. www.ddiscoveries.com
24. www.selectjobs.com

25. www.vjf.com
26. www.hotjobs.com
27. www.cweb.com
28. www.fedworld.gov
29. www.usajobs.opm.gov
30. www.ajb.dni.us
31. www.4work.com
32. www.accountingjobs.com
33. www.bestjobsusa.com
34. www.career.com
35. www.careeravenue.com
36. www.bridgepath.com
37. www.careercity.com
38. www.careercast.com
39. www.careerexchange.com
40. www.careerlinkusa.com
41. www.careershop.com
42. www.careersite.com
43. www.careerweb.com
44. www.computerwork.com
45. www.engineeringjobs.com
46. www.classifieds2000.com
47. www.joboptions.com
48. www.passportaccess.com
49. www.gayworks.com
50. www.cob.ohio-state.edu/~fin/osujobs.htm

Also see
1. www.wetfeet.com
2. www.hoovers.com
3. www.corporateinformation.com
4. www.sec.gov/cgi-bin/srch-edgar
5. www.brint.com/interest.html
6. www.inquisit.com
7. www.networksolutions.com/cgi-bin/whois/whois

Treat **want ads** as sources of information on companies, not jobs. If a company is advertising for a director of procurement for a major civil construction project in Saudi Arabia, you can bet that the company already employs several engineers in the domestic office and will eventually need office assistants, engineering assistants, a warehouse manager, a translator or two, accountants, a computer whiz, and perhaps even a small-plane pilot for the field office. Most entry-level jobs are not advertised anywhere, but an intelligent person can discover and apply for entry-level jobs by extrapolating from newspaper ads for executive personnel. This means want ads that are months old are still pertinent to you.

Newspapers are a particularly poor place for college students and people switching careers to look for job leads. Advertisements usually draw hundreds of applicants, almost all of whom will have more experience than you. As an experiment, I once ran this ad in the Sunday *San Francisco Examiner*: "Hard work. Low pay. Fax your résumé: 415-441-0389." I got 72 résumés! Imagine that. In addition to all this competition for advertised jobs, you need to know that 70 to 85 percent of all jobs that change hands are never advertised in the first place. So newspapers have massive competition and only represent 15 to 30 percent of the total job market. Beware.

Of course, you should apply for advertised positions for which you are qualified. Incidentally, do not ignore small local community papers. Some companies intentionally advertise lower-level and unskilled jobs in small community papers in order to reduce the applicant pool. Other organizations, often nonprofits, political, and arts organizations, advertise in small special interest publications to recruit candidates with an existing interest in their cause.

Many employment professionals have an unwarranted bias against advertised jobs; they fear that they must be low paying and unattractive, or the company would not have had to resort to advertising. In reality, however, many companies have no choice but to advertise their openings in the first place. Small, off-the-beaten-track companies may not have a steady flow of applicants from which to choose, and any company needing an unusual combination of skills may be forced to advertise eventually. Finally, some companies and government agencies are required by policy to advertise all their openings.

Want ads are only one type of **announced opening.** Job openings are also announced on computer bulletin boards, profiled in obscure industry newsletters, listed at your state employment development department, on record at the nearest federal Office of Personnel Management, recorded on company job hotlines, and posted on job bulletin boards in places as diverse as your college office of career planning and the local YMCA. Strategically, these should all be treated the same way as want ads.

Announced openings should be a part of any thorough job search, but they are most often completely overemphasized by job seekers. Use want ads and other announced openings as just another source of ideas. Under no circumstance should you glean more

177

than 25 percent of your leads from newspaper ads. Apply your energy and creativity elsewhere or your odds for success drop through the floor. Ads for entry-level positions often generate hundreds of applicants, and you don't need to face that type of competition. For more on this, see Richard Bolles' *What Color Is Your Parachute?*, which has a section on the success rates of various methods of job-seeking.

Headhunters and employment agencies place a few recent college graduates, but not many. (In most states there is no legal difference between an agency and a headhunting or "executive search" firm. The maxim is, "Headhunters find people for jobs, not jobs for people." In other words, companies contact headhunters with a specific opening, which the headhunter tries to fill. No matter how impressed a headhunter may be with you, she can do nothing for you if you do not fit one of the jobs she has an active search for.) The more specialized the position opening, the more likely some headhunter will be involved in the job search. If you are seeking a fairly specialized position, call some of the headhunters who handle that type of position. The best book ever written on headhunters is John Lucht's *Rites of Passage*. If you're headed for the executive suite, I definitely recommend it, and it's fun to read anyway.

◉ ◉ ◉

Finally, *think categorically!* Lead cards should multiply like amoebae: Every card should suggest two more avenues to research. If one company is interesting, identify every other company like it. You are a sleuth in search of clues, a miner in search of the direction of the vein. If one long-distance phone company is hiring rate analysts, you should immediately guess that there has been some rating change and all the carriers need new rate analysts.

Whenever I think about multiplying lead cards I think of two stories. One of my clients had a new college degree and a background in restaurants, and she wanted a career in sales. She had an uncle in New Jersey who owned a restaurant equipment brokerage. This uncle didn't want to hire her, but he agreed to show her around a day on the job in outside sales. After buying equipment at an auction, getting lost in a massive warehouse, witnessing a fistfight on a loading dock, and meeting with a fussy New York restaurateur—all in the same day—she was hooked. She cracked the yellow pages and called every equipment brokerage in the metro area. Needless to say, she got a position and did very well, until her uncle ended up begging her to come into his business as a partner. If one company is a dead end, call its competitors immediately. You will become a more savvy applicant with every interview.

Another candidate was flown across the continent to interview for a position on the history faculty of a prestigious private college. This college was near several others, so the candidate got on the phone and called the chairs of the history departments at the other schools. "I'm in town to interview at [prestigious college], and while I'm here I'd just like to meet with you and see if you anticipate any openings." He called it the cheap date theory of interviewing, i.e., "I'm here already. . ." The college that paid his airfare did not extend an offer, but in the end one of the other colleges did! I use this same technique on speaking tours. I get one sponsor to pay my airfare, then call everyone else and tell them I'll be there anyway.

Never miss a chance to turn one lead card into several.

Develop Raw Leads into Specific, Targeted Individuals

First of all, work your network. Who in your extended web of contacts works at the company you have targeted? What alumni of your alma mater now work or have ever worked at the company? What peers had internships at a branch of this organization last summer? Who at the career center might have a connection at this company? Who in your family might know someone at or something about this company? What former employer of yours might be able to tell you more about the company? Until you do this, you should not try to approach the company directly.

Then, do a search of recent media citations mentioning your targeted company. These articles will contain the names of people from the company. You should do this anyway, as part of your research of any potential employer. Don't you want to know if your potential future employer has been indicted for polluting the environment or working slave laborers abroad?

If you are interested in a publicly held company, call the investor relations department and ask for the company's latest annual report and other information on what the company does, its product lines, and so on. Just be honest. Tell them you are a college student or a recent college graduate who is interested in the company as a potential employer, and ask for a basic information packet.

These reports will be full of names of senior officers and department heads, as well as good information about how the company views itself, where its growth areas are, and what challenges it faces.

Your reference librarian, or the reference librarian at the nearest business library, can show you dozens of ways to obtain the names of managers at specific companies. Books, however, are probably one of the least efficient sources of names of decision-makers. Remember, any reference book is obsolete before it is printed.

179

The best way to turn a company lead into the specific name of a decision-maker at that company is to pick up your phone and use it. Your telephone should be an integral part of your job-search process. Call up the company and ask! Here is a model script: "Hello. My name is Mary Sullivan. I'm interested in joining your company. My main interests are product development, industrial design, or perhaps project engineering. Who is in charge of these areas? Who would I talk to about this?"

Give people a chance to help you, and they will.

Whenever you write or talk to a representative of a company, use the information you've gleaned from your media search and from your review of the annual report. Every problem they have is an opportunity for you, and the more you know about a company, the better you will be at identifying opportunities there.

Your Goal: Approach and Sell to Individuals

No matter how you generate and develop your leads, you should approach leads in exactly the same way: write first, then call, call, call, call until you get a response.

There are three kinds of leads: people who have the power to offer you a job, people who can refer you to the former, and people who can provide you with background information that will help you in your search. You should know which of these types you are contacting, but always initiate your contact in the same way: Ask for ideas and referrals.

Unless there is an announced opening, you usually do not contact someone about a job with them. You want to "lower the ante," so that they will be more comfortable talking or meeting with you. Point out that you are not applying for a job with them at this time. Ask for their assistance in finding a position, their ideas, advice, and referrals. No one will want to be in the position of having to say no to you or reject you directly. But by lowering the ante, you will put them at their ease.

Your goal is to use the telephone in interactions with the latter two types of contacts (background and referral sources), and to meet in person with the first type (hiring managers). You must be seen by decision-makers who have the power to offer you a job in order to get one. You want to meet them face-to-face whether they are hiring or not. As shocking as this may be to you, hiring an entry-level employee is not a big decision-making process. If they like you, and they think they might be able to use you, they can hire you even if they weren't planning on recruiting anyone. It's no big deal.

Approach your contacts by sending a query letter or a letter and résumé together (see the next chapter for more on query and cover letters). Be sure to state that you will call within two days of receipt of your letter. Then, follow up within thirty-six hours of its receipt with a phone call. To be successful in timing your follow-up calls, you will need to estimate the arrival date of your missive. Call the post office for typical first class posting times between specific cities, or use overnight courier or second day priority mail. After roughly thirty-six hours, your query is dealt with; it is either round filed, delegated, or lost in the usual office shuttle. Timely follow-up is critical!

Do not bother to send anything that won't be followed up with a phone call (with the exceptions of responses to blind box newspaper ads and job announcements that specify "no calls"). Unsolicited mail has less than a 2 percent response rate. If you are happy with that, you'll still be looking for work a year from now. Write first, then call, call, call. In this way, every phone call you make will be a "warm call." You can truthfully say to gatekeepers along the way, "Yes, she is expecting my call." Why? Because in your letter you said you would!

Remember, fewer than seven attempts to complete an unsolicited business telephone contact are too few. Call at least once every day when the person is in town. This is why you will need your 5 x 8 lead cards, to keep detailed notes on the hundreds of contacts you will be making. Soon these cards will be covered with notes like these: "Monday 8-12 8:05 a.m.: Secretary's name is Chris Smythe (male). Roger Cyborg is not in yet. Call back at nine." "Monday 8-12 9:05 a.m.: Cyborg in a meeting. Left message." "Tuesday 8-13 9:05 a.m.: Cyborg out of town until next Monday." "Monday 8-19 9:05: Cyborg couldn't find letter. I said I'd fax another." "Tuesday 8-20 9:05: Cyborg says 'Looks good, let's get together for a chat.' Meeting scheduled for next Monday at 9:00!!"

You don't need a pretext to ask people to meet with you. Be straightforward. You are seeking a job, and want assistance for just a moment in that project. You don't necessarily want to work for your contacts' companies. You are most interested in ideas, leads, referrals, advice, and counsel. It is human nature to want to be helpful. Unless you are rude or inept, which you should take great pains to avoid, people will want to help you.

As an illustration of using a slight pretext to arrange meetings, I know a candidate who was seeking a professional position in residential real estate development. She called every major player in Northern California and introduced herself as a recent graduate and asked if they would take a moment and critique her résumé. She had dozens of meetings over this résumé, and never changed a word of it!

Once you are in a meeting with a decision-maker, be straightforward about asking if there are any places where someone like you could fit into his organization. If you are positive that a decision-maker harbors the exact job that you want, you can be more aggressive. If he has no openings, let him know what you have to offer anyway, "in case something should open up." Then be sure to get leads, ideas, feedback, and referrals.

Ask for referrals to other departments, other divisions, and decision-makers at other companies. Pay attention! If someone offers you a lead, pick it up and follow up on it.

Note that the process of approaching decision-makers described here is not the same thing as informational interviewing. By now you should have decided on a career path, and you should be approaching decision-makers about specific types of jobs. This process of talking to players in the field you have targeted, whether it is financial services or arts administration, is extremely valuable. By circulating, you get a steady flow of helpful information, and, perhaps even more important, you get feedback on your search itself.

I know of one college graduate who wanted to find a job as a property manager. He had almost no experience that could even remotely be construed as related to this career goal, but he had moxie. He called every employer who rejected his candidacy and asked them three questions: what were they looking for in a property manager, what could he do to improve his résumé, and what could he do to improve his chances of getting a job like this in the near future? In this way he sharpened his candidacy, refined his understanding of the targeted employers, improved his résumé, and began to get offers. He eventually got a fantastic job, assistant manager of a 400-unit building, a job he never could have landed when he first started his search.

Your search should be driven by this principle: You are looking for the right fit. You are not looking for any job offer that someone might toss you like a bone. You are looking for the position that will launch your career. Potential employers will respect and value you more if you seem discriminating rather than desperate.

It should be obvious by now that whether a company is hiring or not is irrelevant to you as a job seeker. The phrase, "hidden job market," is nothing more than a reference to the fact that the overwhelming majority of jobs are filled by someone who walks into the right place at the right time. If you circulate in the right places, you will eventually be there at the right time.

Even without the proven track record of these techniques, confirmed by the happy employment of millions of individuals such as yourself, the logic of these strategies should be convincing to you. These methods work; they reduce your competition for announced openings and result in a better match between your skills and the needs of the employer. As mentioned above, most employers have considerable discretion when it comes to entry-level jobs. Particularly in smaller to medium-size firms, hiring can be a one-person decision. If that person is impressed with you, she may suddenly have four new rate analysts instead of three.

One final word of advice: Hard work is always required to launch a career. Too many graduates today want to walk into an important job with a bundle of perks right away. They demand guarantees from their employer without offering any in return. Do not be afraid to take a mundane job that offers the right opportunities for advancement. Be willing to prove yourself. And be sure to reject any job that doesn't advance your career, no matter the pay or perks.

While it is not always true that hard work results in advancement, it is true that advancement is always preceded by hard work.

Follow-Through, Follow-Through, Follow-Through

Your search will generate loose ends and details in great volume. Every new contact is like a comet with a massive tail of follow-through behind it. Your ability to manage that tail is critical to the success of your overall project.

183

Timely and exact execution of follow-through means the difference between success and failure in your search. When a genuine effort does not result in a series of job offers, the reason is most often the timing of that effort. There are two aspects of timing: protocol and momentum.

Job-search **protocol** dictates that you will honor your commitments, be exactly four minutes early for every meeting, and send a brief thank-you letter or note to everyone who assists you in your project. Send thank-you notes immediately after meetings. A thank-you note that arrives a week later is unimpressive. (Sample thank-you notes appear in the next chapter.) If you say you will call on Monday, call before noon. If you say you will call at 9:00 a.m. you must call between 8:59 and 9:01. If your appointment is for 11:00 a.m. at 10:59 you are already late. Every fax and every mailing of your résumé needs a cover letter, however brief. If your résumé or stationery paper has a water mark be sure to print on it right-side up. Employers do notice these details. A sloppy job search is a long one.

Momentum is a much more subtle issue. The placement process has a rhythm of its own, and employers expect a certain ritual dance. If you perform all the steps of that dance well and in time, you can force a decision. If an employer has interviewed you the prescribed number of times and you have performed well, he will feel an obligation and an urge to make a decision. Obviously, the sooner you can force an employer to decide, the better, as more time can only mean more competition as others enter the dance after you.

Many weaker candidates are hired over stronger candidates who do not know how to create momentum. Timely and exact execution of your part of the placement process creates momentum. Laggardly delivery results in loss of momentum and a breaking of the rhythm. In general, deliver the next obligation on your part at the earliest graceful moment. Let the employer know as soon as you are ready to make a commitment.

(Some employers have rather rigid hiring processes and cannot be rushed or controlled. Still, you never lose by being aggressive, timely, and proper.)

Finally, in cases where the decision-making process is drawn out, you need to maintain contact with your prospective employer. Find some reason to call or send something to the employer every three or four business days. Scour the newspapers for articles you think might be of interest to her, then clip them out and send them with a note. Write a letter that begins, "Ever since our meeting I've been thinking about what you said about . . ." Send her your references or, if she already has them, send a new reference that you "just realized" she might be interested in speaking with. Call her, restate your interest in the position, restate that you are ready to make a commitment, and ask how the search is progressing and when she will be ready to extend an offer. You must keep yourself in contact with the decision-maker. Other candidates will pop up and fade away, but you will always be there, like Coca-Cola.

More of these techniques are covered in Chapter 18, "Cold-calling, Interviews, and Closing the Deal."

CHAPTER 17

Cover Letters, Thank-You Letters, and Reference Sheets

COVER LETTERS

The cover letter's importance is overrated. Its main function is to serve as a routing slip for your résumé; its primary job is to get your résumé in front of the targeted individual. In that role, an exceedingly brief cover letter is sufficient:

Dear Ms. Dardanelle:

I am a recent college graduate interested in positions in mechanical engineering. If you could share your career expertise with me, I would certainly appreciate it. I have enclosed my résumé for your review. I will be calling you within two business days to see what ideas and suggestions you may have for me.

Thank you for your consideration.

Sincerely,

Your Name Here

Such a letter is utilitarian, efficient, and to the point. If you use a simple letter like this and employ the job search strategies explained in the last chapter, you will find a position rapidly. Here is a slightly more aggressive version:

Dear Ms. Greers-Ferry:

I am interested in having a short, face-to-face talk with you about opportunities in pharmaceutical sales.

This is not an application for a job. This is an introduction. I'll be calling you shortly to see if we can get together. A moment of your time would be much appreciated, and I'll work my schedule around yours.

Thank you for your time.

Sincerely,

Your Name Here

This last letter is an example of a query letter, which simply announces that you will be calling and/or that you want fairly specific information. Query letters can be used with or without a résumé. By not enclosing a résumé in your initial unsolicited mailing, you reduce the likelihood that your mailing will be routed to the human resources department, and you "lower the ante" with your contact, as well.

⊙ ⊙ ⊙

Incidentally, if after employing every wile and artifice from the last chapter you simply cannot generate the name of a specific person to write to, you can write to a title or department, such as "Chief Engineer" of "Mechanical Engineering Department." The problem with this approach is that most unsolicited résumés that arrive without a definite addressee are discarded without review, and you cannot effectively follow up by phone.

⊙ ⊙ ⊙

If you have been referred by someone, be sure to mention it at the very top of your letter. This will prevent your résumé from being shanghaied before reaching its intended recipient. No clerk or gatekeeper is willing to risk offending a professional acquaintance of his boss. Here is one example:

Dear Mr. Kennedy:

I was discussing remote sensing technologies with Jerome Levinson here at M.I.T., and he suggested that you might be interested in someone with my background. Perhaps by this summer you will have an opening in your company appropriate for me, or you may know someone else who could use an engineer with my training. I'll be calling you on Thursday at 9:00 to see if we can arrange a time to meet.

I look forward to speaking with you soon.

Cordially,

Your Name Here

You should note that the above letter will be quite effective whether your recipient knows Prof. Levinson personally or not.

Short letters are also appropriate when you are dealing with someone whom you have already called:

Dear Ms. Bertschi:

As you requested in our telephone conversation of today, enclosed is my résumé. I will call you by Wednesday afternoon to verify its arrival, and to answer any preliminary questions you may have. I appreciate your assistance, and I look forward to meeting with you on the 12th.

Respectfully,

Your Name Here

Also, should your contacts offer to assist you, be sure to forward extra copies of your résumé to them. As a student or recent graduate, you have a unique opportunity to broadcast your job search from coast to coast. As a practicing professional, you may never again have the opportunity to spread your résumés around with impunity, like so many advertising circulars.

Dear Ms. Lasch:

I truly appreciate your offer of assistance, and I am enclosing several copies of my résumé as you suggested. Please feel free to forward them to interested parties as you deem appropriate. I will call you next week to see if you have any new leads.

Again, thank you!

Sincerely,

Your Name Here

All these short letters can look kind of lonely perched in the center of an 8½ x 11 sheet of typing paper. It might be a good idea to print up some note-sized stationery, either classical monarch size (7¼ x 10½) or even smaller. While you are at it, print up some business cards with your name, address, and a title like "Chemist" or "Job Applicant," and enclose one with each mailing.

187

If you are applying for an announced opening, cite that opening as part of your heading. This way, no one has to actually read your cover letter in order to route your letter and résumé:

> Attn: Ms. Toni Bonetti, Director, Management Recruiting
> Re: Company Representative, Asia/Pacific Markets, advertised in the *WSJ*, 11/20/00

If you are applying for an announced opening, you may want to provide a little more persuasion in your cover letter than if you are strictly using the letter as part of your networking process. Here is an example:

Dear Ms. Li:

I was excited to learn that Management Associate opportunities exist in Indonesia and elsewhere in Asia. Because I am a citizen of Indonesia and fluent in English, Indonesian and Mandarin, I would be particularly interested in discussing these openings.

I was referred to you by [major university's] Career Center. My résumé is enclosed for your review.

As you can see, I will obtain my Master of Business Administration in December of this year. My high grade point average (3.53) and the speed with which I obtained my degree demonstrate my strong work ethic, determination, and ability to excel. My education encompasses a wide range of finance, investment, and banking coursework. I can offer substantial knowledge of Southeast Asian business practices, in addition to hard work, dedication, and future potential.

I am confident that I can make a meaningful and lasting contribution to your firm, and am anxious to discuss this further. Please call me at your earliest convenience to arrange a time. I can be reached at (212) 555-9103.

Thank you. I look forward to our conversation.

Sincerely,

Your Name Here

188

Even though this student asked the prospective employer to call her, she in fact began calling the firm's representative within twenty-four hours of the moment this missive reached Ms. Li's desk. Generally it is best to let an employer know exactly when you will call, and you will want to make that call as soon as possible after they open the letter. The ideal clause would be: "Just as you look up from reading this sentence, the phone will ring. I will be on the other end of the line. You will find it very interesting to speak with me." Barring that, try these two constructions:

"I will call you on Tuesday at precisely 10:30 a.m. You can count on me to be prompt. I look forward to our conversation."

Or, if you are not that prompt, use this version:

"I will call you on Tuesday before noon. You can count on me to be prompt. I look forward to our conversation."

Of course, with comments like these, if you don't follow through by 10:31 or 12:01, respectively, your credibility is shot.

If you need additional experience to become more attractive to employers, get some! Here is how one student obtained valuable exposure that resulted in a breakthrough at a key point in his career development:

Dear Mr. Wainscot:

I am fully aware of your firm's reputation and the competitiveness of your internship program, yet I am willing to volunteer my time or work part-time on your behalf in order to assist you in your business. Surely there is some way that my services could assist you?

My goal is to enter one of the top architectural programs in the United States, and to prepare for this I need your help. It does not matter what you have me do, as long as I am allowed to participate in your business, observe talented designers at work, and gain exposure to a successful architectural practice.

My strength is my art background, which could be of use to you in model construction, mechanical drafting projects, and perspectives and renderings. Is there not a project that you need extra assistance with? Is there not some bid or proposal that you might win if I were to assist you with some modeling or other labor-intensive aspect?

As a recent college graduate seeking experience related to architecture, I offer you an eager and malleable student, solid basic skills, and a desire to please you and your staff.

My résumé is attached for your review. I will be calling you soon to see if we can get together briefly. Even if you do not anticipate that you will be able to provide me with a volunteer position, I would still like to meet with you and hear what ideas you may have for me.

Thank you so much.

Yours sincerely,

Your Name Here

189

This letter resulted in a meeting and almost a year of *paid* work experience in one of the most competitive architectural firms in the country. At the time this book went to press, the candidate was in the act of applying to the top architectural programs in the nation, a career move that was only possible because he has acquired industry experience. (See my *Graduate Admissions Essays: What Works, What Doesn't, and Why* for assistance on graduate applications.)

◎ ◎ ◎

Whenever possible, your letters should be as short as the examples above, with one exception: In the academic world, involved letters of application (two, three, and sometimes even more pages) are common. Academic job placements are usually handled by committee, and have rigid formulae that move along at the pace of a snail. It is not uncommon for an academic search to be open for six months, and sometimes even a year. They are almost always advertised positions, which generate considerable national competition.

Even if you have seen a fairly detailed advertisement for such a position, call and ask for more information—you can usually get a more complete job announcement mailed or faxed to you. Be sure to comply with the terms of the announcement: If the committee asks for four references, three are too few. If the committee asks for a statement of educational philosophy as well as a c.v., you'd better write one. If the announcement requests that you submit transcripts, your magna cum laude status does not exempt you from that requirement. If the deadline is the first of March, your chances may be over by 5:01 p.m. on that day.

In spite of the limited flexibility and the formal application process, successful candidates often mount extensive, involved behind-the-scenes lobbying campaigns to win these positions. They call every connection they have and ask them to "put in a good word" with members of the search committee. If possible, they create a small flow of letters of recommendation from colleagues and professors. Most of all, they learn as much as possible about the targeted institution and opening. I know of one physical geography professor who got a position in Tennessee by conveying that he knew everything, geologically speaking, about the formation of the surrounding area.

190

The following letter is an example of the more formal style typical for entry-level academic or administrative applications. (It also illustrates the appropriate layout and design for any cover letter).

MARTIN PATRICK WALTZ
waltz33@Tulane.edu /alumni
1975 Bayou Road   Telephone /Message: (504) 555-2830
Metairie, Louisiana 70122   Fax, 24/hrs.: (504) 555-8738

August 12, 2000

Office of the President
Special Assistant to the President Search Committee
Ivy University
One Prospect Street
Ithaca, New York 14853

Ladies and Gentlemen of the Committee:

When I originally undertook the juris doctor program from Tulane University School of Law, I intended for it to be, for me, a "liberal arts MBA." Although it is now somewhat trendy to abandon the law before one undertakes it, my goal all along was to enter academia. Ivy University has certainly long been on my list of preferred institutions, the sort of place where I know I could fit in, excel, and contribute. Needless to say, the position of special assistant to the president and assistant secretary to the corporation is quite attractive to me.

My graduate studies were exciting due to content, the analytical structure of the learning, and the discipline required to succeed. Now I am eager to join the university environment in a position of responsibility, drawing upon my combination of administrative, organizational and interpersonal skills. I believe I have a unique blend of talents to bring to a position such as this: a) strong presentation and public speaking skills, b) both expository and persuasive writing skills, c) extensive experience consuming voluminous data and distilling salient points, including summary writing.

In addition to the above, I have specific legal skills that would be of benefit to any college: a) knowledge of contracts, liability, corporation and real property law, and b) perhaps of benefit to the development office, knowledge of wills, estates, and trusts.

Finally, although it is to be expected of everyone, as a resident of one of the more culturally diverse areas in the United States, I am comfortable with all different types of people. I believe I could represent the university well in any capacity, and I would consider it an honor to do so.

Thank you for your consideration. I hope that my application will warrant discussions with the committee. I can be reached by telephone in New Orleans, and I can be available in Ithaca at your convenience.

Sincerely,

Martin P. Waltz

Martin P. Waltz

Enclosure: résumé.

/mw

Thank-You Letters

It is more important that a thank-you letter be timely than that it have any particular content. You should write and post them the same day as the meeting or phone call in reference. A simple note such as the following is sufficient:

Dear Ms. Orr:

Thank you for your time today. I was impressed by Orr Industries, and I hope a tax analyst position opens up before summer. I'll be calling you once every ten days, as you suggested. Also, thanks so much for the referral to Jason T. Colson. We have an appointment already.

Again, thank you, and I'll be in touch.

Sincerely,

Your Name Here

Here is a more expansive model:

Dear Mr. Thompson:

Thank you for the introduction to your office in our meeting of January 28. I am drawn to the professionalism and dedication that you and Ms. Whitney exhibited, and I look forward to learning more about your operations in our next meeting.

I am confident of my skills and abilities related to the position, and I hope I was able to convey those skills to you. I would particularly like to point out my extensive experience in a financial environment.

The sum of my education and my experience, I believe, provides a solid base to meet the demands of this position. I look forward to our next meeting this Thursday, in which I will be happy to answer any additional questions you may have.

Respectfully yours,

Your Name Here

Type thank-you notes on your note-sized stationery, or, if they are quite short, type them on conservative, understated greeting cards, which you can buy at any drugstore or stationers. Do not write out letters by hand; a handwritten letter denotes intimacy, which would be inappropriate. Do not e-mail your thank-you letters. Etiquette has rules, and this is one of them.

☉ ☉ ☉

A thank-you letter is also an excellent place to overcome objections to your candidacy that may have arisen during the interview. Here is one demonstration of this technique:

> You mentioned that several of the candidates you had under consideration had more financial experience than I. After I got home I realized that I had not fully represented my financial abilities (your original ad didn't focus on this requirement). As treasurer I managed capital and operating budgets for my fraternity, controlling almost $100,000 per annum. I was the first treasurer to fully computerize house budgets (using Excel). I also worked on a bylaws amendment to create a depreciation fee to ensure timely long-term maintenance of the house. As part of this, I met with contractors to predict, schedule, and estimate 20 years of maintenance. Then I prepared five years of detailed pro formas for house operations, modeling inflation, cash flow, and trends in construction costs. I think I have more than enough financial skills to excel in the position we discussed.

This type of passage should be couched in the middle of an otherwise entirely positive letter. If you sound defensive in a thank-you letter, you might be better off not sending one at all.

193

Reference Sheets

As a general rule, references should be provided on a separate sheet, not on your résumé. Do not enclose your references with your résumé unless asked to do so. As a matter of etiquette, you should ask for permission before you use someone as a reference. It is a good idea to send a draft of your résumé to your references to remind them of your skills, experience, and aptitudes.

Unless instructed to provide a different number, three to five references is typically sufficient. References should be people in positions of authority who have direct knowledge of your work or study habits. Character references, such as your roommate, your rabbi, or the mayor of your home town, are usually considered worthless.

A reference listing should consist of the person's name, current title and place of employment, and current daytime telephone number. Since references are usually telephoned, a full address is not necessary unless requested. Do not release your references' home telephone numbers or addresses without explicit permission. This is the standard format:

Elizabeth Whinegrove, Ph.D.

Director, Economic Modeling & Analysis

Major Conservative Thinktank

Boston, Massachusettts

(617) 555-1739

If it is unclear what relationship you may have with this person, you can list that in parentheses as part of the reference listing: "(former Chair, Economics Department, Duke University)."

References are not as important at the entry level as they are later on in your career, but they should all be ready to provide glowing reports on your industry and mental acuity. By the way, it is not a good idea to have all male or all female references.

Salary Histories

Occasionally job announcements will ask for your salary history, which is simply a table of your places of employment, dates of employment, official titles, and ending gross income. There are many reasons not to provide this type of information, but they are usually more pertinent to candidates later on in their careers. At the entry level, it is probably just as well to provide the information without further ado. Here is a sample listing:

Global Trade Magazine, New York, New York

Intern (Editorial Assistant), Summer 2000

Salary: $1500 / month (stipend)

If an announcement requests your "salary requirements," simply note that your salary requirements are open to negotiation, or depend upon the exact duties of the position, and put off the issue until you have established a mutual interest in an interview setting.

⇒   ⇒   ⇒   ⇒

CHAPTER 18

Cold-Calling, Interviews, and Closing the Deal

COLD-CALLING

Cold-calling is an integral part of any well-managed job search. While few people are comfortable picking up the phone and calling strangers, the results are overwhelmingly superior to other methods. If you follow up your mailings with a telephone call, your number of interviews will increase dramatically.

I have never seen any research on this specific issue, but anecdotal reports from my clients indicate that your interview ratio will improve by a factor of ten if you are willing to call and ask for an interview. This is as simple as it sounds. Send in your résumé and letter, then call and ask for an interview. Sending out letters and résumés might get you one or two interviews out of one hundred attempts; mailing and then calling until you get a response might get you ten or twenty. Individual results will vary widely, but these figures are compelling.

One of my associates told a recent graduate with a degree in mechanical engineering that he should just open up the yellow pages and call companies and firms that he thought might harbor positions of interest to him. This was in Michigan at a time when every major car manufacturer was laying off all levels of staff. My associate told him to simply call and ask for an interview, whether they were hiring or not. "If they say they're not hiring," my associate advised the candidate, "just tell them you want to talk to them anyway, so they'll know what you have to offer in case an opening should come up." This young man went home and did just that for eight hours a day. Starting without a single lead, he made appointments for eighteen interviews within a week! Experienced engineers were hanging off trees, driving cabs, and learning to macrame at home, yet this candidate landed an engineering job in record time.

Cold-calling works.

You should make your first call before you send out your first mailing. Call and ask to whom exactly you should address your application. Do not get involved in a long conversation on this call.

Your goal is to find out the name, correct title, and exact address of a decision-maker. Find out if they are in town the next few days. If anyone asks why you need this information, just say "I'm going to be mailing him something, and I want to spell his name right." Just get the information if you can and sign off.

Target your follow up calls to this decision-maker. Welcome to the world of gatekeepers, voicemail, and administrative assistants!

Never be anything but extra nice to gatekeepers and administrative assistants. They have incredible power over the information and the people who get through to decision-makers. You want them as allies, not enemies. Still, your goal is to get past them to the hiring authority herself.

Persistence is the number one technique to achieve this goal. Many inexperienced callers abandon their efforts before making a meaningful contact. Remember, fewer than seven phone calls to make an unsolicited business contact are simply too few. Do not be discouraged if people do not return your phone calls. Business people are busy, often very busy, and even your father's best friend may not respond to repeated phone calls. You must be persistent. Polite. Nice. But persistent.

Do not take a lack of a return call personally, and do not mistake it for a lack of interest. Maybe they are quite interested in speaking with you, but they just haven't had a moment to return your call. Call every day if they are in town, at least once a day, the earlier the better. Be polite to the gatekeeper, and leave a message if you don't get through or you get routed onto voicemail.

If after several calls you haven't gotten a return call, ask the gatekeeper for advice. It is a good idea to address gatekeepers by name. Early in the process, ask "May I know your name please?" Most gatekeepers are delighted that you recognize them as human beings. Try saying something like this, "I've been calling Ms. Jaeger for several days, and I haven't been able to get her attention. Do you have any suggestions for me about how I might be more effective in trying to reach her?" This disarming directness has been extremely successful for several of my clients. You may get good advice, even if the advice is to forget it, or you may get put straight through to Ms. Jaeger. As long as you are nice and polite, you have nothing to lose.

197

If you suspect that a particular gatekeeper is screening you out, call early, late, or during lunchtime. The relief gatekeeper is often not as skilled at screening, or may like you better and put you through. Sometimes after hours and early in the morning middle managers and executives pick up incoming calls themselves. This can be a golden opportunity. Most managers don't screen calls at all before patching the caller through.

Also, whenever you are put through to another office or bounced from one gate-keeper to another, make a habit of asking, "What is the direct dial number for that office?" Ask the person patching you through, not the one answering. Record this type of information directly onto your 5 x 8 lead card.

In all these cases, the most successful approach is the most direct. Put a smile in your voice, and speak as if you expect to be put through. "Good morning. Is Ms. Jaeger in? This is Mary Wong calling." As we discussed earlier, if you have mailed Ms. Jaeger a letter, you can say in all honesty, "Yes, she is expecting my call." Do not be coy if the gate-keeper asks you what this is regarding. Say, "I sent her a letter which I believe arrived yesterday, and I am calling to follow up. She is expecting my call before noon today." If pressed, be completely honest about why you are calling, and what you hope to gain by speaking to Ms. Jaeger. Subterfuge and trickery will usually backfire, and are unnecessary anyway.

If you get voicemail, use this script: "This is Dave Wallace. I'm sorry to have missed you. My number is 212-555-1873, but if you're busy there's no need to call me back. I'll be calling again." And again. And again. And again. Once per day until you reach them.

You will not succeed on every attempt, and you should not expect to. Your goal is to improve your odds. You will get better and better at extracting decision-makers' names and titles, penetrating gatekeepers' screens, and getting interviews.

In a strict sense, a lead is dead only when the decision-maker herself tells you to stop bothering her. Otherwise, the lead is live, and it could be the very one that results in the job offer that launches your whole career.

As an old salesman once told me: "Either the guy writes me a check or he throws me out of his office. There is no other possible outcome to a sales call."

Interviews

Some interview books spend scores of pages defining "the six types of interviewers" and "the four types of interviews" and so on. The best advice I can give you is a little more simple:

> Know why you are there

> Know what you have to offer

> Be prepared for the common questions

> Be yourself, but sell yourself

You may be in an interview for many reasons: to find out more about specific types of jobs and career paths; to apply for a specific, announced opening; to get leads and referrals to individuals and companies that harbor jobs you want; or for some more ephemeral reason, such as to follow through on an advisor's recommendation just so that that advisor will continue to assist you in your search. Incidentally, savvy candidates have been known to apply for jobs they know they will decline in order to open up a strategically useful networking conduit. Remember your purpose for arranging the meeting, and try to be sure you don't leave until you achieve it.

If you have properly prepared your résumé, you know what you have to offer. You also know what you want: what type of job, what level of responsibility, and at least a rough idea of your salary expectations. Make a crib sheet of topics and points you want to bring up in the interview. Anticipate your prospective employer's concerns. Make a short list of critical skills necessary to perform in the position you have targeted, and next to each critical skill note what evidence you can offer from your background that demonstrates that you have that skill. (You already did this in Chapter 3, "Know Your Product.") Remember, some of the evidence you may wish to present is material that was eliminated from earlier drafts of your résumé.

We will discuss the most common interview questions and strategies for answering them in following sections. First it is important to consider the interview as an event before you concentrate on answers to questions.

The Interview as an Event: Theater at Its Best
Good theater involves more than just walking the boards; it requires research, costume/wardrobe development, rewriting, rehearsal, and then showtime! Long before the interview itself, your production effort should go into gear.

As mentioned in the last chapter, research the company in any way you can. Before you meet with that representative from Amalgamated Diversified, see if you can dig up any press articles on the company. Ask the company's public relations or investor relations department for brochures and annual reports. Look in various editions of Who's Who and similar references (visit your reference librarian) to see what you can find out about the company's top officers (or maybe even your interviewer). Call the local Better Business Bureau, chamber of commerce, or state consumer affairs board and see if they have any information on the company. Talk to people in your extended network of contacts to see what they know about it. Perform your own market research; call competitors and tell them you are researching their industry, and ask them what advice they would have for someone considering entering this industry; inquire into career paths, reasonable salary expectations, and their impressions of Amalgamated Diversified. You need to understand your motivation and your story line.

You would be shocked to learn how many entry-level applicants have only a vague notion as to what business their prospective employer is in!

Next, cruise by your targeted employer's place of business. If you can, find out how people who hold the position you seek dress. Appearance is critical. I have seen more than one entry-level employee hired because she had the right look or the right suit! You need a perfect costume. Now is not the time to wish you were ten pounds lighter; now is the time to buy, beg, or borrow the exact right costume for the interviews you anticipate. You want to be dressed one step better than your future coworkers' very best everyday outfits. Pay attention to accessories and details. From your shoelaces to your umbrella, your costume should be complementary and coherent.

If this starts to sound like a calculus of appearance, so be it. I know of one candidate who borrowed a herringbone jacket with leather elbow patches to interview for a writing job in the morning, and switched to his own dapper black suit to apply for a financial job in the afternoon. He was invited back for second interviews by both employers. Had he switched his costumes, he would not have been.

There are a thousand "looks" for both men and women, and you must get yours exactly right. Even if you have spent the last four years at Bohemian U., you are about to audition for a part in the real world and you must be willing to look the part to win it! If you are out of touch, read the department store advertisements, study characters on the street, and visit boutiques and haberdashers to catch up.

Most people in business can stand by the front door of any company and tell you who is streaming in every morning: "executive assistant, executive, probably a programmer or computer jock, middle manager, clerk, receptionist, management wannabe, creative type," and so on.

Your appearance tells a lot, whether you like it or not. Make it tell the right things.

◉ ◉ ◉

Your next step is to rewrite and rehearse your script. In addition to your highly targeted résumé and crib sheet of points to make, prepare a list of questions that you expect your interviewer to ask. Then, practice interviewing out loud. Use your roommate or a friend, or tape-record yourself asking questions, whatever it takes to get you to actually rehearse your interview out loud. Most candidates burn through a dozen or so interviews before they get their stage legs. What if your second interview is the one that matters?

It is not enough to know the right answers. You must sound natural, confident, and competent. The right answers need to be right on the tip of your melodious tongue, and only practicing out loud can achieve that.

⊙ ⊙ ⊙

When it is finally showtime: Call to confirm your appointment. Be sure to arrive exactly four minutes early. Have a few extra copies of your résumé. Know as much as you can about your targeted employer. Be exceptionally cordial with the gatekeeper. Be patient and at ease while you wait your turn. Even in the waiting room, your interview has already begun. That gatekeeper is the decision-maker's eyes and ears.

When you finally step into the meeting, look your interviewer in the eye, greet her, commit her name to memory, and shake hands firmly but smoothly. (A handshake should never be a demonstration of strength.) Take a seat only when offered. Sit up straight, and lean slightly forward in your chair. You are on stage. The curtain is up and the lights are on. Now is time to be yourself, but also to sell yourself.

In the first few seconds of your meeting, the interviewer will already have formed an opinion of you. She won't know if she's going to hire you, but within seconds she will know if she is not going to hire you. That is why your appearance and initial demeanor are so darned important.

A Few Rules to Consider
There are a few rules of interviewing etiquette that you will ignore to your peril:

> Make eye contact, but don't stare down your interviewer.

> Never contradict, interrupt, or argue with your interviewer. This is interview suicide.

> Be alert, act interested, and focus on the positive.

> Never, never, never say anything bad about your former employers.

If you have to bite your tongue and speak in codes only you understand, never say anything critical about former employers. "I can't say enough nice things about them" can certainly be taken two ways. Rightly or wrongly, hiring officers usually think another company's bitter, disgruntled employees are the worst hires in the world.

Finally, there is one more rule, and it is a critical one:

> If you want the job, you must state your interest unequivocally.

No matter how interested you are, and how animated you seem about the opportunity under discussion, you absolutely must state that you want the job. Hiring officers will not assume interest on your part short of an explicit statement. Be sure to say something as clear as this: "The job as you have described it to me sounds perfect, Mr. Warren. I am very interested in this opportunity. How do we proceed from here?"

◎ ◎ ◎

There are some interview tips and techniques that fall short of rules, but nevertheless are probably good to observe 100 percent of the time:

> Answer the question that was asked.

Interviewers hate it when respondents fail to answer the question that was asked. No matter how harmless the communication error, the fault will always lie with the candidate. If you don't understand the question, restate it. "Do you mean . . .?" or ask a clarifying question: "I'm sorry, I'm not sure I understand your question. Are you referring to classroom experience or work experience?"

You can also just punt. "I'm sorry. I'm not sure I understand your question. Could you rephrase that?"

Never be afraid to say those three magic words, "I don't know." Other important phrases to have in your repertoire are "I'll have to think about that. Could we come back to this in a moment?" and more simply, "I'll have to get back to you on that."

> Always find out what happens next in the hiring process.

Be sure to ask about their hiring cycle, how many interviews to expect, when the decision will be made and by whom, what the competition is like, what the selection criteria are, and other information on the hiring process itself that will help you to excel as a candidate. Many otherwise good candidates create a disadvantage for themselves by failing to make such inquiries.

> Ask your own questions to evaluate the job.

You definitely want to know as much as possible about your job duties, to whom you will report, how morale is among your future peers, how long it takes to get a promotion, what happened to the last person to hold this position, what challenges face the company, and the company's plans for the division/department/team. Some companies treat new hires like fodder, and you don't want to be the last one hired before the whole unit is reorganized.

(Unfortunately, entry-level new hires cannot negotiate guarantees and contingencies into their hiring contracts. Yet. If your intuition tells you something is amiss, pay attention to it.)

> Avoid discussions of salary and perks until late in the hiring process.

If you seem more interested in the perks than the job, you will be out of contention. On the other hand, if you agree to a low-ball range before the employer is committed to you, it is very hard to build that range back up later. If salary comes up prematurely, ask your contact what salary they had in mind for the position. Then use lines like these: "We're in the same ballpark, but I am really more interested in the job and what it entails. Can we come back to this later?" Or, "That seems a little low for what you are expecting from this position, but let's talk further because I really like the company and the people I've met so far." You have no leverage over salary negotiations until the company has a definite interest in hiring you.

> Never burn a lead or a source.

Even if the job or the company is absurdly wrong for you, be graceful. If you find you are not interested in a position, be forthcoming with that fact. "This job doesn't seem exactly right for me, Ms. Collins. I really had in mind more of a customer service or public relations function than a direct outside sales position. I feel that my strengths are teamwork and collaboration, and it sounds to me like what you need is more of a lone-eagle type. I appreciate the opportunity to meet with you and learn about Amalgamated Diversified, however. You know, I have a friend who I think would be perfect for this position. Let me give you her name and number, and I'll call her and let her know about the opening, as well."

If an interview doesn't lead to candidacy for an opening, get leads and referrals instead. Collect business cards from everyone you contact in your search. Every contact is a contact that can lead to your perfect career job. Check back in with all your referral sources once every two weeks, at least. Just a quick call to see if they have any new leads, rumors, or referrals is sufficient.

This process of checking back can be highly productive. Employers who initially reject or deflect you can be very receptive to your candidacy when something does open up. If you check in with them on a regular basis, they will feel as if they already know you.

Warning: Do not press for leads when you are a contender for a known opening. This is an indicator that you either lack confidence in your candidacy or don't actually want the position.

203

The Most Common Interview Questions

As stated earlier, the most common interview is a line by line review and discussion of your education and experience as presented in your résumé. Know your résumé by heart! In addition, you should be ready for the following questions:

> Tell me about yourself.

This little command causes more trouble than any other single phrase. First of all, remember to couch your response in a business context. This is not a request to discuss your home town or your childhood pets. The best way to answer this question is to discuss the evolution of your career interests leading to the ultimate, inevitable conclusion that you should work for them.

Anyone graduating from college today should be able to make a one- to two-minute presentation of who he is, what he wants, and how he has prepared himself for this move. Practice until you can do it smoothly.

> What are your strengths?

Similar questions are "What adjectives describe you?" or "How would you describe yourself?" These are a piece of cake. Describe your strengths relative to the ideal candidate, and in order of importance to the position you are applying for.

> What are your weaknesses?

This is a bona fide trick question. Your weaknesses must be strengths in disguise. Here is an example: "I have this passion for detail. Sometimes I'll spend hours getting something just right. But as you can see from my recommendations and transcripts, I still manage to get plenty of work completed, too. As a matter of fact. . . ."

> What kind of work environment do you like best?

There are dozens of ways to ask this same question. "Do you like to work alone or in a team?" "Do you like to work on a computer or with people?" "Can you work with close supervision or do you prefer to work independently?" "Would you rather do bookkeeping or edit letters?" "Tell me about your prior job. What aspects did you enjoy most? Least?" And so on. The correct answer is more or less the true one. Put everything in a positive light, but why lie to get a job sitting behind a computer screen eight hours a day if what you really want to do is deal with people, or vice versa? Be yourself, but sell yourself.

> What other types of positions are you applying for?

You may be applying to be a church organist and a nude dancer at the same time, but you better tell the pastor that you are applying only for other organist jobs and the club manager that you are applying only for other dancing jobs, if you get what I mean. Be careful that you not let disparate interests lead a potential employer to the conclusion that your real interests lie elsewhere. I once knew a college professor who was a bartender. He had two résumés without one single overlapping job.

> What do you do with your leisure time?

This is definitely a trick question. This is an attempt to learn what sort of person you are. Most people on this continent watch TV in their leisure time, but that has to be one of the worst answers you could give. Be ready to describe leisure activities that would complement the career path you have chosen, or activities that are so inherently interesting that the interviewer is disarmed. "I play sax for a club band every Friday and Saturday night" might be interesting, maybe too interesting. "I am researching a book on the history of transistors" might be better. Avoid controversial items, like "I get arrested in front of abortion clinics nationwide." Saying, "I spend time with my family," might be true, but is not a good choice. Most employers fear that family obligations are a direct competitor for the employee's loyalty, for mothers *and* fathers. Prepare an answer to this one in advance, or you may find yourself stammering, "What leisure time?"

> What are your long-term goals?

Other questions like this are "Where do you see yourself in five years?" and "How does this job fit into your overall plans?" By now you should see a pattern to these answers: The correct answer is five years further along the career path that leads out of this position. It is your job as a candidate to know what that typical career path is. Contrary to what some think, excessive ambition is not really impressive to employers. Saying, "I want to be making $250,000 within five years," is probably going to cause the interviewer to think you are naïve or immature or both. Saying, "I would expect at least two or three promotions by then, which would make me a senior account manager," is probably a lot smarter.

> Describe a problem you had with a former supervisor, and how you dealt with it.

205

Some interviewers will goad you into saying bad things about former employers. Resist the bait. Answer this question without slurring your last boss. Try something like this:

"I had this boss who had a habit of delegating assignments to me and then taking them back before I had a chance to complete them. I sat down with him and told him what he was doing, and that I thought it robbed me of a chance to develop my skills and kept him from getting the effective support I was capable of providing. So he agreed to let me do a major contract proposal if I would get it ready three days early. I did, and he didn't change a word of it. I got a bonus because we won the contract."

Trained interviewers will ask many questions like this:

> Tell me about a time when . . .

> What would you do if . . . ?

This is called behavioral interviewing. The interviewer wants you to model future behavior, using potential incidents that might really come up in the workplace, or they want you to model past behavior, which industrial/organizational psychologists have established is the best indicator of your future workplace behavior. The best way to answer these is to recount a specific incident, to tell a specific story that answers the questions. Do not blather on in generalities, because the interviewing really wants a specific response.

Prepare answers to these questions before you go into any interview. Although there are thousands of variations, these are the most common types of interview questions you will face. With practice, you will become smooth and confident and able to handle the really weird questions like "Why are manhole covers round?" or "How many golf balls would fit into a 747?"

Interview Follow-Up

After each interview, you should immediately summarize the meeting on your 5 x 8 lead card. Pay particular attention to recording the employer's key concerns. Try to infer his motivating factors. For example, his last assistant may have been great at spreadsheets and reports, but she was lousy on the phone and a sloppy dresser. Even if spreadsheets comprise 90 percent of the job, the "hot buttons" for this hiring authority may be customer service skills and personal appearance. This human factor must be taken into account in your efforts to cinch this job.

A full-scale job search will involve hundreds of contacts, and in no time at all you will need such notes as these to refresh your memory.

Of course, you should record the date of your next planned contact, such as "Get references to Dave by Friday," or, "Decision to be made by next Wednesday. Call Dave Wednesday after lunch if he hasn't called me first."

Next, write that thank-you note or letter and get it in the mail!

What Interviewers and Hiring Authorities Want

You might think that researching companies/jobs/career paths, customizing your résumés, scripting interview topics, rehearsing, and following through with thank-you letters is a lot of effort for one lead. You may ask, Why not just buy a mailing list, lick more stamps, and see what happens?

The problem is that no matter how many stamps you lick, there is some other candidate out there doing a bang-up job of applying for the position you want. While you are spreading yourself thin, she is researching the company/position/career path, networking her way into an appointment, coming off ultra-prepared in the interview, and beating the pants off your strategy.

In spite of all that you may have heard, the job search is not a numbers game! It is not a matter of making a certain number of applications before one "clicks." If you do not use intensive search tactics, you will always find yourself the company's second or third choice, if you are in the running at all. "I'm sorry, Jim. If we could hire two, we'd take you both, but the other candidate just knew more about the business and our needs." Don't be Jim.

It may sound funny, but companies want candidates who want them. It's like the dating game. Dates want suitors who want them, not suitors who just want a date.

You must realize it is better to make one tenth the number of applications and do ten times as good a job of applying, than it is to lick a lot of stamps and wait. Job searching is a qualitative sport, not a numbers game.

I once shadowed a corporate recruiter on a full day of interviews at a major university—twelve scheduled interviews, eleven of which took place. On his interview form he reduced each meeting to a terse sentence or two, a paragraph at most. He was interviewing for an engineering position. "All these students," he told me, "are prescreened. They are all technically qualified for this position." Yet he found that four of the eleven interviewed needed "improved career focus." That is, they were in an interview for an announced job with a known company and they failed to convince the recruiter of their interest.

Two failed the interview on communication grounds. One was "too nervous, didn't sell himself," and one "could sell herself more aggressively, not confident." Seven of twelve were out of contention. (Interestingly enough, the recruiter referred the two poor communicators for further interview counseling at the career center. Their participation in the interviews didn't pay off in a job offer, but it did generate some much-needed criticism. This is one of the reasons I say everyone should participate in on-campus hiring programs.)

207

Three of the candidates were rejected as "not a match at this time." In the interview, by mutual agreement or by decision of the interviewer, these candidates were judged to be qualified, but not appropriate for the position. The reasons varied, but were not recorded.

Two candidates were judged worthy of further consideration. These two candidates odds went from 1:12 to 1:2. Here is the table:

> 1 was a no show for his scheduled interview

> 4 did not have sufficient "career focus" to impress the recruiter

> 2 failed their interviews on communication grounds

> 3 were judged "not a match at this time"

> 2 were rated "well prepared" and "potential fit" and were scheduled for follow-up

The point of this story is that by being prepared, interview savvy, and focused, two or these candidates reduced their competition by over 90 percent!

Maybe one of the ten disqualified candidates was in fact tremendously better qualified than the two finalists, but that doesn't matter. The finalists gave the recruiter what he was looking for.

Although you cannot extrapolate statistically from this particular interview series, the recruiter gave every indication that he thought it was typical. If a 90 percent reduction in competition is possible in a prescreened applicant pool, just imagine the benefits in a wide open field with a proportion of unqualified candidates.

Employers have many complaints about college job seekers. Here are two, pulled at random from a recent message exchange on a listserv for human resources professionals:

Last spring I hired a part-time office assistant. The position was perfect for a college student, and given our location near several large NYC colleges, I called their student employment offices and submitted listings. The position required the ability to do accurate data entry (speed wasn't the issue, accuracy was), answer phones and speak to callers professionally, and handle a variety of other clerical tasks. I really didn't think it was that complicated. I had a similar position in high school.

The résumés started to come in, full of misspellings, poor grammar, and typos. There were a couple of applicants that seemed fine on paper, but once I had them on the phone I realized they were incapable of using standard business English.

Once the interviews began, it got even worse. Applicants came in not dressed for an interview; one looked (and smelled) like she had just gotten out of bed after a night of pub hopping the evening before.

One "gentleman" was really pushy about getting an interview. He became belligerent during the interview, and then began to outright lie when asked about his skills. According to him, Access is a word processing program, PowerPoint is used to create spreadsheets, and Word and WordPerfect are "exactly the same program; some people call it one thing, and some people call it the other."

I had more or less settled on an applicant. However, when I called to check her references, she had been terminated from her previous job after not showing up or calling in for three days with no excuse other than she didn't feel like coming to work. Luckily, the person who had hired her replacement had received a couple of résumés from other candidates that looked pretty good. She faxed them over to me, and I hired one of them.

I just couldn't believe it. It took over 100 résumés, 13 interviews, and almost 4 weeks to hire a part-time office assistant!

I just finished a hiring cycle, too, and I was amazed at how ill prepared for the working world most of these applicants were. They didn't know how to create a reasonably well done résumé (I wasn't looking for a slick presentation, but logical formatting would have been nice); the résumés were full of typos and poor grammar. Many didn't know how to write an intelligent cover letter. Over half misspelled my name! They didn't dress appropriately for an interview (jeans, wads of chewing gum, one came in in a shirt which revealed her tattooed midriff! {BTW, the person I did hire had a pierced tongue, but she had the wisdom to keep it out of sight until a couple of weeks after I hired her!}). One was so fearful that she was shaking through the entire process (it was beyond nervous!). One never looked at me. One used several off color words on a regular basis throughout the interview. What an experience!

Obviously, you can beat this type of competition.

209

Negotiations and Closing the Deal

If you follow the suggestions in this book and you get out of bed and look for work for forty hours per week, from Sunday afternoon until Friday noon, you will start to get offers. What do you do with them?

First of all, anticipate them. You need to know your salary expectations, your feasible start dates, and any special terms of employment you need. You don't want to find yourself in some meeting where the employer is ready to hammer out a deal and you are saying to yourself, "Gosh, what do I want?" Talk to people in your network. Know what would be an appropriate salary for the type of job you are pursuing.

Most important of all, make sure you are actually getting an offer, not a teaser. Sentences like these don't mean a thing: "If we were to hire you today, when could you be ready to start?" Even worse are the well-meaning people who all but promise you the job. "It looks like you'd be great; I just want you to meet one more person . . ." It's great to get excited about a job prospect, but watch out! You don't have an offer and you don't have a deal. A job search is not over until you get something in writing or get through your first day on the job without getting fired before quitting time. Until then, keep making new applications and don't fall in love with an opportunity that may dissolve into a heartbreaking mist.

Recent graduates are common victims of this scenario. Keep some detachment all the way through negotiating terms of employment. This protects you two ways: you will not be emotionally destroyed if the offer doesn't materialize, and you will be in a better negotiating position if it does.

If you think you are getting an offer, stop and verify it explicitly: "Are you offering me the position?" If you get a yes answer to such a direct question, only then should you begin to negotiate terms. Terms of employment are usually quite simple at the entry level: salary level and incept date. Always negotiate raw salary first, before you introduce any troubling details. Your brother's wedding in six weeks and your pre-existing health condition are just the kind of problems that weaken your position for salary negotiations.

Do not be shy about asking how their salary offer was determined. If all the other new sales reps start at 15 percent, you can bet there's not going to be much room for negotiation. If you are the only Webmaster in the company, however, there might be considerable room to manipulate your salary and perks.

In addition to salary and incept date, be sure to firm up the details of insurance coverage, relocation allowances (if applicable), signing bonus (if any), probationary periods, vacation and sick day policies, car allowances (if applicable) and the like. Try not to do this with a line manager; it is better to review such details with a human resources professional. Then, even if you have to write it on the back of a napkin, write down exactly what you have been told and what you have agreed to and get the hiring authority to initial it. Don't worry about the admissibility of your napkin as evidence, you want to avoid a misunderstanding. (Recent employment law cases have upheld the binding nature of oral contracts, but let me assure you that you don't want to be in a court of law trying to enforce one.)

When you have terms written out and initialed and an exact incept date, you have a **firm offer.** Until then, you do not. Job offers without the details are not a done deal.

Stalling and Accepting

Stalling an offer is an art form. Some candidates take particular pride in playing one prospective employer off against another. You can stall for a few days simply by saying that you need time to think about it. As a matter of fact, it is a good idea to sleep on an offer, but make sure it is a standing offer. If you do not accept fairly promptly, some employers retract the offer, with or without telling you.

Again, be very explicit with your hiring authority. "I would like to take three days to consider this, Walter. May I let you know my decision on Friday morning?"

Once you have an offer, it is perfectly fair to call up all your other hot prospects and let them know that you have one. This may force them to tip their hands and make an offer. Then you can go back to the first company and try to jack up their offer.

This is brinkmanship, and it is a dangerous game. In general, if an offer is not attractive to you, decline it gracefully and go on. If it is, negotiate fair terms and accept it. If you are unsure about an offer, don't accept it; stall gracefully while you evaluate it and test your alternatives. Be sure to get advice from your campus career office. They know typical starting salaries in your region and standard hiring practices, and their advice is often invaluable at the negotiations stage.

Once you decide to accept, get your napkin turned into a letter from the employer stating the same terms. Don't use the word "contract"; it scares people. Such a letter is all you need to protect your interests. Until you get such a letter or start your first day of work, you do not have a done deal. Keep making new applications and thinking of your alternatives in case the deal falls through.

As a matter of honor, once you accept an offer you cannot accept another.

Immediately call any other standing offers and decline, then send a note to every soul involved in your search and thank them warmly. Announce your appointment and provide your new business phone number. Offer your services to help them in any way you can, should they ever need it.

Congratulations! You're hired!

Selling Yourself . . . Literally

The job market is a free market, and it often appears to be a chaotic, inefficient, disorganized, unregulated, unstructured mess. Before you lament that fact, consider this: Free markets ideally work to the advantage of both buyer and seller.

The job market can be tamed and understood. You can provide the structure to control your experience in this economic trading ground. You are the product, and it is your responsibility to market and sell that product. You are free to strike almost any deal you want with any buyer you want.*

Besides, who could sell you better than yourself? Who else really knows what you have to offer, and even more important, what you want? The risks of a free market are borne by the individual but so are the rewards, including the ability to sell your skills and abilities to the bidder who offers a mix of cash and quality of life that appeals to you.

Our society benefits when individuals are given the skills to excel in navigating the job market. Since Richard Bolle's first edition of *What Color is Your Parachute?* over 20 years ago started a revolution in thinking about how we change jobs, there has been an agonizingly slow but steady improvement in scholarship, thinking, and writing on the topic of the job market and job-search process. Today you can benefit from scores of excellent books containing good advice.

---

*Federal and state labor laws and regulations in this country are not excessive, being intended to protect against discrimination and allow individuals to sell their skills without hindrance by matters unrelated to job performance. Such restrictions generally increase the job market's contribution to the ideal of meritocracy.

The ability to find a job is a skill that can be learned, improved upon, and perfected like any other. You cannot avoid the responsibility of managing your own career. Over the span of your life you will change careers and locales more often than people of any prior generation.

As your career progresses, continue to read books and articles on the job market and the job-search process. Things change rapidly and the hottest résumé style or job search tactic from ten years ago might fail miserably today, and the same will be true in the future.

Employers rightfully assume that candidates who remain ignorant of developments in the job-search process are likely to remain similarly ignorant of developments in their field. Since fewer and fewer people can expect a long career with one company, or would want one, you need to become a flexible careerist with a constantly developing bag of skills. One of the most important of those skills is the ability to sell the rest of your skills.

Even inside a company you may be called upon to constantly create, re-create, and justify your assignments. This is the way of the new world, and you can either be aggressively a part of it or watch it pass you by. Since I started writing résumés there have seen several small revolutions in business. Older secretaries who refused to learn computers were displaced. Overpaid middle managers with vague "people" skills but no area of technical expertise were replaced by computerized information processing and flatter organizational charts. Generalist computer programmers, the original cowboys of Silicon Valley, were replaced by specialist whiz kids fresh out of college and eager to work for half the pay. Master craftsmen found their jobs exported or automated, leaving them without a single transferable skill. Managers who insisted on having secretaries were replaced by younger, faster managers who could babysit themselves. Similar changes are in progress even as you read this sentence.

As your career progresses keep looking ahead. Have a plan and a back-up plan, complete with all the little intermediate steps you will need to take to realize those plans. Be sure to incorporate continuing education (perhaps one or more graduate degrees or, possibly even more important, specialized study and certification programs). Don't fight tidal changes in employment; anticipate and embrace them. (If all the companies in your field are laying off people right and left, become an expert in downsizing.)

Life ≠ Work

Having worked with so many aggressive careerists over the years, it is tempting to make generalizations and proffer advice even when none is requested. At the risk of offending a few, but with the hope of influencing a greater number, I will offer a few observations that may be of benefit to you in your life and career planning.

My career-coaching practice has traditionally focused on assisting aggressive career-oriented individuals, almost every one of them smart, motivated, and savvy. Nevertheless, I noticed that some of them were unidimensional. All they cared about and all they knew about was business—and only their own narrow segment of it at that. Although highly educated in one specialized field, they were often totally ignorant of the world as a whole.

As you pursue success, remember to keep outside interests. Read, participate in the arts, have a hobby, make your family a priority, learn deeply about something outside your career. This is not just so that you will be more interesting to bump into at a party, but also so that you will have intellectual and emotional enrichment separate from your working life. If you do face a setback in your career, these interests will help you weather it better than someone whose whole life is defined by a job. In fact, they can even provide a financial cushion.

A physician once gave me some interesting advice: "Make part of your money from your job, part of your money from your hobby, and part of your money from your money." He was constantly dabbling in some little venture, and often made considerable income from his hobbies. For example, he used to import beer steins from Germany, in part to deduct the occasional trip to Europe. He bought cast-off hospital gowns for pennies and sold them mailorder to high school kids for huge profits.

An avocation or a second interest can provide you with an emotional anchor against your primary career, and can even become a second career.

One college professor I know of decided to see if he could make any money out of a lifetime interest in fly fishing. Within a few years he had a factory in China turning out zillions of little hand-tied perfections. He made more money in retirement that he ever made in his academic career, and his entrepreneurial profits were a welcome addition to his meager pension.

Unlike Americans, most of the people in the world do not equate their worth and identity with their jobs. There are solid social, emotional, intellectual, and financial reasons to cultivate outside interests.

As a related point, you should have enough self-confidence and enough money to quit whenever you want. You will enjoy your job more when it's your choice to stay, and you will not be afraid of or beholden to your employer. This requires that you save enough money to carry you through a job search, and that you take care of yourself enough to know that you really deserve enriching and meaningful employment.

215

Finally, you should never put up with harassment or discrimination. Protest such treatment, record and document offenses carefully, do your best to recruit witnesses, and initiate formal internal procedures whenever you have a bona fide case.

It is true that many employers are plagued by petulant whiners who think work should be completely painless, and who complain about everything from the lighting to the flavor of the free coffee. I hope that you would not contribute to this plague. On the other hand, business has hardly come to terms with the deep problems of harassment and discrimination, nor will it until it is forced to. Nevertheless, I do not recommend that you sue your employer unless you have totally exhausted internal procedures.

If you ever do have to sue an employer, thoroughly document the problem and discuss it with an attorney before you leave the company, but don't actually file a lawsuit until you are securely employed in your next position. A job candidate with an active lawsuit is a career pariah.

UNABLE TO ANSWER QUESTION 23, "WHAT PERSONAL GOALS DO YOU HAVE TO GIVE YOUR OWN LIFE MEANING," FENTON PEEKS AT HIS NEIGHBOR'S PAPER.

Good Luck!

For many of us, a good career is without question the most satisfying thing in our lives. I hope this book has been of some benefit to you in considering your career and in some small way contributes to your happiness, whether you decide to pursue a position as a blues singer or a tax attorney.

I would like to know what you liked or didn't like about this book, what you found particularly useful, what you thought was superfluous, and what you would like to see covered in greater detail.

Most of all, I am eager to hear your job-search stories. Although I would love to see the résumés you might create with this book (especially technical and scientific résumés), I am more interested in your stories—creative strategies, tricks to get in to see employers, or "just dumb luck" tales about how you got your most important lead or interview.

If you have a comment or a story to tell, please write me a letter:

Donald Asher
From College to Career
c/o WetFeet.com
609 Mission Street, Suite 400
San Francisco, California 94105

Bibliography and Useful Resources

15 Questions: More Practice to Help You Ace Your Consulting Case. San Francisco: WetFeet.com, Inc., 1998.

Ace Your Case™ The Essential Management Consulting Case Workbook. San Francisco: WetFeet.com, Inc., 1998.

Asher, Don. *Asher's Bible of Executive Résumés and How to Write Them.* Berkeley: Ten Speed Press, 1996.

Asher, Don. *Graduate Admissions Essays: What Works, What Doesn't and Why.* Berkeley: Ten Speed Press, 1991.

Asher, Don. *The Foolproof Job Search Strategy.* Berkeley: Ten Speed Press, 1995.

Asher, Don. *The Overnight Job Change Strategy.* Berkeley: Ten Speed Press, 1993.

Asher, Don, and Dan Asher. *The Overnight Résumé.* 2nd ed. Berkeley: Ten Speed Press, 1999.

Beat The Street: The WetFeet Insider's Guide to Acing Your I-Banking Interviews. San Francisco: WetFeet.com, Inc., 1998.

Bolles, Richard Nelson. *What Color Is your Parachute? 2000.* 30th Rev. ed. Berkeley: Ten Speed Press, 1999.

Careers in Aerospace: Within Your Lifetime. $3.00 (plus 4.95 S&H). Washington: American Institute of Aeronautics and Astronautics, 1999. Contact: Publications Customer Service, PO Box 753, Waldorf, MD 20602.

Careers in Public Relations. $3.50. New York: The Public Relations Society of America, 1999. Contact: Dept. PPG, 3rd Floor, 33 Irving Place, New York, NY 10003-2376.

Consulting for PhDs, Lawyers, and Doctors. San Francisco: WetFeet.com, Inc., 1999.

Encyclopedia of Associations. 2nd ed. Volume 1 and 2. Farmington Hills, MI: Gale Research, 1990.

The Gale Directory of Publications and Broadcast Media. 135th ed. Edited by Kristen B. Mallegg. Farmington Hills, MI: Gale Research, 1999.

Getting Your Ideal Job: Networking, Interviewing, and Landing Your Job Offer. San Francisco: WetFeet.com, Inc., 1999.

The Insider Guide to Jobs in the Biotech and Pharmaceuticals Industry. San Francisco: WetFeet.com, Inc., 1999.

The Insider Guide to Jobs in the Computer Hardware Industry. San Francisco: WetFeet.com, Inc., 1999.

The Insider Guide to Jobs in the Computer Software Industry. San Francisco: WetFeet.com, Inc., 1999.

The Insider Guide to Jobs in the Entertainment Industry. San Francisco: WetFeet.com, Inc., 1999.

The Insider Guide to Jobs in the Insurance Industry. San Francisco: WetFeet.com, Inc., 1999.

The Insider Guide to Jobs in the Telecommunications Industry. San Francisco: WetFeet.com, Inc., 1999.

The Insider Guide to Jobs on Capitol Hill. San Francisco: WetFeet.com, Inc., 1998.

The Insider Guide to Venture Capital. San Francisco: WetFeet.com, Inc., 1998.

Is That Your Best Offer? How to Negotiate a Higher Salary and More Perks. San Francisco: WetFeet.com, Inc., 1999.

Killer Consulting Résumés. San Francisco: WetFeet.com, Inc., 1997.

Lucht, John. *Rites of Passage at $100,000+ : The Insider's Lifetime Guide to Executive Job-Changing and Faster Career Progress.* Rev. ed. New York: Viceroy Press, 1993.

Making Yourself Heard: Communications That Get You Interviews and Offers. San Francisco: WetFeet.com, Inc., 1998.

Malnig, Lawrence R. *What Can I Do with a Major In . . . ? How to Choose and Use Your College Major.* Leicestershire, England: Abbot Press, 1984.

The Mutual Fund Industry: The WetFeet.com Insider Guide. San Francisco: WetFeet.com, Inc., 1999.

Paetro, Maxine, and Giff Crosby (Illustrator). *How to Get Your Book Together and Get a Job in Advertising.* Chicago: Copy Workshop, 1998.

Parker, Yana. *Damn Good Résumé Guide: A Crash Course in Resume Writing.* 3rd ed. Berkeley: Ten Speed Press, 1996.

So, You Want To Be a Brand Manager: The Essential Guide. San Francisco: WetFeet.com, Inc., 1998.

So, You Want to Be a Management Consultant: The Essential Guide to the Management Consulting Industry. San Francisco: WetFeet.com, Inc., 1999.

So, You Want to Be an Investment Banker: The WetFeet Insider's Guide To Landing a Job on Wall Street. San Francisco: WetFeet.com, Inc., 1999.

So, You Want to Be in Advertising. San Francisco: WetFeet.com, Inc., 1999.

Social Entrepreneurship: Non-Profits for Profit. San Francisco: WetFeet.com, Inc., 1997.

U.S. Department of Labor. *Dictionary of Occupational Titles, 1991: 2 Volumes in 1.* 4th ed. Indianapolis: Jist Works, Inc., 1999.

WetFeet.com's Industry Insider Guide. San Francisco: Jossey-Bass Publishers, 1999.

Wright, John J. *The American Almanac of Jobs and Salaries 1997–1998.* New York: Avon Books, 1998.

Young Professional's Aerospace Handbook. $9.95 (plus $4.95 S&H) Washington: American Institute of Aeronautics and Astronautics, 1999. Contact: Publications Customer Service, PO Box 753, Waldorf, MD 20602.

Artwork Credits

Page 6: Cartoon reprinted with permission from artist, Kirk Anderson, Pioneer Press.

Page 14: "Luann" cartoon, by Greg Evans. Reprinted with permission from United Media.

Page 16: "Dilbert" cartoon, by Scott Adams. Reprinted with permission from United Media.

Page 31: "For Better or For Worse" cartoon, by Lynn Johnston. Reprinted with permission from United Media.

Page 72: "Off the Mark" cartoon, by Mark Parisi. Reprinted with permission from Atlantic Feature.

Page 89: "Off the Mark" cartoon, by Mark Parisi. Reprinted with permission from Atlantic Feature.

Page 182: Cartoon reprinted with permission from artist, Kirk Anderson, Pioneer Press.

Page 193: "Off the Mark" cartoon, by Mark Parisi. Reprinted with permission from Atlantic Feature.

Page 216: Cartoon reprinted with permission from artist, Kirk Anderson, Pioneer Press.

Get the Inside scoop on the job you want with WetFeet.com's Insider Guides!

Save time in your job search with WetFeet.com's series of comprehensive reports on what it's REALLY like to work for the top firms. This acclaimed series has helped hundreds of thousands of job seekers get the jobs they want. Each rigorously researched 50-to-100-page Insider is a concise yet detailed report on a particular company or industry. You'll learn:

> **what's happened in the past, what's hot right now, and where things are going**

> **about the work you'll be doing—and the culture you'll be doing it in**

> **the inside scoop on compensation, interviewing, and more**

WetFeet.com is committed to providing you with the most up-to-date, top quality, information to help you ace your interviews. WetFeet.com stands behind all of our research with a 100% satisfaction guarantee! Please contact our Member Happiness team for more details. In the U.S. call (800) 926-4JOB, outside the U.S. call (415) 284-7900 or e-mail comments@wetfeet.com.

Management Consulting

So, You Want to Be a Management Consultant
Ace Your Case™ The Essential Management Consulting Case Workbook
Fifteen Questions: More Practice Questions to Help You Ace Your Case
Killer Consulting Résumés
Consulting for PhDs, Lawyers, and Doctors

A.D. Little
Andersen Consulting
Arthur Andersen
A.T. Kearney
Bain & Co.
The Boston Consulting Group
Booz·Allen & Hamilton
Deloitte Consulting
Ernst & Young Consulting
KPMG
McKinsey & Co.
Mercer Mgmt. Consulting
Mitchell Madison Group
Monitor Company
PricewaterhouseCoopers

Financial Services

So, You Want to Be an Investment Banker

Beat the Street™: The WetFeet Insider Guide to Acing Your I-Banking Interviews

The Mutual Fund Industry

The Insider Guide to Jobs in Venture Capital

Bear Stearns

Bank of America

Charles Schwab & Co., Inc.

Chase Manhattan

Citibank

Credit Suisse First Boston

Donaldson, Lufkin & Jenrette

Ernst & Young Accounting

First USA

Goldman, Sachs & Co.

J.P. Morgan

Lehman Brothers

Merrill Lynch

Morgan Stanley Dean Witter

Salomon Smith Barney

The Toronto-Dominion Bank

Warburg Dillon Read

General Career Prep

Making Yourself Heard: Communications That Get You Interviews and Offers

Getting Your Ideal Job: Networking, Interviewing, and Landing Your Job Offer

Is That Your Best Offer? How to Negotiate a Higher Salary and More Perks

High Technology

The Insider's Guide to Jobs in the Computer Hardware Industry

The Insider's Guide to Jobs in the Computer Software Industry

Amazon.com

Hewlett-Packard Company

Intel Corporation

Microsoft Corporation

Oracle Corporation

PeopleSoft

Brand Management

So, You Want to Be a Brand Manager: The Essential Guide

The Clorox Company

General Mills Inc.

Nike

Procter & Gamble

The Walt Disney Company

Additional Titles

Careers in Traditional and Interactive Book Publishing

So, You Want to Be in Advertising

The Insider Guide to Jobs in the Entertainment Industry

The Insider Guide to Jobs on Capitol Hill

The Insider Guide to Jobs in the Insurance Industry

The Insider Guide to Jobs in the Biotech and Pharmaceuticals Industry

The Insider Guide to Jobs in the Telecommunications Industry

Nonprofits for Profit: The WetFeet Guide to Social Entrepreneurship

WetFeet.com is the leading career research site on the Web. Our job is to make your job search easier by gathering and presenting rigorously researched insider information on companies, industries, and broader career issues so that you can make your job search efficient, effective, and even fun. We aim to be your most-trusted partner in the job search and give you the critical competitive edge you'll need to identify opportunities, land job offers, negotiate a great compensation package, and then excel on the job.

Now go get your feet wet!

Visit us:

(800) 926-4JOB in the U.S.
(415) 284-7900 outside the U.S.

comments@WetFeet.com

fax: (415) 284-7910

Visit WetFeet.com today!

Become a WetFeet.com member and receive discounts and more!

Notes